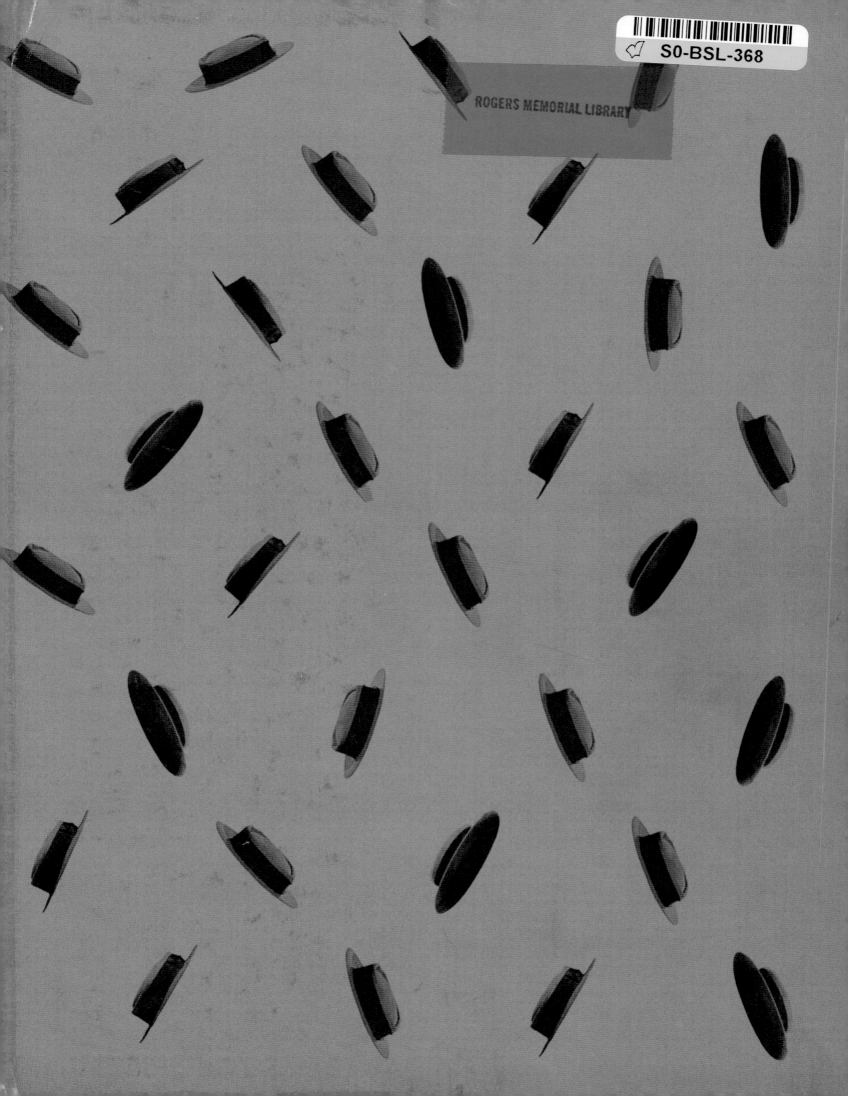

Buster Keaton *Remembered*

Buster

Eleanor Keaton *and* Jeffrey Vance

Keaton
Remembered

Afterword by Kevin Brownlow

Manoah Bowman, Photographic Editor

Photographs from the collection of the

Academy of Motion Picture Arts and Sciences

Harry N. Abrams, Inc., Publishers

Contents

Page 1: A 35mm frame enlargement from THE
SAPHEAD (1920), showing Bertie after he had been
tossed off of the floor of the stock exchange.

Page 2: One of Buster's earliest publicity photographs
upon entering films, 1917.

Page 4: Buster consults his script on an M-G-M sound
stage used for SPEAK EASILY (1932).

Above: The hapless projectionist is surrounded by film
in SHERLOCK JR. (1924).

IN EARLY 1998, WHEN THIS BOOK WAS ONLY A TENTATIVE PROJECT STILL IN
the talking stages, I found myself taking a very close look at our holdings of still photographs relating to Buster Keaton at
the Margaret Herrick Library of the Academy of Motion Picture Arts and Sciences. The Library owns, in its various collections, by far the largest and most comprehensive body of Keaton photographs known to exist in any library or archive on the
planet. In terms of quantity, quality, range, and variety, the Academy's holdings are truly extraordinary, numbering somewhere in the area of seven thousand individual items.

By far the largest concentration of Keaton photographs is found in the Metro-Goldwyn-Mayer Collection, donated to
the Library by M-G-M in 1978, which arrived in 969 uninventoried and unorganized record storage boxes. The collection
had remained virtually inaccessible in deep storage in a New Jersey warehouse since the 1950s. Twelve years later, when we
completed the sorting, processing, and inventorying of the massive collection, we finally knew precisely what it contained.
Among the nearly one million items, there are nearly complete files of all seven of Keaton's M-G-M talkies, as well as large
files on *Spite Marriage* (1929), *The Cameraman* (1928), *Battling Butler* (1926), *Seven Chances* (1925), and, miraculously, *The
Navigator* (1924). (I say miraculously because there was very little in the collection prior to 1925, and *The Navigator* was not
produced, but merely distributed, by Metro-Goldwyn—before the Mayer was tacked on to the company name.) Aside from
these production files, the M-G-M Collection also contains a biographical file of Keaton stills, numbering more than three
hundred prints.

Another significant group of Keaton photographs is located in the Jules White Collection. White was the head of the
Columbia short subjects department from 1933 to 1958, and he donated the collection to the Library in 1975. The collection
consists of stills (and scripts) from 522 films and includes photographs from nine of Keaton's ten Columbia shorts
(1939–41), containing a total of 220 prints.

A third, and possibly the rarest, large cache of Keaton stills came to the Library as a gift in the 1950s. Shortly after I started working for the Academy in 1972, I found these prints in the basement of our former premises at 9038 Melrose Avenue,
an old theater that the Academy had made its headquarters in the 1940s. The stills were in a box and were dirty and
extremely curled—I quickly dubbed them "Keaton's Dead Sea Scrolls," which should give a clear impression of their condition at that point. Although severely curled, they had luckily suffered no moisture damage, which would have caused them
to stick together. This made it possible for us to rewash and regloss the prints, restoring them to their original condition. We
achieved excellent results, and the photographs have since resided in the Library's Core Collection Production Files. The
Keaton box proved to contain more than twelve hundred stills, including prints from nine of Keaton's silent features, dating

from 1923 to 1928, and from ten of Keaton's silent shorts, dating from 1920 to 1922. Original stills from the short films are exceptionally rare, and most of these prints are probably unique.

Our most recent acquisition of a large body of Keaton photographs came from Keaton's widow, Eleanor Keaton, who donated the photos to the Library in June 1998, thanks largely to the efforts of Jeffrey Vance, who believed it was of paramount importance that the materials be preserved and maintained in perpetuity by an archive and not fall into the hands of private individuals or, worse, end up on the auction block. Jeffrey was instrumental in bringing Eleanor to agree with the wisdom of that belief.

Eleanor's material dates primarily from the time she met Buster (1938) through his death (1966), and so it was the perfect complement to the Academy's holdings, which were strong on the earlier period but weak on the later period. She also had some very early original vintage photographs from Keaton's infancy, childhood, and vaudeville days, as well as a Keaton family photo album of snapshots dating from 1909 to 1917. Certainly the Academy previously had nothing like this !

Eleanor's collection consists of more than nine hundred items and provides a rich representation of Buster's last three decades. It comprises many personal photographs, candids, and snapshots, as well as good material documenting his later film, stage, and television work.

A happy by-product of Eleanor's donation was that it inspired Jeffrey Vance, Manoah Bowman (this book's photographic editor and creator of the prints herein), and me to pursue outside sources and unearth additional Keaton material for the Academy Library, with the goal of making our Keaton holdings as comprehensive as possible. Of particular help along these lines were Marc Wanamaker, James Karen, and Robert S. Birchard, who generously and freely let us copy anything we wanted from their own personal collections. Richard W. Bann and Kevin Brownlow also allowed us to copy several of their Keaton stills.

So, I can cheerfully conclude that the Academy Library's photographic holdings on Buster Keaton are now even greater due to the generosity of Eleanor Keaton, this book, and all the help we have had along the way. But we are always looking for more!

Robert Cushman
Beverly Hills

"INVENTIVE" WAS THE KEY WORD USED BY CELEBRITY PHOTOGRAPHER SID AVERY about one of his favorite subjects, Buster Keaton, when I asked him about his photo shoot with the great comedian for U.S. Steel in 1964. As one of the few photographers still living who actually knew Keaton and photographed him, his comments reinforce a fact that is not always readily apparent: that Buster Keaton showed just as much imagination and creativity for the still photographer as he did for the cinematographer.

For his silent films, Keaton often used his inventiveness to create a cartoonlike effect in his still photographs. He wanted many of his publicity photographs to be as amusing and entertaining as possible so that the popular film magazines of the time, such as *Photoplay* and *Motion Picture Classic*, would publish them.

In light of this fact, Jeffrey Vance and I, following the advice of the late Eleanor Keaton, selected many of the photographs that display Buster's creativity and imagination. This was not an easy process, as there were literally thousands of images from which to choose. Imagine the difficulty of having to narrow down more than seven thousand photographs to a mere 225 (this book's limit). This process was complicated by the knowledge that some of the most famous stills of Keaton were cartoonish "gag" shots that did not even appear in the films they were supposedly representing. For example, two of the most instantly recognizable photographs of Keaton from *The Navigator* (Keaton sitting stoically on the steamship, and Keaton hanging off the rigging ropes looking out at the sea) are nowhere to be found in the film.

Our ultimate goal became to make this book as comprehensive as possible, by mixing the most famous and iconic images of Keaton with behind-the-scenes and scene stills that best represented the films themselves, and finally by adding many previously unpublished personal photos of Keaton, in an effort to create a unique and hopefully definitive photographic book on his life and films.

Determining the identity of the photographers proved to be an obstacle. As is typical of the silent era, most of the various still photographers for the films remain unknown. This is unfortunate because many of the photographs that appear in this book are masterpieces of composition for which their creators deserve proper credit. We know that Byron Houck was the still photographer for Keaton's greatest film *The General*, and that he worked with two still cameras—an 8 x 10 Eastman for the stationary and posed shots and a 5 x 7 Graflex for the more difficult action sequences, as well as for the candid behind-the-scenes photographs. Sadly, our ability to make an attribution to a particular photographer is an anomaly.

Although the identity of most of the scene still photographers is a mystery, the portrait still photographers of the period are well documented. Keaton posed for some of the world's finest photographic artists, including Nelson Evans, Arthur

Rice, Melbourne Spurr, Clarence Sinclair Bull, Ruth Harriet Louise, George Hurrell, Richard Avedon, and, of course, Sid Avery. Within these pages you will find at least one portrait by most of these photographers—some credited for the first time.

Choosing the images and identifying the photographers was only one part of assembling this book. Apart from serving as the photographic editor of this book, I also decided to create the prints in the darkroom myself. The process of making the photographic prints was a long and arduous one, which I accomplished over a period of about one year. In many cases we had access to the original nitrate 8 x 10 camera negatives, from which I always printed when available. For the other images, we had original vintage prints as the primary source material. From these, Producers and Quantity Photo, Inc. of Hollywood produced splendid 8 x 10 copy negatives, following our specific instructions as to exposure, filtration, and polarization.

As for the prints from original negatives appearing in this book, the earliest is the shot from *Cops* (1922) on page 89, and the latest is the still of Keaton and Charles Chaplin at their dressing tables from *Limelight* (1952) on page 204. In creating the prints from the negatives, I attempted to make them all look better than they had ever looked before. In the darkroom, this involved paying careful attention to varying degrees of contrast, tonal values, and all necessary burning and dodging to bring out and retain all the detail possible. Normally, I made at least three prints of each image and chose from these. All the prints were archivally processed and made, direct contact, on Ilford double-weight fiber paper. I truly strove for perfection in the creation of these images and hope that I got as close to it as is humanly possible.

Although the Academy offered a wealth of material from which to choose, it should be noted that there are some small gaps. In the case of Keaton's film *The Saphead*, the Academy seems to have the only extant vintage still. We were lucky that Buster was in it! In many instances, when searching for images from each short film, we had only two or three stills from which to make our selection.

Because the Buster Keaton Collection that Eleanor donated to the Academy largely contained images of a personal nature, we had to look elsewhere to fill some of our gaps. Until the mid-1950s Keaton himself held the best collection of his own film stills. However, as a result of his and Eleanor's generosity to various authors, researchers, newsletters, and other publications, many of the original photographs they lent out were subsequently lost or never returned. Hence, one of the most daunting challenges in preparing this book was to locate some of this material or to find other similar first-generation images from which to work.

Also, the reader might notice that there are films or appearances that are not represented in these pages. Some of these have been omitted because Eleanor counted them among Buster's lesser efforts and did not wish to commemorate them in this book. For example, there are no photos included of Keaton's last starring feature film, the 1946 low-budget Mexican production *El Moderno Barba Azul* (a.k.a. *The Modern Bluebeard* or *Boom in the Moon*). We readily concur with Eleanor that this one will probably not be missed.

It is our final hope that this book will lend credence to the idea that the best of the still photographs of Buster Keaton can stand as great works in their own right, alongside his monumental achievements on the motion-picture screen. These images can stand alone not only because they are such wonderful photographs, but also because of Keaton's own compelling personal mystique—a mystique so powerful that it transcends the era in which it was created and succeeds in withstanding the test of time.

Manoah Bowman

Los Angeles

I would like to thank the following people whose assistance with the photography for this book was invaluable: Robert Cushman, Photograph Curator at the Academy of Motion Picture Arts and Sciences' Margaret Herrick Library, who gave me special and repeated access to the Library's vast holdings of Keaton photographs. Peter Avellino and Michael Whitfield for their dedicated darkroom assistance in the production of many of the photographic prints herein reproduced. A special thanks to Laura Nix and Windham Beacham for helping me out in a pinch. Finally, I would like to express my gratitude to Jasmine Brunsuzyan and Shahe Melelian of Producers and Quantity Photo for having the reserves of patience it must take to deal with me and all my special requests.

M.B.

INTRODUCTION *by Jeffrey Vance*

Buster Keaton, c. 1920. Photograph by Hoover.

ON MAY 29, 1940, AT CITY HALL IN DOWNTOWN LOS ANGELES, CALIFORNIA, an unassuming young bride named Eleanor Ruth Norris said "I do" and became the third wife of a man twice her age, who just happened to be the legendary film comedian Buster Keaton. None of the small group of family and friends present, and perhaps not even the groom himself, realized that Eleanor would prove to be no less than Buster Keaton's savior.

Keaton's tremendously successful career of the 1920s had derailed in the 1930s when, following the advent of talking pictures, his artistic creativity and ingenuity were quashed by the burgeoning studio system. Private adversity, the result of an unhappy first marriage, also contributed to his professional decline. Keaton, who had once enjoyed great critical acclaim and the fruits of being a top box-office draw, had become a chronic alcoholic and, by all accounts, was finished in the motion-picture industry. Enter Eleanor Keaton. Eleanor kept her husband away from alcohol, remained with him until he died, and helped him rebuild his career, his reputation, and his status as one of the great artists of the cinema. This book, upon which Eleanor worked consistently until the day she died, represents not only her final tribute to the man she loved but also her final contribution to the Keaton legacy.

* * *

Born Joseph Frank Keaton in Piqua, Kansas, on October 4, 1895, Buster Keaton was as old as the cinema when he began his career in motion pictures at the age of twenty-one. Within a few years, Keaton would be known all over the world. Eventually, his frozen visage would be as recognizable an American face as Abraham Lincoln's.

Keaton had spent a lifetime as a performer before he was captured on even a single frame of celluloid. His first appearance on stage was at the age of nine months and, at the age of five, he became the newest member of his parents' vaudeville act. The Three Keatons was among the most violent and raucous vaudeville acts in the history of the American theater. Like any other prop, Buster was routinely thrown about the stage, and occasionally into the audience, by his irascible father, Joe Keaton. Buster Keaton always maintained that it was the great escape artist, Harry Houdini, who gave him his nickname, "Buster," after seeing the child take a fall down a flight of stairs with little or no collateral damage. "That's sure a buster!" Houdini told Joe Keaton. From such a legend the name Buster Keaton was born.

Buster Keaton learned that his wild acrobatics made people laugh. He also learned that the more seriously he took his comedy, the more hilariously the audience regarded it. Night after night, even at

Top: Buster greets some of his young fans while on location, c. 1921. Eddie Cline is the man wearing the cap.

Center: Buster, Alf Reeves (Charlie Chaplin's business manager), Charlie Chaplin, H. O. Stechhan, H. M. Horkheimer, an unidentified man, and Lou Anger at the Horkheimer Brothers' Balboa Amusement Producing Company studio, Long Beach, California, c. 1918. Photograph attributed to Cudney.

Bottom: The Keaton family in Hollywood, 1920. Louise, Myra, Harry "Jingles," Buster, and Joe Keaton.

Opposite: Buster in the abandoned first version of THE ELECTRIC HOUSE, 1921.

an early age, Buster faced whatever travails were foisted upon him with a kind of stoic diligence. Although many of his early film shorts with Roscoe "Fatty" Arbuckle include fleeting moments of Keaton experimenting with smiling, laughing, or mugging for the camera, by the time Keaton broke into the movies in 1917, his immovable face was already part of the package.

By the end of their vaudeville run in 1917, there was no question as to which of The Three Keatons was now the star. Even as early as 1901 the act was billed in the *Dramatic Mirror* simply as "BUSTER, And his assistants . . . ."[1] Despite its success, the act ultimately broke up because of the erratic and often unpredictable behavior of the elder Keaton, whose onstage violence increasingly spilled over into his offstage family life.

On his own in 1917, Buster was quickly offered the sum of two hundred fifty dollars a week to headline at New York's Winter Garden Theater. Displaying some of the exquisite timing for which he would become famous, Buster did the unthinkable and turned down the theater to try his hand at motion pictures for a mere forty dollars per week.[2] He was fascinated with the technical aspects of film and believed he could succeed in the movies as he had on the stage. Motion pictures had transformed other vaudevillians into world-famous figures with enormous wealth in a very short time.

Above: Buster (out of costume) and a group of unknown women ham it up for the camera on the open-air stage of the Keaton studio during the production of **THE PLAYHOUSE** (1921). The heavy motion-picture make-up worn by all the women suggests that they were gathered for a screen test or film scene and not for a gag still.

Opposite: A dinner party held by Joe Schenck to welcome Rudolph Valentino into United Artists, 1925. Clockwise from left: Natalie Talmadge, William S. Hart, Norma Talmadge, Hiram Abrams, Douglas Fairbanks, Peg Talmadge, Allan Forrest, James Hood MacFarland, Buster, Mary Pickford, Charlie Chaplin, Charlotte Pickford, Joe Schenck, Natacha Rambova, Sydney Chaplin, Rudolph Valentino, Constance Talmadge, John Considine, Lottie Pickford, and Arthur Kelly. Photograph by Weaver.

Keaton began working, first in New York and later in Los Angeles, with Roscoe "Fatty" Arbuckle, a rotund, baby-faced man who was one of the most beloved comedians in the cinema. He was regarded as the best comedy director in films next to Charles Chaplin. Like Chaplin, Arbuckle had learned film comedy from pioneer film producer Mack Sennett at the Keystone Film Company, where his film career began in earnest in 1913.[3] Arbuckle, in turn, formed Keaton's conception of film. Once Arbuckle saw what a brilliant craftsman as well as talented comedian he had in Keaton, he soon had him codirecting as well as acting in the Arbuckle films. They began working out gag routines together, and in a short time Arbuckle's work began to bear an unmistakably Keatonian touch.

Two hallmarks of Keaton's style of comedy — mechanical precision and outguessing his audience (the audience expects one result and the comedian gives them another) — first appear in the Arbuckle series. In *Back Stage* (1919), one of the best of the Arbuckle-Keaton films, Arbuckle is unharmed as a balcony facade collapses and falls around him while he stands protected within an open window that passes over him. The precision of this gag would be replicated by Keaton in *One Week* (1920), *The Blacksmith* (1922), and most memorably in *Steamboat Bill, Jr.* (1928). Also in *Back Stage*, the audience thinks Buster's bedroom is coming apart around him as he lies in bed until it is revealed that this is not Buster's bedroom at all but a stage set being struck. The scene would be re-created in Keaton's *The Playhouse* (1921). This surprise effect, in which a situation appears one way but is then revealed in its total context to disclose that the viewer has been fooled, would be employed by Keaton throughout his film career.

Keaton worked with Arbuckle in fifteen comedies between 1917 and 1920 (the run was interrupted

Buster with a wooden statue of himself on the steps of his M-G-M bungalow, c. 1930. The statue was a gift from a German woodcarver.

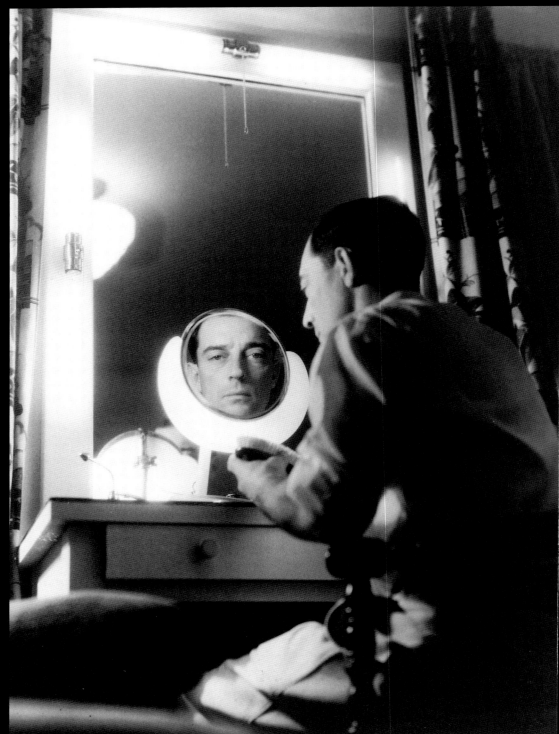

Buster in his bungalow at M-G-M, c. 1929. Photograph by George Hurrell.

MGMP-4594

MGMP·9396

Buster takes time out from his favorite sport of baseball to pose for the still photographer in September 1928.

Opposite: Photograph by George Hurrell, c. 1929.

when Keaton served in World War I in 1918–1919).
After this, Joseph M. Schenck, who produced the
films of Norma Talmadge as well as those of
Arbuckle, began production of two-reel comedies
with Keaton as the principal star. As Arbuckle went
to Paramount to make feature-length comedies,
Schenck provided Keaton his own studio and free
rein to create, direct, and star in his own films. This
arrangement resulted in nineteen shorts that afforded
Keaton a laboratory in which he enjoyed the freedom to experiment with and explore his own
comedic impulses, as well as to refine his screen
character, his conceptions of film structure, and his
use of the camera and editing as comedy devices.

Keaton once said that had he not become an
actor, he might have been a civil engineer. His first
independent release, *One Week* (1920), in which
Buster attempts to build a prefabricated house, is a
brilliant film that demonstrates his engineering skills.
One Week also takes a dramatic leap in story construction, cinema technique, and comic invention—
away from the films he had made with Arbuckle just
a short time before.

Keaton always thought in terms of the camera
when devising comic situations. His films from this
period are especially remarkable because of his ability
to tell a story with the camera instead of merely plac-
ing the camera in a stationary position and perform-

ing in front of it. Keaton's understanding of the camera as his partner, his high level of craftsmanship, his
engineering brilliance, and his unique performance
skills are apparent in even his earliest independent
comedy.

Some of these early films, such as *The Paleface*
(1922) and *The Frozen North* (1922), reveal Keaton's
propensity to juxtapose his comedy against grand
landscapes, a technique employed to full effect in
the classics *Our Hospitality* (1923) and *The General*
(1926). *One Week, The Boat* (1921), *The Electric
House* (1922), and *The Balloonatic* (1923) show
Keaton's attention to minute detail and obsession
with complicated mechanical props. *The Playhouse*
displays an experimentalism that bent the film medium beyond just capturing a performance. In one
sequence Keaton brilliantly plays every character in a
vaudeville theater, an effect achieved by using multi-
ple exposures. *The Playhouse* was surpassed only by

*Opposite: Photograph by
Ruth Harriet Louise, c. 1928.*

Above: GO WEST *(1925)
was the last silent feature film
in which Buster wore his
porkpie hat.*

23

his similarly innovative feature, *Sherlock Jr.* (1924). And the *Damfino* of *The Boat*, a prop with endless mechanical possibilities, presages one of Keaton's most inspired films, *The Navigator* (1924).

Keaton benefited also from a superb team of people who were able to transfer his vision to film. Eddie Cline codirected with Keaton most of the Keaton shorts. His technical director was Fred Gabourie, who was responsible for building the sets and planning special stunts and effects. His cinematographer was the highly skilled Elgin Lessley, a Mack Sennett veteran. Jean Havez and Clyde Bruckman (both of whom had worked for Arbuckle), along with Joseph Mitchell, were his three top gagmen. The system Keaton adopted was to plan everything beforehand while leaving room to improvise performance details and unexpected touches that could never be prepared in advance.

Buoyed by the success of the Keaton shorts, in 1923, Schenck determined that Keaton was ready to star in his own features.[4] Between

Upper left: Photograph by George Hurrell, c. 1930.

Above: Photograph by Clarence Sinclair Bull, c. 1928.

Opposite: Photograph by Melbourne Spurr, c. 1924.

1923 and 1928, Keaton made ten independent feature-length comedies: *Three Ages* (1923), *Our Hospitality, Sherlock Jr., The Navigator, Seven Chances* (1925), *Go West* (1925), *Battling Butler* (1926), *The General, College* (1927), and *Steamboat Bill, Jr.* (1928). These ten films showcase Keaton's incredible imagination at its greatest heights, stretching silent comedy to its outermost boundaries and ensuring his place as one of the artistic geniuses of the twentieth century.

Receiving the requisite bumps and bruises during the execution of his physically challenging brand of comedy had always been commonplace for Keaton, but his feature films of the 1920s nearly killed him.

Despite careful planning, Keaton missed a jump, hit a wall, and plunged two stories during the filming of *Three Ages*. While filming *Our Hospitality*, Keaton's hold-back wire snapped, and he was propelled down a raging river, almost drowning in the mishap. When executing a stunt for *Sherlock Jr.*, Keaton broke his neck (although, incredibly, he did not realize he had broken his neck until he had a complete physical examination years later). The footage of the accidents proved so effective that Keaton kept the shots in the final versions of the films. Never has a filmmaker physically suffered so much for his art as did Buster Keaton during the filming of his silent comedies, and the films possess a realism that clearly reflects that fact.

Buster as "the three wise monkeys," c. 1921. Photograph attributed to Arthur Rice.

A two-headed Buster, c. 1921. Double-exposure photograph by Arthur Rice.

By the time Keaton completed *Steamboat Bill, Jr.*, Al Jolson had sung in *The Jazz Singer* (1927), and talkies had burst onto the movie scene. Large, monolithic studios had already supplanted many of the smaller independent filmmakers. Keaton's last three independent films, *The General*, *College*, and *Steamboat Bill, Jr.*, were critical and commercial disappointments at the time—although today *The General* is considered one of the greatest films ever made, and *Steamboat Bill, Jr.* is viewed as one of Keaton's finest achievements. With the Keaton pictures failing commercially, and in an effort to stay ahead of the shift in film production, Joe Schenck convinced Keaton to abandon his own studio and join Metro-Goldwyn-Mayer's stable of stars. Keaton's first comedy for M-G-M, *The Cameraman* (1928), is a masterpiece and one of Keaton's funniest comedies. The film that followed, *Spite Marriage* (1929), was Keaton's last silent film and the last of his films to display the intrinsic Keaton style of comedy. Both films were commercially successful.

At M-G-M, Keaton no longer enjoyed the artistic freedom he had as an independent filmmaker. Keaton, an instinctual artist, did not fare well in the regimented M-G-M workplace with its carefully prepared scripts and endless timetables. Worse still, the

studio chose stories for Keaton without consulting with him. In the first talking film in which he starred, *Free and Easy* (1930), Keaton suffered the indignities of having to work with less talented gag men and of being forced to adhere to a detailed script in advance, allowing less opportunity to improvise. As he ceased to be a creative filmmaker and was reduced to a mere comic performer, Keaton resorted, as he had done on earlier difficult occasions, to drink. Further adding to his unhappiness was the deterioration of his marriage to Natalie Talmadge. The resultant erratic behavior and long absences from the studio caused costly delays in the production of his films. After seven commercially successful but artistically abysmal sound films at M-G-M, which were plagued behind the scenes with Keaton's drinking, Louis B. Mayer terminated Keaton's contract.

At only thirty-seven years old, the legendary comedian was out of work, an alcoholic, and a shell of his former self. He was divorced from Talmadge. (The marriage had ended with such rancor that she legally changed their sons' names from Keaton to Talmadge.) What followed were a disastrous second marriage, forgettable short comedies for Educational and Columbia, and relegation to the status of a gag man and supporting player. Keaton was convinced his days at the top were over.

Buster Keaton's marriage to Eleanor Norris in 1940 reversed this seemingly desperate personal and professional downward spiral. Eleanor encouraged Buster to appear on stage in summer stock, to take supporting roles in feature films, and, starting in 1947, to play the Cirque Medrano in Paris, reclaiming his rightful place as a great clown. However, it was television that allowed Keaton to emerge from obscurity in America. His introduction to the new medium was an appearance on the initial

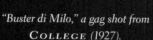

"Buster di Milo," a gag shot from COLLEGE *(1927).*

Opposite: Buster, Harpo Marx, James Cagney, and George Burns at a charity event benefiting the Motion Picture Relief Fund, April 1949.

broadcast of the *Ed Wynn Show*, which aired in December 1949. Two weeks later, Keaton had his own local half-hour television program, *The Buster Keaton Show* (later followed by a half-hour syndicated comedy series in 1950). It was also in 1949 that James Agee wrote his influential *Life* magazine article, "Comedy's Greatest Era," which officially rediscovered Keaton and established him with the other major silent clowns as cinematic greats. Keaton did not think himself a great artist and was embarrassed by and mistrustful of those who did. He saw himself as a vaudevillian who had been fortunate enough in silent films to have had the opportunity to make pictures the way he wanted them; but he was now an actor for hire, and he made himself available for virtually anything. When asked, Keaton was also willing to contribute gag ideas and direction. Yet Agee's article was important for Keaton, as it was published at a time when Keaton was the only one of the great silent-film comedians available for employment. Chaplin produced only occasionally and after 1940 made only four films. Harold Lloyd had retired. During the 1950s, the Keatons' partnership with Raymond Rohauer helped preserve and eventually re-release Keaton's classic silent films, introducing him to new generations of film-goers who had become interested in Keaton through his various guest appearances on film and television, and through Agee's article. Just a decade later, by the early 1960s, Keaton's rehabilitation was complete. He received an honorary Academy Award in 1960, and in 1962 a tribute at the Cinémathèque Française. In 1965, the year before his death, Keaton enjoyed a successful final tribute to his life and work at the Venice Film Festival.

Keaton worked almost until the day he died, appearing in a wide range of motion pictures and television productions, including important films such as Billy Wilder's *Sunset Boulevard* (1950), Charles Chaplin's *Limelight* (1952), Michael Todd's *Around the World in 80 Days* (1956), and Samuel Beckett's *Film* (1965). His work spanned the entire development of twentieth-century American comedy. A performer who came from turn-of-the-century vaudeville, Keaton kept adapting, making the transition from vaudeville to silent movies, to talking films, to television, and even to commercials. In 1956, Paramount Pictures paid Keaton fifty thousand dollars for the rights to make *The Buster Keaton Story* (1957). He used the money to purchase his beloved ranch in Woodland Hills, California, where he raised chickens, grew an orchard, tinkered with his Rube Goldberg-like gadgets, played cards, and lived out his last years happily with Eleanor.

Top: Buster, Jacques Tati, and Harold Lloyd, 1959.

Below: With Raymond Rohauer en route to the Venice Film Festival, September 1965. Photograph by Chris K. Economakis.

Opposite: Buster and Eleanor Keaton at their Woodland Hills ranch, c. 1956. Photograph by Charles Schneider.

Buster Keaton died on February 1, 1966, at the age of seventy, at his home in Woodland Hills. He was buried at Forest Lawn Memorial Park-Hollywood Hills with a rosary in one pocket and a deck of cards in the other. "That way," remembered Eleanor, "wherever he was going, he was ready."

* * *

In the 1920s, Buster Keaton stood a distant third to Charles Chaplin and Harold Lloyd in both box office receipts and public adoration. Owing in large part to the work of his third wife, Eleanor Keaton, by the time of his death, Keaton's reputation had been restored to the rank of the great film comedians, alongside Chaplin and Lloyd. In 1995, the centenary of his birth, Keaton tributes and film festivals were held all over the world.

Buster Keaton's comedy endures not just because he had a face that belongs on Mount Rushmore, at once hauntingly immovable and classically American, but because that face was attached to one of the most gifted actors and directors who ever graced the screen. Evolved from the knockabout upbringing of the vaudeville stage, Keaton's comedy is a whirlwind of hilarious, technically precise, adroitly executed, and surprising gags, very often set against a backdrop of visually stunning set pieces and locations—all this masked behind his unflinching, stoic veneer.

Eleanor Keaton died on October 19, 1998, at the age of eighty after battling lung cancer, the same disease that killed her husband. This book is Eleanor Keaton's final tribute to the man she adored, the artist she admired, and the legend she devoted her adult life to advancing. The following pages reveal the Buster Keaton she knew, told through loving remembrances and through cherished photographs, many reproduced from her personal collection.

Buster and Eleanor Keaton at their Woodland Hills ranch in 1965. Photograph by Roddy McDowall.

Opposite: Buster in 1955.

MY LIFE WITH BUSTER *by Eleanor Keaton*

Buster and me at Heathrow airport, London, 1959.

MY LIFE WITH BUSTER BEGAN WITH A DISAGREEMENT OVER A GAME OF CARDS.

In 1938, I was working at M-G-M, where I had a contract all through the war years, as a dancer in musicals. I was there until the "purge" when everybody—writers, directors, actors—was let go; television had come in and they stopped making musicals.

At M-G-M, all the kids used to play cards during the long waits between takes. I had played card games of all kinds—go fish, gin rummy, pinochle—but one day, I saw some people playing bridge. I became fascinated with the game and wanted to learn it. Art Whitney, one of the dancers, volunteered to take me to a place where there was "always a bridge game all day every day and a good teacher." Whitney was Harry Keaton's best friend; the bridge game was at Buster's house on Queensbury Drive in Cheviot Hills; and the "good teacher" was Buster.

Before long I was going to Buster's house twice a week to play bridge, whenever I was not working or Buster was not working. At first, I just watched and learned the game. Back in the 1920s, Buster used to play for a quarter a point, which can turn into a lot of money. Some nights up to three thousand dollars changed hands. Buster's mother, Myra, his brother, Harry "Jingles," and his sister, Louise, lived with him in the 1930s, and all played cards. It seemed like a bridge game was being played all the time in that house. After a while, I felt confident enough to join in, but not without making a lot of mistakes.

For months, there was nothing between Buster and me. I was just a pair of hands to hold cards. I had been playing in the game for about six months when someone yelled at me for playing a wrong card or for bidding wrong. I got angry and yelled back. That was the first time, Buster told me later, that he noticed me. I guess that is when my life with Buster really began.

At the time, Buster's lady friend was Dorothy Sebastian, his leading lady in *Spite Marriage*. She was also a regular at the bridge games. Although Buster had begun to feel something for me, he did not dare break it off with Dorothy. He was worried it would cause too much trauma for her. Instead, he hatched a plan. We used to go as a group to the wrestling matches at the Hollywood Legion Stadium. One evening, Buster invited one of the good-looking wrestlers and his manager over for dinner. That was all it took. Dorothy fell for the wrestler, and Buster was clear to date me.

Our first date was at Earl Carroll's supper club Vanities on Sunset Boulevard across from the Palladium in Hollywood. That was the first time we had ever been alone. Our typical date, however, was doing what Buster loved—playing bridge at his house. We did not go out very often. We dated a full year before I asked Buster to marry me. We had gone to Palm Springs for New Year's Eve. After midnight, while Buster and I were dancing to the orchestra, I looked at him and asked, "When are we going to get married?" And he replied, "Tomorrow?" I said, "Well, not really quite that quick." He suggested that May 31st would be a good day: "That's easy for me to remember because that's when I was married the first time." I said something to the effect of, "Up yours!" and we settled on two days earlier, May 29th.

Buster caught smiling on our wedding day, May 29, 1940, at Los Angeles City Hall. Judge Edward R. Brand is on the right.

No one thought the marriage would last. Even before we were married, several of Buster's friends (such as his doctor, Jack Shuman, and A. C. Freud) sat me down and tried to talk me out of going through with it. I was a polite girl, so I listened to them. Then I did exactly as I pleased, and Buster and I were married on May 29, 1940.

We were married at City Hall in downtown Los Angeles. My sister, Jane, was my maid of honor and Leo Morrison, Buster's agent, was his best man. Eddie Brand, who was Harry Brand's (Buster's former publicity agent and production supervisor on *College* and *Steamboat Bill, Jr.*) son, had just been made a judge, and he performed the ceremony. It was his

first wedding, and he was very nervous. Looking back on it, the whole thing was very funny. Eddie had the shakes so bad you could hear his papers rattling. When we first arrived and started to get organized, Eddie tried to marry Buster to my mother (she was nearer his age than I was). Once we did get started, the entire fire department unexpectedly came up out of the basement. Everybody except Eddie, Buster, and me ran to the window to see where the fire was. Eddie called me "Eleanor Morris," instead of my real name, "Eleanor Norris." He also switched back and forth between "Do you, Joseph Frank?" (Buster's real name) and "Do you, Buster?" After it was all over, I never was certain whether we were ever married at all.

We left that afternoon for our honeymoon, a fishing trip on June Lake. Buster was making two-reel comedy shorts for Columbia at the time, so we squeezed in a week between shorts. The rest of our guests stayed behind at Buster's house, where our St. Bernard puppy, Elmer II, ate our wedding cake and was sick for three days. Quite a beginning for twenty-six years of marriage!

Before I began dating Buster, I had never seen a Buster Keaton film. I knew that he had been a star in the 1920s, but I have no memory of seeing any of his films as a child. My experience with movies in the 1920s was an occasional big feature such as *The King of Kings* (1927) and Saturday matinees when mostly shorts were shown. I watched Laurel and Hardy shorts and Charley Chase, but no Buster Keaton. The first time I ever saw a Keaton film, Buster himself showed it to me. It was before we were married, and the film was *Battling Butler*, the only film of which a print could be easily located, for whatever reason. The two of us watched it while Ernie Orsatti, an old friend of Buster's, projected the film in the little projection room at the Orsatti talent agency.

I have often thought that Buster and I were loners who found each other. Without being conscious of it at the time of our marriage, I suppose Buster was a kind of father figure to me (after we married, I even called him "Father"). My own father, Ralph Norris, who worked as an electrician at Warner Brothers, was

Buster and me arriving in Southampton, England, aboard the MAURENTANIA, *June 14, 1951.*

killed in an accident at the studio when I was ten. After his death, I grew up fast. When I started dating, I had no interest in men my age. It was like taking out a child. Buster was different from any other man I had known.

Buster and I lived in Cheviot Hills until the outbreak of World War II. At that time, everyone was worried about a possible attack by the Japanese. Buster did not want his mother living alone, and when we could not persuade her to move in with us, we sold the Cheviot Hills house and moved into her home on Victoria Avenue. We stayed there until 1956 when we bought the ranch in Woodland Hills.

Buster and I met Raymond Rohauer, his future business partner, at the Coronet Theater on La Cienega Boulevard in Los Angeles in the summer of 1954. Raymond ran a film society that was showing *The General*, and Buster wanted me to see the film. After the screening, we told Raymond that we had 35mm prints of some of Buster's silent films stored in our garage. Raymond later came to the house to see what we had, and this led to a business arrangement whereby Raymond would preserve the films and clear the rights to exhibit them in exchange for fifty percent of the profits. About the same time, James Mason, who then owned Buster's Italian Villa, found many 35mm prints of Buster's silent films in an aban-

doned shed on the estate. Buster had used the shed as an editing room, and the prints had been untouched for over twenty years. These prints were eventually given to Raymond, who preserved them as well. Raymond spent seventeen years and lots of money to reclaim copyrights and preserve the films before he made a profit. If it were not for the efforts of Raymond Rohauer, many of Buster's silent films might not exist at all.

An important acknowledgment of Buster's work in silent films was given to him in November 1955 by the George Eastman House in Rochester, New York. A museum and research center of photography and film, Eastman House gave gold plaques (called the George Award) to those who had made an important contribution to the advancement of motion pictures between 1915 and 1925. Buster considered it more prestigious than an Oscar because it was a one-time award. He enjoyed the event in Rochester and seeing old friends and fellow recipients such as Harold Lloyd and Mary Pickford. He was drinking more than usual, and he had a bad chest cold and was coughing a lot. Soon after we returned to California, Buster ruptured a vein in his esophagus and started hemor-

Buster and me on the liner QUEEN ELIZABETH II *upon our arrival in New York City, October 27, 1952.*

rhaging. I took him to the U.S. Veteran's General Hospital where he almost died. The doctor told me, "if he lives five days I'll let you know what I think." It took twenty-seven hours to stop the bleeding, and Buster had to have blood transfusions. By the time his condition stabilized, he looked like an octopus with all the tubes coming out of him. He was in the hospital for a total of four weeks. Smoking two packs of cigarettes a day surely landed him in the hospital, but alcohol contributed to his condition as well.

A lot has been made of Buster's drinking, but in reality it only went on for about five years, from 1931 to 1935. Buster had been dry for about three years before I met him. He had occasional drinking binges during the first fifteen years of our marriage. But after his health scare in 1955, he never had more than a beer or two before dinner every night. That was his "cocktail."

As a result of his television work and roles in films such as *Sunset Boulevard, Limelight,* and *Around the World in Eighty Days,* the film industry took an interest in Buster again. Paramount Pictures paid Buster fifty thousand dollars for the screen rights to his life story, with him agreeing also to work as technical adviser on the film. The director was Sidney Sheldon, the best-selling novelist, and Donald O'Connor was cast as Buster. For eight weeks Buster helped Donald with the comedy sequences, and he had a wonderful time working with him. However, the finished film, *The Buster Keaton Story* (1957), was awful. Buster and I attended a studio preview screening, and we felt like crawling out on our hands and knees. It was outrageous the way they fictionalized his life and magnified his drinking.

The wonderful thing that happened as a result of

The Buster Keaton Story was that it enabled us to buy a six-room house on one and a half acres of land located at 22612 Sylvan Street in Woodland Hills, California. We moved into the "ranch," as Buster called it, in June 1956. Buster had a swimming pool built, and, since he wanted to raise chickens, he built a chicken coop, which looked like a schoolhouse, behind the house. Woodland Hills, which is north of Hollywood in the San Fernando Valley, did not have many residents at that time. As he was the only famous homeowner in the area, Buster was named honorary mayor of Woodland Hills.

The house in Woodland Hills was something we both adored, and when Buster was not working we enjoyed being at the "ranch." We liked having friends over for barbecues and bridge games, and we treasured our quiet moments alone. Buster had a vegetable garden and fruit trees and would spend hours watering them. He liked collecting walnuts from our nine walnut trees and enjoyed finding four-leaf clovers, something he had a talent for spotting quickly since childhood. He had a dozen Rhode Island Red hens that he called his "girls." He gave them names like Zsa Zsa, Marilyn, and Ava. He had a rooster too. Buster swam every day and enjoyed cooking, playing his ukulele, and watching television, which fascinated him. Buster loved trains. His favorite film of his own was *The General*, and he had a toy train that ran on tracks around our picnic table and back into the

Grandpa Buster joins grandchildren Jim, Mike, and Melissa Talmadge in a children's swimming pool at home on Victoria Avenue, 1952.

garage. The cars were big enough to hold a Coca-Cola or a hot dog, and Buster used to drive food around to our guests whenever we had a picnic. And, of course, he loved to play bridge for hours on end.

Buster and me playing in the snow after a blizzard in Rochester, New York, where Buster received the George Award at the first Festival of Film Artists held by the George Eastman House in November 1955.

Buster was always working on gags, no matter where we were—at home, on the road, wherever something came to him. Once after dinner on the *Ile de France* ocean liner, while people were dancing, I noticed Buster was gone. I looked around and finally found him outside in the foyer standing in front of a huge window, wiping a tiny spot with a handkerchief. I watched him carefully clean the glass, admire his work, and put his handkerchief away. Of course, there was no glass in the window. Buster was always doing things like that.

At home, it was the same. Buster would be in the den, sitting on the floor, working something out in his head. That was the way he "wrote." He never put anything down on paper; he just kept it all in his head. No matter what the project was—television, commercials, movies—that is the way he worked. He would put it all together in his head and, instead of handing someone a script, he would simply explain

39

Feeding the chickens outside the coop Buster built at our Woodland Hills ranch, c. 1956. Buster thought every chicken coop he ever saw was an eyesore, so he built one that did not look like a chicken coop. It looked like a little schoolhouse. Photograph by Charles Schneider.

to them how the scene or the gag should go. I suppose that is the way he worked in the silent days. Somebody like Buster does not change the way he operates so easily.

As a result of the inaccuracies and distortions in *The Buster Keaton Story*, Buster wanted to set the record straight with an autobiography. Writer Charles Samuels met us in Las Vegas in 1958, where Buster and I were performing at the Desert Inn in a show called *Newcomers of 1928*, to work with Buster on his book. Charlie took an apartment next to us, and they spent practically all day every day for eight weeks working. When *Newcomers of 1928* ended, Charlie came back with us to Woodland Hills and worked with Buster for another three weeks until he was finished. Charlie did not use a tape recorder; Buster talked and Charlie typed. The finished book was published by Doubleday in January 1960 as *My Wonderful World of Slapstick*. It is a simple, straightforward book with a title indicating Buster's devotion to his work.

Since the publication of *My Wonderful World of Slapstick*, a lot of academics have written about Buster's films and his so-called stoic approach to filmmaking. I do not think Buster ever knew what these people were talking about. Someone once asked Buster what was his "philosophy," or what he was thinking when he made a certain scene in a film. Buster answered simply, "To be funny." What better "philosophy" is there than that?

One of the most meaningful events of Buster's last years was receiving an honorary Academy Award in April 1960. Although I knew he was going to receive the award, Buster did not. He thought the only reason we were invited to attend the Academy Awards was as a result of his performing as comic relief with Robert Cummings in an Oscar show taped at the Hollywood Brown Derby just before the awards ceremony at the Pantages Theater. Buster received his award at the Governors' Ball held at the Beverly Hilton Hotel after the telecast. The citation on the statuette reads, "To Buster Keaton for his unique talents which brought immortal comedies to the screen." Tears were in his eyes when Buster reached the podium to receive the award, and all he managed to say was "thank you."

The most frequent question I am asked is, "Did Buster ever smile?" Because he rarely changed his deadpan expression, people just cannot visualize him smiling. And, if there was a camera around, you would never catch him smiling. He thought it was bad for his image if he was caught smiling or laughing for the camera. But if there was no camera around, and if something funny happened, he smiled. If it was really funny, he laughed. Buster had a wonderful laugh.

Buster loved to make audiences laugh, but rarely attended a screening of his own films to hear the laughter firsthand. He was actually very shy and deathly afraid of crowds. At a 1962 retrospective showing of his films at the Cinémathèque Française in Paris, when the lights went up and he saw a large group coming toward him, he took off in a panic up the aisle as fast as he could run. When I finally

Buster, dressed as a waiter (shown here at the table of Jimmy McHugh and Jane Russell), stole the show at the Hollywood Brown Derby in a live half-hour television program that immediately preceded the Academy of Motion Picture Arts and Sciences' third Oscar telecast in April, 1960. Buster had no idea at the time he would be receiving an honorary Oscar later that evening.

caught up to him, he was in an alley, vomiting. Also in 1962 we went on a tour of twenty German cities with *The General.* Buster drove a special train, made to look like the *General* of the film, into each city stop for publicity purposes. We were supposed to go to a screening of *The General* in Munich. Buster chickened out and decided to stay back at the hotel, so Raymond Rohauer and I went to the opening night alone. While we were standing in the lobby with the theater manager, all of a sudden we heard this scream of laughter. I thought to myself, "What is that laughter all about? *The General* is not that funny at the beginning." Raymond and I ran up the stairs to our seats in the balcony and discovered what all the racket was about. It was Buster's short, *Cops,* which they had decided to show before *The General,* and the audience just loved it. When we went back to the hotel later that night, we told Buster about the audience's reaction. He was very pleased, although he

Buster's train set at our ranch in Woodland Hills, September 1959. The toy train came out from the kitchen on a track that ran the length of the pool alongside the fence, and curved over a trestle to a round table. We used it to deliver soft drinks and hot dogs to guests. As Buster said, "It saves having waiters." Photograph by James Karen.

could not bear to go to the theater to hear it himself.

Buster and I flew to Europe in the summer of 1965 to make two feature films. The first was *War Italian Style,* the best-forgotten low-budget American International Pictures feature with Buster playing a Nazi general. During the six-week shoot of *War Italian Style,* Raymond Rohauer arranged for Buster to appear briefly at the Venice Film Festival. Before we left for Europe, Buster had been given a complete physical and was diagnosed with bronchitis. By the time we arrived in Venice in early September, his breathing was unusually heavy; he was tired, sick to his stomach, and weak. The tremendous reception he received in Venice seemed to reinvigorate him somewhat for *A Funny Thing Happened on the Way to the Forum,* which was shot just outside of Madrid in September. It was directed by Richard Lester, and Buster enjoyed working with Zero Mostel, Jack Gilford, and Phil Silvers. He was unable to do anything that required much physical exertion, and a double had to be used for the long shots of Buster running. The weather during the three weeks we

With Bimbo the elephant in a photo shoot for a U.S. Steel advertisement, 1964. Photograph by Sid Avery.

houses or yachts, just three square meals a day. That was the most he ever said about me, but I knew what he meant. Whenever I would get all gussied up for a premiere or formal event, and I would come into the room wearing a long gown with my hair done and my make-up fixed, all ready to go, I would ask him, "How do I look?" And he would say, "You'll do." I knew that was his best compliment.

More than thirty years after his death, I can still say that Buster Keaton was the kindest, gentlest man I have ever known. Everybody who knew him loved him, and I suppose that somewhere along the line I just joined the rest of the group. I think that these qualities come through in his films, and I trust that these pictures will remind everyone of what a wonderful soul he was.

Left: Buster was the subject of THIS IS YOUR LIFE, *which originally aired nationally on April 3, 1957. Ralph Edwards, host of the series, watches as I adjust Buster's tie.*

Below: Buster and me with our 180-pound Saint Bernard, Elmer III (whom we called "Junior"), at our Woodland Hills ranch, 1965.

were in Madrid was unseasonably cold, and it rained most of the time. I looked after Buster, who was weak from what we thought was exhaustion. However, he was determined to go directly to Canada, as planned, to make *The Scribe*, an industrial safety film.

Buster became so short of breath that he had to be given oxygen on the airplane all the way home and taken in a wheelchair from the plane to the car after completing work on *The Scribe*. I took him straight to the hospital where he was diagnosed with lung cancer. He had half of one lung functioning. The doctor said he would live anywhere from one week to three months.

No one ever told Buster he had lung cancer for fear of scaring him, but he knew he was ill. We played bridge until five o'clock on January 30, 1966, the night we took him to the hospital. He came home the next day, and in the morning of February 1, 1966, the cancer that had started in his lungs from a lifetime of smoking and had metastasized to his brain took his life. I have missed him every day since.

Whether at home or on the road, I was almost always with him during our twenty-eight years together. I was his babysitter, secretary, bookkeeper, mother—whatever he needed. Buster once told my mother that I did not want diamonds or pearls or

Buster Keaton

Remembered

Eleanor Keaton and Jeffrey Vance

BUSTER WAS A CHILD OF THE theater from birth. He was born barely offstage between shows on October 4, 1895, in Piqua, Kansas. His parents were both medicine-show entertainers. His father was Joe Keaton, a comedian and eccentric dancer with a great pair of long legs, who was known for his hitch kick, a high kick that he performed in later years in Buster's films. His mother, Myra, sang and played several musical instruments. He was christened Joseph Frank Keaton, as five earlier generations of first-born sons before him had been called Joseph Keaton.

Buster's father was born Joseph Hallie Keaton in 1867, in Prairie Creek Township, near Terre Haute, Indiana. The Keaton forebears were Quakers of Irish and Scottish descent. Joe, the son of a gristmill owner, was a dreamer and a drifter who supported himself with menial jobs. According to Keaton family legend, the twenty-six-year-old Joe participated in the Oklahoma land rush of 1893, staking a homestead claim near Perry, Oklahoma, which he gave over to his father and mother.

Buster's mother was born Myra Edith Cutler in 1877 in Modale, Iowa. Her father, Frank L. Cutler, owned the Cutler Comedy Company, a traveling medicine show. Medicine shows, a form of entertainment popular in the nineteenth century, were usually open-air revues that combined simple singing, dancing, and recitation with the selling of quack medicine (called "Kickapoo elixir," it promised to do just about anything and everything), which was the show's only source of revenue. Myra, of English and German parentage, performed in her father's medicine show, where she played piano, double bass, and the cornet.

Joe Keaton joined the Cutler Comedy Company, working as both a bouncer for the show and knockabout comedian. He and Myra soon fell in love, and

Joseph Frank Keaton at six months of age. Photograph taken in Davenport, Iowa, on April 4, 1896.

the couple quietly eloped and were married on May 31, 1894 in Lincoln, Nebraska. Myra's family was not happy with her choice of a husband, and the newlyweds were not welcomed back into the Cutler Comedy Company. Joe and Myra went on their own, working in various rival medicine shows.

It was while they were performing with the Mohawk Indian Medicine Company on a one-night stand in Piqua, Kansas, that Buster was born in the home of Jacob and Barbara Haen, whose house was nearest to the church hall where Joe and Myra were performing and where the expectant mother went into labor. Myra stayed with the Haens for two weeks after Buster's birth, after which both mother and child rejoined the show.

In 1897 Joe and Myra found work in a traveling medicine show called the California Concert Company with Harry Houdini, who would become the great escape artist. Buster always said that it was Houdini who gave him his nickname, "Buster," after seeing him take a fall down a flight of stairs unhurt at the small hotel where they were staying. "That's sure a buster!" Houdini proclaimed. "That's a good name for him," responded Joe. There are several variations to this story, but Buster was consistent in his version.[1] Whether it was Houdini or some other family friend who gave Buster the name he would use for the rest of his life, one thing appears to be certain: Buster was the first person to use it as a nickname.

Buster underneath his father at the time of Buster's first stage appearance at nine months of age, July 1896.

Previously, "buster" was only vaudeville slang for a stage fall. The name Buster Keaton even predates R. F. Outcault's "Buster Brown" comic strip.

Joe and Myra kept the infant Buster in an open costume trunk offstage while they were performing. As soon as he was able to crawl, Buster wanted to join his parents onstage. His first appearance was at nine months, when Buster managed to get out of the trunk and crawl onto the stage to join his father, who was performing a black-face monologue. Buster's entrance received more applause than the mono-

logue. At eleven months of age, Buster nearly suffocated when the lid of the costume trunk (which served as both playpen and crib) was accidentally closed by a stagehand while Joe and Myra were working onstage. Buster's early life was fraught with such accidents. The most adventurous day of his childhood took place in July 1898 in Kansas, when he was just twenty months old. Buster wandered out into the backyard of the boardinghouse where the family was staying. He stuck his right index finger into a nearby clothes wringer and crushed it. The local doctor was quickly summoned, and he amputated Buster's finger at the first joint. He cried himself to sleep, but as soon as he woke up a few hours later he was outside again, trying to knock a peach loose from a tree using a rock. The rock hit his head, and the doctor was called again to sew three stitches in his scalp. Finally, that evening, Buster was awakened by the sound of a cyclone. He went to the open window of the second-story bedroom to investigate and was literally sucked out by the storm and whirled away into the air about one block from the house. A man saw Buster, grabbed him, and carried him to safety. Joe and Myra decided quickly afterward that it would be safer if Buster was onstage where they could keep an eye on him.

Joe and Myra soon left medicine shows for small-time vaudeville. The act they created, The Two Keatons, had little to set it apart from other knock-about comedy acts and was notable only for the slapstick Joe would perform on and around a prop table (Joe billed himself in advertisements as "The Man with the Table"). The act received bookings, but it was not a great success. All that changed with Buster's professional debut at William Lee Dockstader's Wonderland Theater in Wilmington, Delaware, the week of October 15, 1900, when The Two Keatons became The Three Keatons. Dockstader encouraged Joe and Myra to put Buster into the act, so Joe improvised some comic roughhousing with five-year-old Buster.

The act that was improvised in Delaware became the standard situation used for the entire career of

At age four, 1899.

The Three Keatons in vaudeville: Joe would try to show the audience how to bring up children correctly by making them "mind." Buster was the high-spirited child, and Joe was the pestered parent. Buster would throw a basketball at Joe, trip him up and then step on top of him, and hit him with a broom. Joe would then retaliate by throwing Buster around the length of the stage, through chairs, tables, scenery, and sometimes into the audience. Buster's stage coat had a harness built inside it with a suitcase handle between the shoulders, and Joe would pick him up by the handle and throw him with accuracy and precision. Myra did not participate in any knockabout comedy. She played the alto saxophone or some other instrument between the antics of father and son.

The nightly act was never the same, and it never had a script. The Three Keatons performed in theaters that had two shows a day, and the act was constantly evolving during performances and was measured against the reactions of the audience.

The success of The Three Keatons was based on Buster's ability to take spectacular falls unscathed. Buster had learned stage acrobatics and comic falls by watching his father and other vaudeville acts. He always maintained that because he started performing at an early age, his body control was completely instinctual. He also quickly developed an instinct for comic invention, technique, timing of comedy rou-

tines, and what made people laugh, which would serve him well when he started making films.

The Three Keatons quickly became one of the funniest and most talked-about acts in vaudeville. As grotesque comedians, Joe and Buster were costumed more as clowns than the stereotypical immigrant Irishmen they resembled; Buster was dressed as a perfect miniature of Joe, complete with bald-headed red wig, Irish beard, baggy trousers, and slapshoes. Audiences did not take the physical danger of the knockabout comedy seriously because they could see that no one was being hurt. A clever public relations representative for The Three Keatons, Joe created a public image of Buster as a tough kid who survived hotel fires, cyclones, and train wrecks. He was nicknamed by Joe "The Human Mop"—so called because Joe would literally mop up the stage with him—and "The Little Boy Who Can't Be Damaged."

It was also during his years in vaudeville that Buster began to develop the stone-faced manner he later used in films. Joe and Buster both realized that Buster received more laughs from the audience when he was serious. If Buster started to smile or laugh during the act, Joe would say, "Face! Face!" which

The Three Keatons in New York, 1900. Photograph by Feinberg.

meant he should become deadpan. As Buster later remembered in his autobiography, *My Wonderful World of Slapstick*:

> *One of the first things I noticed was that whenever I smiled or let the audience suspect how much I was enjoying myself they didn't seem to laugh as much as usual. I guess people just never do expect any human mop, dishrag, beanbag, or football to be pleased by what is being done to him. At any rate it was on purpose that I started looking miserable, humiliated, hounded, and haunted, bedeviled, bewildered, and at my wit's end.[2]*

By 1902 The Three Keatons was considered the roughest knockabout comedy act in the history of the stage. They became a second headliner, an important act in vaudeville. However, with success, The Three Keatons attracted the attention of the Society for the Prevention of Cruelty to Children, also known as the Gerry Society, a private organization formed to stop the exploitation of children. The family was constantly being summoned before authorities who were convinced Buster was being abused. Buster later recalled:

> *The law read that a child can't do acrobatics, can't walk a wire, can't juggle—a lot of those things—but there was nothing said in the law that you can't kick him in the face or throw him through a piece of scenery. On that technicality, we were allowed to work, although we'd get called into court every other week.*
>
> *Once they took me to the mayor of New York City, into his private office, with the city physicians here in New York, and they stripped me to examine me for broken bones and bruises. Finding none, the mayor*

Top: *The Three Keatons in San Francisco, 1901.*

Left: *Family portrait of The Three Keatons, c. 1905.*

Opposite: *The Four Keatons: Joe, Myra, Buster, and Harry "Jingles," c. 1907.*

gave me permission to work. The next time it hap-
pened, the following year, they sent me to Albany,
to the governor of the state. Then in his office, same
thing: state physicians examined me, and they
gave me permission to work in New York state.
Massachusetts thought I was a midget.[3]

The Gerry Society never found any evidence of child abuse in Buster's case. If they had, he would not have been allowed to perform onstage. However, accusations that Buster was an abused child have been put forward by several biographers, despite Buster's account and all evidence to the contrary.

According to Buster, his years in vaudeville were some of the happiest days of his life. In his silent comedies he used his vaudeville routines and fre-

quently employed his father to appear in his films, which suggests that he liked his father and what he did in vaudeville.

The unfortunate aspect of Buster's life in vaudeville was that he never went to school or had the opportunity to have lasting friendships with children his own age. Although Buster had a tutor for a time who taught him in the mornings, he received most of his schooling from Myra. He spent only one day of his life—when he was six years old—in a Jersey City, New Jersey, public school room. He was expelled on his very first day for answering the teacher's questions with punch lines he had learned from the stage. He was very self-conscious in later years about never having gone to school and felt inferior to most people as a result. Buster's shyness around people outside his

Joe and Buster proudly show off a fish caught in Muskegon Lake,
with Louise and Harry "Jingles" along for the ride, c. 1910.

immediate circle or show business had to do in large measure with his stunted childhood.

The Three Keatons soon became four and later five Keatons when Myra bore Harry (after Houdini) Stanley Keaton in 1904 (who was nicknamed "Jingles" because of the noise he made with his toys) and Louise Dresser (after Louise Dresser, a vaudevillian who later acted in silent films) Keaton in 1906. Buster's younger brother and sister joined the act for a short time, and the entire family paraded onto the stage dressed in identical costumes. However, Jingles and Louise never became a lasting part of the act. Buster was the star and the family's main support. As soon as they were old enough, Jingles and Louise were sent to boarding schools in Michigan while Buster and his parents continued to tour in vaudeville.

The family did not normally work in the summer. For eight years, from 1909 to 1917, the entire family spent summers together in Bluffton, Michigan, an actors' colony adjacent to Muskegon, where many vaudeville performers owned summer homes. The family would look back on this period as the happiest summers of their lives. The cottage they owned was called "Jingle's Jungle." There they would spend their summers fishing and swimming on Lake Muskegon, playing cards, and socializing with fellow vaudevillians. During these summers Buster played baseball like other kids and dressed his age (on tour in vaudeville he had to dress like an adult and act like one to

With a neighbor's dog at the Actor's Colony at Bluffton, Michigan, c. 1911.

avoid problems with the Gerry Society). The popular hangout was a tavern called Pascoe's Place, which was famous for its beer and fried perch.

As Buster grew up, Joe was unable to throw him around. The act was still rough, with kicks, chases, and hitting each other with brooms. Buster developed new routines in which he would swirl a basketball at the end of a rope at Joe or pull a broom out of a knothole in the stage floor. Buster also began incorporating parodies of the other acts on the bill. During this period he also developed a love of parodying popular songs, for which he had a reputation for the rest of his life.

The success of the act could have gone on indefinitely. However, Joe's drinking steadily increased as he became older, and he found it more difficult to do the physically demanding act with Buster. His alcoholism began to impair an act that depended on precision timing, and his abusive behavior on- and offstage soon alienated Joe from employers as well as his family. In January 1917, Buster broke up the act to make a new start on his own. Although he was just twenty-one years of age, he was a veteran of the theater with many opportunities before him. He quickly found work with the Shuberts in the musical comedy revue, *The Passing Show*, at the Winter Garden Theater in New York, but he never made it to the first rehearsal. He would instead go into the movies, working with Roscoe "Fatty" Arbuckle.

PARAMOUNT-ARBUCKLE COMEDY

CHLOROFORM

ROSCOE "FATTY" ARBUCKLE
IN
"OH DOCTOR!"

"PATIENCE, PATIENT" SAID FATTY CUTTINGLY.

BUSTER HAD ENJOYED MOTION pictures from his earliest days in vaudeville, when short films were shown as "chasers," the last presentation in an evening of vaudeville entertainment. However, two films in particular, Mack Sennett's *Tillie's Punctured Romance* (1914), the first comedy feature, and D. W. Griffith's *The Birth of a Nation* (1915), greatly impressed him. During all the Keatons' years in vaudeville, Joe Keaton had nothing but contempt for films. When newspaper magnate William Randolph Hearst proposed in 1913 to bring The Three Keatons to the screen in a series of shorts based on the George McManus comic strip "Bringing Up Father," Joe responded, "We work

Above: Buster, an unidentified player, and Arbuckle in a scene that either was deleted or does not survive in extant prints of OH, DOCTOR! *(1917).*

for years perfecting an act, and you want to show it, a nickel a head, on a dirty sheet?"[4]

In March 1917, ten days before he was to start rehearsals for *The Passing Show*, Buster was walking down Broadway when he met Lou Anger, an acquaintance from vaudeville, who was with Roscoe Arbuckle, the screen comedian. Arbuckle invited Buster to visit the Colony Studio, where he was about to begin a series of two-reel comedies for producer Joseph M. Schenck. Buster gladly accepted the invitation.

Roscoe Arbuckle was known as "Fatty" to the public, so called because of his large size. He too had been a stage performer, but started in motion pictures in 1909 for the Selig Polyscope Company and joined Keystone in 1913 as a Keystone Kop for comedy producer Mack Sennett. By 1917, Joe Schenck had lured Arbuckle away from Sennett with a contract that gave him a higher salary and his own company—which Arbuckle named the Comique Film Corporation—where he had greater creative control over the films. Arbuckle was, at the time, second only to Chaplin among film comedians in world popularity.

Buster visited Arbuckle at the Colony Studio at 318 East 48th Street, between Second and Third Avenues. The studio was a converted livery stable leased by Schenck, where the films of dramatic actress Norma Talmadge (Schenck's wife), Norma's sister Constance Talmadge, and Arbuckle were made. Buster was invited that day to play a scene in a film, which became his first film, *The Butcher Boy*

(1917). In his very first film sequence, Buster walks into a rural grocery store and immediately improvises with a barrel full of brooms—he was an expert at improvising comedy with brooms, as this was a prop frequently used in his vaudeville act. He buys a bucket of molasses from Arbuckle and becomes completely stuck in the gooey substance. It is a classic comedy sequence, and Buster remembered it with great affection, later restaging it for his television debut in 1949 and performing it on subsequent television appearances.

Arbuckle was impressed with Buster. His debut performance was perfect and done without a single retake. He was especially impressed by how well Buster reacted to being hit by a sack of flour, which put his head where his feet had been. Arbuckle saw immediately that Buster was not only a great comic actor but also a storehouse of vaudeville routines who could do spectacular comic pratfalls. He invited Buster to join the company at a salary of forty dollars per week. Buster canceled his contract with *The Passing Show* at two hundred fifty dollars a week to work with Arbuckle. Buster left the stage, as he was immediately captivated by the possibilities of motion

Buster (far right) makes his screen debut in THE BUTCHER BOY *(1917). Al St. John wields the pitchfork with Roscoe Arbuckle on the receiving end. Leading lady Josephine Stevens is at center.*

Alice Mann, Arbuckle, and Buster in CONEY ISLAND *(1917).*

Buster, Al St. John, Arbuckle, and Alice Lake in A COUNTRY HERO *(1917).*

Buster, Arbuckle, and Al St. John in OUT WEST *(1918).*

pictures, particularly the technical aspects; films immediately did away with the physical limitations of theater.

For his first screen appearance, Buster kept the deadpan expression he had developed in vaudeville. It became his trademark, later giving rise to nicknames such as "The Great Stone Face." Amazingly, the porkpie hat he would use for the next fifty years was

first worn in *The Butcher Boy.* Although Buster would frequently experiment with both laughing and crying broadly in the Arbuckle films, he most often reacts in the deadpan manner for which he is known.

The titles of the comedies Buster made with Arbuckle—*The Butcher Boy, Oh, Doctor!* (1917), *Coney Island* (1917), *Out West* (1918), *The Bell Boy* (1918), *The Cook* (1918)—indicate Arbuckle's working

Above: Buster and Arbuckle on location in California's San Gabriel Mountains for MOONSHINE *(1918).*

Opposite: Alice Lake, Arbuckle, and Buster (above) in THE BELL BOY *(1918).*

method. Arbuckle chose a particular role or setting, and gags evolved from the premise. The Arbuckle films are pure slapstick, rich in gags that contain as their focal point Arbuckle himself, who had a warm and charming comic personality that captivated audiences. Despite his large size, he was very graceful and able to perform great comic falls.

Buster and Arbuckle had an instant rapport both on and off the screen; they shared a generous nature, a love of practical jokes, and a devotion to their work. Buster first played second-string comedy roles, along

with Al St. John (an original member of the Keystone Kops and Arbuckle's nephew). He soon graduated to the role of Arbuckle's comedy partner, both in front of and behind the camera. Buster began to be his assistant director and contributed many of the gags, along with gagmen Herbert Warren, Jean Havez, and Clyde Bruckman. Arbuckle became Buster's mentor, and Buster learned from Arbuckle the technical side of filmmaking, everything from setting up shots, to operating the camera, to editing film.

According to Buster, he and Arbuckle had only

Arbuckle, Al St. John, Buster, and Arbuckle's dog, Luke, on the beach in Santa Monica, California, c. 1918.

Opposite top: Buster, Arbuckle, Kate Price, and Alice Lake in GOOD NIGHT, NURSE! (1918).

Opposite bottom: Buster and Arbuckle in BACK STAGE (1919). Also pictured are Molly Malone (far left), Buddy Post (large man in top hat), and Jack Coogan (in background wearing a straw hat).

one friendly disagreement in all their years of friendship. Arbuckle maintained that the average mentality of movie audiences was twelve years. Buster disagreed. He felt that anyone making pictures who believed that movie audiences had a twelve-year-old mind would not be in the motion-picture business very long.

Arbuckle's Comique company soon moved from the Colony Studio to the Biograph Studio at 796 East 176th Street in the Bronx, and in October 1917 moved to California. They rented space at the Horkheimer Brothers' Balboa Amusement Producing Company on Sixth and Alamitos Streets in Long Beach and later used the Henry Lehrman Studio in Culver City.

Buster had made twelve films with Arbuckle when World War I broke out. He was inducted into the army in June 1918 and assigned to Company C of the 159th Infantry, 40th (nicknamed "Sunshine") Division. He left for France in August and served for about four months before the war ended. However, he stayed overseas for nearly eight months. He worked as a cryptographer, but he mainly entertained the troops. His most popular act was his "Princess Rajah" snake-dance routine, based on a vaudeville act that had once played on the same bill with him. His skirt

"OH DOCTOR, FEEL MY PULSE!"

Roscoe Fatty Arbuckle
in
Good night Nurse

GARAGE

GENERAL MERCHANDISE

MG27150

With Arbuckle in the team's last two-reeler, THE GARAGE (1920).

was assembled from mess-kit utensils, his brassiere was made of army dog tags, and the "snake" he charmed was a hot dog. (When Buster returned to California, he adapted the routine in *Back Stage* [1919], one of the best films he made with Arbuckle.) Buster's antics were such a hit that he remained in France long after his friends had sailed, entertaining soldiers waiting for transportation back home.

Buster contracted a chronic ear infection while in France, and when he returned to the United States in April 1919 the army sent him to Johns Hopkins Hospital in Baltimore for observation. The infection resulted in some hearing loss that he never recovered, and that worsened every time he would get a bad cold.

Buster kept this photograph of Roscoe Arbuckle (c. 1918) in the den of his Woodland Hills ranch. Photograph by Witzel.

Upon his return to California, Buster threw himself into his work with Arbuckle and the Comique company, which at that time was his entire life. They worked six days a week and loved every minute of what they were doing. Buster made three more films with Arbuckle. The last Arbuckle-Keaton collaboration, *The Garage* (1920), Buster thought the best of the series. The film has the two men running a combination garage and fire station. It is filled with Buster's gags and looks forward to *The Scarecrow* (1920) and *The Blacksmith* (1922).

Joe Schenck sold Arbuckle's contract to Paramount Pictures, where Arbuckle was to make feature-length comedies under a contract that guaranteed him three million dollars over a three-year period. Schenck gave Buster a contract to make his own two-reel comedies. This marked the beginning of Buster's great career and the beginning of the end of Arbuckle's. Arbuckle's first features were not a great success. His salary was virtually the whole budget, so the studio attempted to recoup their investment by using him cheaply in remakes of old Paramount properties that were inappropriate for him. The studio also had Arbuckle make more than one film at a time. However, what really ended Arbuckle's film career was the aftermath of what took place in the course of a bootleg liquor party in Arbuckle's hotel suite at the St. Francis Hotel in San Francisco over Labor Day weekend in September 1921, when a bit player named Virginia Rappe became ill and died four days later of a ruptured bladder. Arbuckle was accused of brutally raping her and was tried three times for manslaughter. He was eventually exonerated with an unprecedented apology from the jury. However, by that time it was too late. Public opinion turned against him, his contract with Paramount was canceled, and for a time he was banned from appearing on the screen by the newly formed Motion Picture Producers and Distributors of America (later renamed the Motion Picture Association of America). Arbuckle was devastated, his great screen career ruined. Eventually he worked as a director under his father's name, William Goodrich, and in the early 1930s he appeared in films under his own name in a few Warner Brothers' Vitaphone comedy shorts.

Buster loved Arbuckle, and the two remained the best of friends until Arbuckle died in 1933. Buster kept a smiling portrait of his friend and mentor on the wall of his den at the Woodland Hills home, his final residence, until the end of his life.

THE SAPHEAD WAS A FILM VERSION of the play *The New Henrietta*, a success in 1887 as *The Henrietta*, and revived on Broadway in 1913 with William H. Crane and Douglas Fairbanks. The film was Buster's first appearance in a feature film and established him as a film star in his own right.

Marcus Loew, whose Metro Pictures was to distribute the new Keaton two-reelers, wanted to make a prestige production in an attempt to improve the quality of Metro's films. Loew bought the famous play from John Goulden, a leading theatrical producer, and set out to make a seven-reel feature film at a time when Metro's biggest productions were only five-reel films.

Joe Schenck encouraged Loew to cast Buster in the role of Bertie "The Lamb" Van Alstyne, the role Fairbanks had played onstage in 1913 and in his first film, *The Lamb* (1915). Feature films were given more space by reviewers than comedy shorts, and Schenck knew that a high-quality feature-film role—and the marketing of such a special production—would

greatly increase interest in the Keaton two-reelers. Loew agreed and arranged to borrow Buster from Schenck. According to Buster, it helped that Fairbanks himself had recommended Buster to Loew for his old role.

The New Henrietta was rewritten to make Buster's role of Bertie the main character. Retitled *The Saphead*, the film was directed by Herbert Blaché, assisted by the stage director of the 1913 Broadway revival, Winchell Smith (who also served as the film's producer). William H. Crane, who created the character of Bertie's father, Nicholas Van Alstyne, onstage in the original production and in the 1913 revival, reprised his role for the film.

Buster plays the pampered Bertie Van Alstyne, son of millionaire Nicholas Van Alstyne, known as the "Wolf of Wall Street." Bertie, in an attempt to make it on his own, buys a seat on Wall Street. (The sheltered Bertie believes he is actually buying a *seat*, as in chair.) However, on his very first visit to the Stock Exchange, Bertie thwarts the scheme of the villainous Mark Turner and saves the family's fortune in the Henrietta gold mine.

The experience of creating a fully developed character influenced Buster's formulation of the later Keaton characters Rollo Treadway in *The Navigator* and Alfred Butler in *Battling Butler*. *The Saphead* also served as a model for all the Keaton features: the transformation of a bumbling, incompetent young man into an athletic, graceful hero who proves himself became the basic feature of all of Buster's major films.

Buster gives an excellent performance in *The Saphead*. Although he had no hand in the direction, he did suggest a few tumbles and gags in what is essentially melodrama mixed with high comedy. The film was well received, and Buster proved that he was an actor and not just a comedian. *Variety* wrote of his performance: "As for Buster, a cyclone when called upon, his quiet work in this picture is a revelation."[5] Buster enjoyed the experience of *The Saphead* so much that he suggested to Schenck that he make fea-

tures in the future instead of two-reel comedies.
Schenck did not agree.

While Buster was making *The Saphead*, Schenck
bought him his own studio, at 1025 Lillian Way, at the
corner of Eleanor Avenue in Hollywood. The studio
was originally the Climax Studio and later the Lone
Star Studio, the "lone star" being Charlie Chaplin,
who made his twelve two-reel comedies for the
Mutual Film Corporation there in 1916–1917.
Renamed the Buster Keaton Studio, it was adjacent
to the Metro studios on Romaine Street. Buster shut-
tled between the two studios toward the end of *The
Saphead*, as he was making his first two-reel shorts
while completing the feature film.

Opposite: Buster as he looked at the time of
THE SAPHEAD, *his feature film debut.*
In his prime, Buster stood five feet five inches
tall. He had dark brown hair and hazel-
colored eyes. Photograph by Nelson Evans.

Below: In THE SAPHEAD, *Buster as*
Bertie Van Alstyne has his wedding to Agnes
Gates postponed upon the arrival of some
incriminating love letters delivered by an
anonymous messenger. With William H.
Crane, Irving Cummings, Katherine Albert,
Carol Holloway, Edward Jobson, Buster, and
Beulah Booker.

THE NINETEEN INDEPENDENT shorts Buster made between 1920 and 1923 allowed him complete creative freedom. There is an amazing variety to them, and in terms of comic invention and technical ingenuity, no one was making comedy shorts better than Buster Keaton at this time. The spontaneity of these shorts is in part what has kept these films so wonderfully fresh to modern viewers. Buster and his team were totally committed to their work; nothing else mattered so much. As Buster once said, "When we made pictures, we ate, slept, and dreamed them."[6] Buster received one thousand dollars a week plus a twenty-five percent share of the net profits from the films. In his first year, he made eight two-reel comedies for release through Metro. He went on to make eleven more two-reelers for release through First National.

As producer, Joe Schenck did not interfere with the new studio's operations; the Keaton shorts were so successful that Schenck simply paid the bills and relieved Buster of all business worries to make films. Everyone was happy with this arrangement, including the small group of impressive stockholders of the Comique Film Company (which changed its name to Buster Keaton Productions in 1922), comprising Joe Schenck as president, his brother Nicholas Schenck as vice-president, David Bernstein as secretary-treasurer (Bernstein was also secretary-treasurer of Loew's, Incorporated), Marcus Loew, A. P. Giannini (president of the Bank of Italy, later renamed the Bank of America), and Irving Berlin.

Buster also had an impressive creative team. Eddie Cline codirected most of the shorts with Buster. Cline was a Mack Sennett veteran: a onetime Keystone Kop, gagman, and director who also appeared in many of the Keaton shorts as an actor in bit parts. From Roscoe Arbuckle's unit Buster retained Lou Anger as studio manager. Also brought in were technical director Fred Gabourie, who was responsible for the building of the sets and for the mechanical planning of special stunts and effects, and head cameraman Elgin Lessley, another Mack Sennett veteran. J. Sherman Kell (whom everyone called "Father Sherman" because he looked like a priest) was film editor. The scenarios and gags for the shorts in the first year were created by Buster and Eddie Cline. By 1921 Joseph Mitchell (who was in charge of the Keaton scenario department) along with Jean Havez and Clyde Bruckman (both of whom had worked for Arbuckle) worked as Buster's three top gagmen. Buster's father, Joe, acted in several of the films, and Joe Roberts, a vaudevillian and old family friend from Buster's boyhood summers on Lake Muskegon, Michigan, was a comic heavy.

Buster supervised every phase of his films. When developing a scenario, the daily story conferences were held from 10 A.M. to 6 P.M. six days a week. Buster, Eddie Cline, Lou Anger, the gagmen, the cameramen, and the property men all participated in the story conferences. Buster later remembered how they would develop a story for a comedy:

> When the three writers [Bruckman, Havez, and Mitchell] and I had decided on a plot, we could start. We always looked for the story first, and the minute somebody came up with a good start, we always jumped the middle. We never paid any attention to that. We jumped to the finish. A man gets into this situation; how does he get out of it? As soon as we found out how to get out of it, then we went back and worked on the middle. We always figured the middle would take care of itself.[7]

Although no formal script was prepared, the plot and the logistics of each film were all carefully planned in advance at the story conferences. However, the freedom to improvise was very important to Buster. He did not like to have performances carefully scripted. He used to walk or talk through scenes briefly just to block out the basic action before filming. Unlike Chaplin, Buster did not film his rehearsals or film many takes of any particular shot. He may have photographed a scene three or four times, but Buster would very often use the first take.

He also had his cameramen keep filming even if something went wrong because that was when Buster did some of his best improvisation. Buster liked to keep it looking and feeling fresh. The cast was small enough—there were usually just three principals: the villain, the girl, and Buster—for him to work this way. Although his studio was one city block in size—perfect for any of his needs—he frequently went on location, as real surroundings always produced the unexpected. When he did not feel like filming or when he had a creative block, Buster and the crew would play baseball.

Buster never repeated a gag or a story idea in any of the nineteen independent silent shorts. The best of them—*One Week*, *The Goat*, *The Playhouse*, *The Boat*, and *Cops*—are some of his finest comedies.

An unidentified actor as "Tiny Tim," Buster, and Bartine Burkett in THE HIGH SIGN (1921).

ALTHOUGH ONE WEEK WAS THE first of Buster's independent shorts to be released, *The High Sign* was the first independent comedy Buster produced. Dissatisfied with the film, he shelved it for more than a year, releasing it only after he broke his ankle while filming the abandoned first version of *The Electric House* and the company needed a film to release. *The High Sign* begins with the title: "Our Hero came from Nowhere—he wasn't going Anywhere but he got off Somewhere." Buster is first seen thrown from a passing train. Relocated at a seaside amusement park, he helps himself to the newspaper of a man passing by on a merry-go-round. Buster sits on a bench and opens the newspaper. He unfolds it and unfolds it. Its large size forces him to sit on the back of the bench. The newspaper opens up to a size as big as a bed sheet and envelops him. He topples backward, and his head tears through the paper. It is the first of many Keatonesque gags— bizarre and surreal—that mark the difference between Buster's dry and quiet comedy style and the violent slapstick of Arbuckle. (In fact, unfolding the oversized newspaper was one of Buster's favorite gags, and he would return to it for live performances in his later years.) In the giant newspaper he finds a small help-wanted advertisement for an attendant at a shooting gallery, where he gets the job by a trick that allows him to masquerade as an expert marksman.

Buster is hired both by an underworld gang called the Blinking Buzzards and as a bodyguard by the man the Blinking Buzzards want to murder, all convinced Buster is a sharpshooter. The climax has

Buster being chased by the Blinking Buzzards through an elaborately rigged house, filled with secret corridors, trap doors, and revolving panels. The chase through the house was photographed on a cutaway set, which reveals the intricate inventiveness of the house as the backdrop to the frenzied pace of the action.

The film is filled with brilliant gags. However, Buster thought the gags were too ridiculous and clever for their own sake. He felt the film was too similar in style to the films he had made with Arbuckle (Buster even had Al St. John appear in a cameo) and he wanted to make his first release special. *One Week*, the film he made next, would be a much stronger film, consistent with his own style of comedy.

*Buster and his crew on **THE HIGH SIGN** signal for the still photographer aboard a boat on location off the coast of Venice Beach, California. Eddie Cline is in the wide-brimmed hat on the left with cameraman Elgin Lessley seated immediately behind him.*

ONE WEEK WAS BUSTER'S FIRST masterpiece, and many consider the film the finest short comedy he ever made. The story line is tighter than *The High Sign*, and a distinct visual style (such as the use of long takes filmed in long shots) and Buster's unique sense of the absurd are clearly evident. The film was inspired by a Ford Motor Company documentary, *Home Made* (1919), an educational short about prefabricated housing. Buster saw this obscure little film and decided to do a sort of parody of it. *One Week* has many of the devices used in *Home Made*, including the wedding, the Model T, and the use of the pages from a daily calendar to show the house being built in one week.

The film opens with newly-weds Buster and Sybil Seely (an unknown actress in her first film with Buster) leaving the church. As a wedding gift, the couple is given a build-it-yourself house kit and a plot of land. Handy Hank, Buster's disappointed rival, changes the numbers on the boxes containing the house. The structure Buster assembles is a joke unto itself; an irregular and confused mess. After a disastrous house-warming party, in which the house is nearly ruined by rain, the newlyweds discover they have built the house on the wrong lot. They try to tow the house behind their Model T, but it breaks loose and stops on a railroad track. A train comes racing toward the house, but it passes by on a parallel track. As they breathe a sigh of relief, from the opposite direction another train smashes the house to oblivion. Buster places a "For Sale" sign on what little is left of their house—along with the build-it-yourself instructions—before the two walk away into the distance.

The excellent production values of this and many of the subsequent Keaton two-reelers were almost unsurpassed by anyone in comedy. The house set for *One Week* was very elaborate; it was built on a turntable so that it could spin around for the violent rainstorm scene.

The fall Buster takes when he steps out the bath-room door into air was one of the few occasions when Buster really hurt himself making films. The impact of the fall was such that his arms and back swelled up very badly just a few hours later. Al Gilmore, his physical trainer, had to put him in hot and cold showers and then apply olive oil and later horse lini-ment to eventually get the swelling down.

One Week showcased the essential Buster, with two of his favorite elements—violent storms and a train—worked into the story. He believed that the film would be a good first release. He was right: *One Week* was hailed as the comedy sensation of the year.

Opposite: Buster looks askance at the house he has assembled in One Week *(1920).*

Above: With Sybil Seely.

BUSTER'S SECOND RELEASE BEGINS with him on the golf links with a socialite, Sybil Seely, with whom he is enamored. Buster is an inept golfer, and he manages to hit himself on the head with his golf ball. Unconscious, he dreams of being mistaken for escaped convict No.13 and then taken to prison where he narrowly escapes being hanged (thanks to the help of the warden's daughter, also played by Seely). He changes clothes with a prison guard, quells a prison-yard riot, and defeats a giant convict (Joe Roberts). The film ends with Buster awakening from his dream on the golf links in the arms of the consoling Sybil Seely.

Convict 13 contains black comedy, particularly the scene in which Buster is about to be hanged while the prisoners sit as spectators cheering on the proceedings and concessions are sold as if it were a ball game. As the giant convict, Joe Roberts is memorable in his first major role in a Keaton film. He played the heavy in all of Buster's remaining independent shorts. His scenes with Buster in this film are very much in the David and Goliath manner. Buster appears dressed in a prison warden's uniform only to discover that Roberts has knocked out an entire procession of prison guards as they entered the yard. Roberts in this film is reminiscent of Eric Campbell, the huge comic villain Chaplin used in his Mutual comedies, and certain moments of *Convict 13* resemble the most famous of the Chaplin Mutuals, *Easy Street* (1917).

One scene in the film is a reworking of a routine Buster did in vaudeville with his father. Onstage, Joe would sing while Buster stood on a table swinging a basketball on the end of a long rope in a circular motion around his Father's head. Buster would whirl the rope closer and closer to Joe until the ball hit Joe smack in the face. In the climax of *Convict 13*, Buster swings a ball and chain to stop a prison riot, knocking the prisoners unconscious. The first convict hit in the film is none other than Joe Keaton.

With Joe Roberts in CONVICT 13 *(1920). Buster's younger brother, Harry "Jingles," is the prison guard on the far right.*

71

BUSTER AND JOE ROBERTS PLAY farmhands who share a one-room house that is filled with surprising time- and space-saving devices: the phonograph doubles as a stove; the bookcase also serves as the icebox; and the bed converts into an upright piano. Breakfast involves a series of strings dangling from the ceiling, which pull down to an assortment of condiments that the two men swing back and forth to each other over the breakfast table. Buster had built similar Rube Goldberg-like contraptions as a boy at his summer home on Lake Muskegon, Michigan. He made them for his own amusement, as well as for a lazy vaudevillian neighbor named Ed Gray, who hated to make any unnecessary movements. The devices created in *The Scarecrow* are similar to those he built as a boy, and this scene is the film's cleverest routine.

Domestic harmony changes to rivalry as the two men both try to win the affection of the farmer's daughter, played by Sybil Seely. Buster is soon diverted from romance when he is chased by a dog (Arbuckle's Staffordshire Bull Terrier, Luke) and gets thrown into a hay-processing machine, which tears away his clothes. Borrowing the clothes of a nearby scarecrow, Buster kneels down to tie his shoe when the farmer's daughter encounters him. She mistakes his kneeling position for a formal marriage proposal, which she accepts. As the two race off on a motorcycle to elope, they accidentally take on an extra passenger—a parson who pronounces the couple husband and wife as the motorcycle is accidentally driven straight into a lake.

Buster kneels to tie his shoe and ends up engaged to Sybil Seely in THE SCARECROW *(1920).*

NEIGHBORS BEGINS WITH THE title "The Flower of Love could find no more romantic spot in which to blossom than in this poet's Dream Garden." This fades into a backyard in a slum. Buster and his girl (Virginia Fox) are a 1921 Romeo and Juliet, their romance impeded at every turn by the antagonism between their feuding families. The girl's father is played by Joe Roberts, and Buster's father is played by his real-life father, Joe Keaton. The story ends with the young lovers finally united in marriage.

The simple story is just a loose framework for many memorable gags and stunts. The acrobatics of the three-man pyramid stunt, with Buster on top, were performed by Buster and his vaudevillian friends the Flying Escalantes, who he would use again in the Educational comedy *Allez Oop* (1934). However, the most interesting scenes feature Buster and his father doing routines similar to those they had performed together onstage. In one sequence, Buster drops into a bottomless barrel, his head stuck into the muddy tenement courtyard. Joe pulls away the barrel and then yanks Buster by the legs, trying to dislodge his head from the mud. At one point Joe stands on Buster's arms as he pulls Buster by the legs. Joe says in a title, "He's *my* son and I'll break his neck any way I please."

Neighbors was the first Keaton film that featured Virginia Fox, his most frequent leading lady, a former Mack Sennett player who appeared in nine of Buster's silent comedy shorts. In 1923, she married Darryl F. Zanuck and retired from films.

Buster and Virginia Fox are star-crossed lovers trying to quietly elope in NEIGHBORS (1920). Buster is standing on the head of Joe Roberts, who plays the girl's father.

IN THIS FILM, BUSTER IS FALSELY
accused of being a hold-up man at the bank where he
works as a clerk. On the run, he hides out in an abandoned house, where a visiting opera company of
Faust also seeks refuge. The house, in fact, is the
hideout of the real hold-up men and the corrupt
bank teller (Joe Roberts), who have rigged the place
as a haunted house to frighten people away. A fast
series of clever haunted-house gags follow—the focal
point being a staircase that flattens into a ramp, sending Buster and others sliding—before Buster thwarts
the villains. The film ends with Buster in the arms of
the bank president's pretty daughter (Virginia Fox).

Ironically, the best moments in *The Haunted
House* take place outside the haunted house.
Particularly funny is the routine of Buster as a bank
clerk accidentally spilling a bottle of glue all over his
counter and creating chaos, a sequence that borrows
from the molasses scene in *The Butcher Boy*, Buster's
first film. Perhaps the most memorable moment
comes when Buster is hit over the head after subdu-
ing the bank robbers. He dreams he is an angel
ascending to heaven. When Saint Peter rejects him at
the gates, he then slides down into hell where he
finds that the devil has been expecting him.

The best sequence in THE HAUNTED
HOUSE *(1921) has Buster as a bank
clerk spilling a bottle of glue, which
results in bank notes stuck to his hands,
the floor, and everything around him.*

HARD LUCK WAS BUSTER'S PERSONAL favorite of his own silent shorts, not because he thought it better than the rest but because the film contained the greatest laugh-getting sequence of any of his pictures. The film itself was considered lost for more than sixty years until it was partially reconstructed from extant footage acquired by Raymond Rohauer and assembled by Kevin Brownlow and David Gill in 1987.

In the film, Buster loses his job and his girl. Down on his luck, he tries to commit suicide. All of his inept attempts to do away with himself meet with failure. These hilarious suicide-attempt gags are similar to those Harold Lloyd did in his comedy shorts *Haunted Spooks* (1920) and *Never Weaken* (1921). The second half of the film finds Buster hired by the local zoo to capture the one animal they do not have: an armadillo. Needless to say, he fails, and he is also unsuccessful as a fisherman and horseman. The aforementioned hilarious sequence comes at the end: rejected by Virginia Fox, Buster climbs up to the high-diving platform of an open-air swimming pool. On the platform he poses and struts for the benefit of the girls lounging around the pool. He then performs a great swan dive and misses the pool completely. Landing on the cement walk next to the pool, he leaves a large hole in the pavement. The scene fades and is followed by a title, "Years later." The scene fades back to the abandoned pool, the hole still visible. Buster emerges from it, dressed in Oriental clothes, followed by his Chinese wife and two children. Unfortunately, this sequence was not among the footage uncovered for the film's reconstruction, and only still photographs from the scene are known to exist.

With a Chinese wife and children in the missing sequence that concludes HARD LUCK *(1921). According to Buster, this sequence evoked the greatest laugh of any scene he ever did.*

FILLED WITH COMPLEX AND inventive gags, *The Goat* is one of Buster's cleverest two-reel comedies. The film opens with Buster standing in a bread line, waiting for a handout he never gets. He next stops and stares through the barred window of a police station as a photographer prepares to take a mug shot of the murderer Dead Shot Dan (played by Mal St. Clair, who codirected the film with Buster). The crafty Dan, seeing Buster, bends down out of camera range and triggers the camera, photographing Buster behind bars. Later, when Dan escapes, the "Wanted" posters put up by the police and the newspaper photos show Buster as the escaped criminal.

The rest of *The Goat* revolves around Buster being mistaken for Dead Shot Dan. One of the film's best scenes has Buster, on the run in a park, hiding under the tarpaulin covering a sculptor's full-size model of a statue that is about to be unveiled. When the statue is revealed in a public ceremony, Buster is seen posing on the back of a full-scale clay horse. The horse gradually sags at the knees under Buster's weight, but Buster continues to hold his pose.

The Goat also features one of Buster's most memorable moments with a train. Pursued by the police, Buster jumps a train and in some complicated and very funny maneuvers manages to make his escape. The film then irises out and in again. In an extreme long shot the train is coming toward the camera. As it comes into a close-up, we see Buster sitting on the front of the engine looking straight into the camera. It is a wonderful moment—slow, simple, and effective—unlike anything else in the otherwise complex, fast-paced comedy. Buster had a lifelong love affair with trains. He loved trains so much that he would often try to work one into his comedies just to make something different from what anyone else might do with a train in motion pictures.

Buster is mistaken for the murderer Dead Shot Dan in THE GOAT *(1921), one of his finest comedies.*

BUSTER BROKE AN ANKLE WHILE working on the film he started to make just before *The Playhouse*, the abandoned first version of *The Electric House* (which he would entirely remake and release the following year). During his absence from film production, Buster married Natalie Talmadge in Long Island, New York. Returning to California, he needed a comedy that would demand none of his usual physical stunts. The resulting film is *The Playhouse*, the most visually spectacular of all his short films. Aside from its technical virtuosity and Buster's amazing performance in the film, *The Playhouse* is also fascinating for its numerous references to his years in vaudeville.

Buster found the idea for this strongly cinematic film from vaudeville: the famous swimming and diving star Annette Kellerman and her one hundred mirrors, which created for the audience the illusion of one hundred Annette Kellermans. The film begins with a dream sequence in which Buster plays every role in a vaudeville theater: the conductor and every member of the orchestra, the members of the audi-

ence—men and women—all have Buster's face, as well as the minstrel performers onstage. The effect is astonishing when one sees nine Busters all at once in the same frame. In these early days of motion pictures, all of the special effects were created inside the camera on one piece of film. For the scene in which nine Busters dance in a minstrel act, the same film was exposed nine times. Elgin Lessley would block out the entire frame except for the small space occupied by Buster as that one character and crank the camera at an exact speed. Lessley would then rewind the film to the precise point, and Buster would do his performance exactly the same again. To make sure each time he did the dance it would be in synchronization with his other performances, Buster danced to banjo music played to a metronome.

In the film, the program for the vaudeville show lists all the credits as being performed by Buster Keaton. This sequence was a playful jab at Thomas H. Ince, the pioneer film producer who took credit for everything in his productions, sometimes even a directing credit when he no longer directed the films he produced.

Buster later regretted not having made the entire film with him playing all the parts, but he was unsure at the time whether audiences might tire of the joke or think he made it as a demonstration of his acting virtuosity. In the second part of the film, Buster awakens from his dream to find he is a stagehand at a vaudeville theater. In this part of the film Buster reworks gags from *Back Stage* and performs vaudeville routines from The Three Keatons act: pulling a broom out of a knothole in the stage floor and also diving through the backdrop, the Original Aboriginal Australian Splash (which was a parody of Annette Kellerman's famous dive). Buster also does an

In one of his most remarkable performances, Buster substitutes for a performing ape in THE PLAYHOUSE *(1921). Eddie Cline plays the trainer.*

Opposite: Buster becomes his own triptych in THE PLAYHOUSE, *his most visually spectacular comedy short, which uses the multiplicity of a single image as one of the film's comic devices.*

astounding number of variations on gags involving twins, which he tops each time. The most remarkable moment in the second half of the film comes when Buster at the last minute substitutes for a performing orangutan when the real orangutan escapes. Buster's impersonation of the ape is one of the best things he ever did as an actor. The performing ape is another direct reference to his vaudeville days: Buster had performed on the same bill in 1909 in London, England, with "Peter the Great," a performing monkey who could do nearly anything his human trainer could do.

THE BOAT WAS BUSTER'S SECOND favorite of his short films and one of the finest comedies he ever made. The film begins with Buster, who has built a boat in his basement, attempting to tow the oversized vessel out of the narrow door of his house. He attaches the boat to his Model T, and as the boat pulls through the doorway, the foundation of the house tears apart, and the house collapses. Undeterred, Buster, his wife (Sybil Seely), and two children (wearing little porkpie hats) take the boat, named the *Damfino*, to the harbor.

The launch of the *Damfino* is one of Buster's most celebrated sequences. He stands proudly on the deck as the boat slides slowly down the ramp to the bottom of the harbor. It took three days to get the scene to go the way it was intended. Fred Gabourie constructed two thirty-five-foot boats for the film—one to float and one to sink—but each boat managed to perform the function intended for the other. To get the boat to slide properly to the bottom of Balboa Bay, Gabourie dropped a sea anchor into the bay with cables attached to the stern of the boat and a rigged pulley that pulled the boat under water.

The title "You can't keep a good boat down" opens the next scene of the film, with Buster making repairs to the boat. The maiden voyage is a disaster for the entire family. When a storm rises, Buster radios the coast guard for help. When asked to identify the name of the vessel, Buster's response of "*Damfino*" gets the sharp reply: "Neither do I."

The boat sinks in the storm, and the family is set adrift in their lifeboat (a small bathtub). When they realize that they are floating in water just a few feet deep near land, they leave the tub and walk to shore. "Where are we?" asks Sybil Seely in a title as they walk ashore. "Damfino" mouths Buster, and the film ends as the family disappears into the darkness of night.

As perfect and self-contained as *The Boat* is as a two-reeler, Buster had the idea of combining *One Week* and *The Boat* as a four-reel feature involving the adventures of a husband and wife, with Buster and Sybil Seely. (Seely, who had been replaced by Virginia Fox as Buster's leading lady, was rehired to do *The Boat*.) However, the feature never materialized.

Buster stands proudly next to his hand-made boat, named **DAMFINO**, *in* **THE BOAT** *(1921). The launch of the* **DAMFINO** *is one of his most celebrated sequences.*

uster Keaton in " The Boat"

K-N-3-3

THE PALEFACE IS BUSTER'S PLAYFUL look at the Western films that were popular at the time. The film begins with some lengthy scenes of exposition that show a group of oil prospectors cheating some native Americans out of their own lands. The Indian chief (Joe Roberts) proclaims to his tribe: "Kill the first white man who comes through the gate."

Buster, of course, is the first white man to pass through the gate of the reservation. Managing to thwart the desire of the Indians to burn him at the stake, Buster is made their leader and organizes a successful raid on the oil prospectors' office. All eventually ends well with Buster marrying the chief's daughter.

The Paleface is wonderfully ridiculous, full of very funny cartoonish gags, perhaps the best being when Buster makes himself asbestos underwear that enables him to calmly wait out the blaze at the stake unharmed. The film is also filled with some spectacular stunts by Buster, including an incredible leap into a tree and a terrific fall from a suspension bridge into a ravine. To achieve the stunt, Buster first had to fall eighty-five feet from the bridge into a net. The next camera setup shows Buster from twenty feet up but out of camera range, and the shot was of him falling into the ravine. The special effects used are convincing, and the grand outdoor settings of *The Paleface*, mixed with gags fraught with danger, anticipate *Our Hospitality* and *The General*.

As "Little Chief Paleface" in a gag still from **THE PALEFACE** *(1922).*

COPS (1922)

COPS IS ONE OF BUSTER'S BEST and best-known comedies. Its chase scene, in which Buster is pursued by hundreds of cops, is regarded as a classic sequence of screen comedy. The film opens with a surprise-effect gag. Buster is first seen looking very sad behind bars, leading the audience to think he is in prison. The next shot, however, reveals him to be a free man standing behind the bars of the front gate to the home of his sweetheart (Virginia Fox). It is a clever visual gag, so good in fact that Harold Lloyd would open his most famous film, *Safety Last* (1923), in a very similar way.

Scorned by his girl as a failure in business, Buster sets out to make good. Almost immediately, he gets into trouble when he accidentally finds and ultimately pockets the money from the wallet of a burly plainclothes policeman. He next becomes the victim of a con-man who sells Buster the furniture from someone else's house. The real owner happens to be a policeman in the process of moving into a new home. Buster acquires a horse-cart to load his newly acquired furniture and drives his broken-down horse and cart into the middle of a police parade. An anarchist on the roof of a nearby building throws down a bomb, which lands right next to Buster. The scene with the bomb was actually daring for its time, for it directly refers to the Wall Street bomb explosion that killed thirty people and injured many more in 1919, one of many bomb scares immediately following World War I.

Buster lights his cigarette from the burning fuse, and then casually throws it aside, not realizing it is a bomb ready to explode. The explosion ruins the parade, and the chase is on by the entire police force to capture Buster. The frenzy of the chase itself was carefully staged, and it is photographed and edited beautifully. The chase ends with Buster running into the police station, an army of policemen close behind. The doors to the station close behind them. A solitary uniformed figure emerges from the station house and locks the door: Buster. His girl passes by and snubs him completely. He unlocks the door to the police station and enters. A "The End" title is chiseled on a gravestone, on top of which rests Buster's porkpie hat. The strange ending of the film is similar to the effect Buster would later achieve in the ending of *College*.

Buster is chased by the entire police force in a classic moment from COPS *(1922).*

My Wife's Relations and the six films that followed did not equal the quality of the best of the earlier shorts. By this time, Buster had mastered the two-reeler and was anxious to start making features, as Chaplin and Harold Lloyd had already done. All of these remaining shorts have wonderful moments, but the comic invention is not sustained as in the earlier films. They give one the feeling that Buster and his team were in need of new challenges and were growing restless with the two-reel form.

In *My Wife's Relations* Buster is falsely accused of breaking a window. A large, rugged Irishwoman (Kate Price) hauls him into court where the judge—who does not speak English—marries them by mistake. She takes him home to her father and four brothers, who treat him with contempt until they mistakenly believe he is about to inherit one hundred thousand dollars. The family then loans the bewildered Buster money to move the entire clan into an expensive apartment, and there they live a life of luxury until it is discovered that Buster's inheritance is nonexistent.

The film ends with Buster making his getaway on a train bound for Reno.

The scene Buster liked best in the film is the family dinner: Buster is not fast enough to get anything but empty serving plates until he changes the calendar to Friday, providing him his only opportunity to get a steak from the devout Irish Catholic family. Buster would rework this same material for his Educational comedy *Palooka from Paducah* (1935), with his own father, mother, and sister in the cast.

Kate Price, who plays the virago wife in *My Wife's Relations*, was in fact a sweet character actress who had worked with Arbuckle and Mary Pickford, and with whom Buster enjoyed working. She had a good sense of humor, and caused the cast and crew to burst into laughter in the scene in which she brings Buster home to meet her family, and as they enter through the door her hungry family asks her for dinner. She shouted, "Dinner my ass! Look what I married!" Unfortunately, Kate's line did not make it into the film's intertitles.

Buster meets his new in-laws in My Wife's Relations *(1922). Harry Madison, Tom Wilson, Buster, Wheezer Dell, and Joe Roberts.*

THE BLACKSMITH (1922)

THE BLACKSMITH, WHICH BUSTER directed in collaboration with Mal St. Clair (who had codirected *The Goat*), is similar to the type of films Buster made with Roscoe Arbuckle, particularly *A Country Hero*, *The Hayseed*, and *The Garage*. The film opens with titles from the famous Henry Wadsworth Longfellow poem, "The Village Blacksmith" (a poem Buster knew since childhood, and which he used in a comic recitation onstage in vaudeville). There are some funny moments with Buster as an assistant smithy, such as the scene in which he fits a beautiful white horse with new shoes as if he were a kindly salesman in a shoe store.

One scene, involving a gleaming white Rolls-Royce in need of minor repairs that Buster manages to completely ruin, he later admitted was a mistake. Audiences do not enjoy watching something valuable—something that they themselves wish to own—being destroyed. Owing to the failure of this scene, Buster did not enjoy the film very much and did not rate it high among his films. The film concludes with Buster eloping with the owner of the white horse (Virginia Fox). As we see the two depart on a train, a title reads "Many a honeymoon express has ended thusly," and a small train derails and falls from a bridge. In a surprise ending, the train is revealed to be but a toy train, and Buster and Virginia are shown as contented parents of a small child.

Buster and Joe Roberts in THE BLACKSMITH (1922).

THE FROZEN NORTH IS A PARODY
of Western melodramas and of their famous star,
William S. Hart. The opening shots of the film were
photographed on location at Donner Lake outside
Truckee, California, in mid-winter.[8] Buster is first
seen coming out of a New York subway station into a
big bank of snow in the middle of frozen Donner
Lake. The film abounds with silly slapstick involving
snow and is given a mock-serious tone by the opening
intertitles, which are from "The Shooting of Dan
McGrew" by Robert W. Service.

The film's best scene is Buster's parody of two-gun
Bill Hart arriving home to discover a couple embrac-
ing. Wearing a small version of Hart's campaign hat
from the Spanish-American War and a six-shooter on
each thigh, Buster is convinced he has discovered his
wife with a lover. He is devastated. Glycerin tears roll
down his face (Hart nearly always managed to have
at least one scene in each film in which tears rolled
out of one eye and down his cheek). Enraged at the
man who has wrecked his home and the wife who has
betrayed him, Buster pulls out both guns and shoots
them; they spin around in the style of a poorly acted
melodrama before collapsing onto the floor. Buster
walks over to look at the lifeless forms and discovers
that the woman is, in fact, not his wife. An intertitle
reads, "My God! I'm in the wrong house."

Audiences of the 1920s recognized the parody and
thought the film hysterically funny. However, Hart
himself was not amused by Buster's antics—particularly the crying scene—and did not speak to Buster
for two years after he saw the picture.

*Buster assumes the famous two-gun stance of William S. Hart,
the silent-screen Western star, in his parody* THE FROZEN
NORTH *(1922).*

DAYDREAMS (1922)

In DAYDREAMS (1922), Buster writes letters to his sweetheart in a way that allows her to misinterpret his adventures as successes. She imagines him as a surgeon at a hospital, a Wall Street tycoon, a great actor, and a chief of police. Surviving prints of the film are incomplete, and the scenes depicting the surgeon, the Wall Street tycoon, and the police chief are missing from extant prints.

DAYDREAMS BEGINS WITH A SHORT scene of country-boy Buster resolving to leave for the big city and make good in order to marry his girl (Renée Adorée, one of the few actresses of note to play in a Keaton film), who waits back home for him to become a success. Throughout the rest of the film, Buster writes letters to his girl that allow her to misinterpret his adventures as successes: she imagines him as a surgeon at a hospital, a Wall Street tycoon, a great actor, and a chief of police, when in actuality he works at a dog and cat hospital, as a street sweeper, and in the chorus of a show, and then ends up a fugitive from the law.

The sequence in which Buster is on the run contains a chase similar to the one in *Cops*, but it ends with one of Buster's most memorable images. Buster thinks he has eluded the police by jumping aboard a ferry boat. However, the boat is not going out but rather coming into port. He escapes from the deck of the boat and onto the ferry's great paddlewheel, which begins to rotate. To avoid going under water, he climbs inside the paddlewheel and walks in place as the wheel turns, like a hamster on a treadmill. It eventually speeds up to the point that Buster tumbles and rolls within it, and the scene ends with him clasping onto one of the blades and twirling around the outside of the wheel.

BUSTER BROKE HIS ANKLE WHEN his foot was caught on the top of the escalator while filming the abandoned first version of *The Electric House*. When he returned to the idea of the film, none of the old footage was used and new sets were created by Fred Gabourie.

The film begins with Buster receiving the wrong diploma at his college commencement. Believed to be a qualified electrical engineer, he is commissioned by the college dean (Joe Roberts) to modernize his home with an assortment of electrical conveniences while he and his family are away. Upon their return, Buster demonstrates the electric staircase, sliding doors, mechanical ball rack for the billiard table, and automatic swimming-pool drain. The family is pleased with Buster's work until the house is eventually sabotaged by his fellow graduate—the real electrical engineer—who creates chaos by switching the wires. Booted out of the electric house and into the automatic swimming pool, Buster is sucked down the plug-hole and floats out a drain pipe.

The exteriors of the house were filmed at Buster's own Tudor-style home on Westmoreland Place. Although Buster did not have fond memories of this film, owing to his broken ankle (he thought it a lack of professionalism to be hurt on such a routine stunt and to cause a halt to production), he loved the scenes of the electrical inventions. Buster re-created the little dinner-table railway in the film for the picnic table at his Woodland Hills ranch thirty-five years later.

Even the floor is not safe when Buster's mechanical creations go berserk in **THE ELECTRIC HOUSE** *(1922).*

THE BALLOONATIC BEGINS WITH
Buster idle in an amusement park, where he follows a
pretty young woman (Phyllis Haver) into the Tunnel
of Love and comes out with a black eye. He then
wanders over to where a hot-air balloon is to be
launched. The balloon breaks free, with the intended
passenger on the ground and Buster onboard. He
lands in mountain country where the young woman
who gave him the black eye is camping. Despite their
initial antagonism, love blossoms, and the two set sail
in his canoe. Their romance appears to be short-
lived, as the canoe heads toward a dangerous water-

fall. All ends well as the two lovers sail safely beyond
the brink of the waterfall and float into the sky, a long
shot revealing that the canoe is attached to the hot-air
balloon.

The Balloonatic is notable for the appearance of
Phyllis Haver as Buster's leading lady. Haver, a former
Mack Sennett player, enjoyed noteworthy success in
silent films and brought to *The Balloonatic* an interesting and well-developed characterization; the film
is the only one of the nineteen independent shorts in
which the interplay between Buster and his leading
lady is wholly successful.

Opposite: On location for THE BALLOONATIC *(1923). Fred Gabourie is seated between Buster and leading lady Phyllis Haver, with Eddie Cline directly behind Buster. The use of two Bell and Howell 2709 Studio Model cameras pictured follow the standard silent-era practice of creating two original negatives, one for domestic and one for foreign distribution.*

Above: A balloon launch. The Keaton Studio is just visible in this still, only a few blocks behind and to the left of Buster.

R E J E C T E D   B Y   H I S   G I R L F R I E N D
(Virginia Fox), Buster resolves to set sail alone in his
little boat, named *Cupid*. Days later he is exhausted
and starving, hopelessly adrift at sea. He is picked up
by a whaling ship named *The Love Nest*, on which
the captain of the ship (Joe Roberts) punishes minor
offenses among his crew by throwing them perma-
nently overboard. Buster quickly becomes the last
surviving mate, eventually abandoning ship on its
lifeboat, *The Little Love Nest*. His adventures on the
high seas prove to be just a dream, and the film ends
with Buster awakened in his little boat, still tied to
the dock.

The Love Nest has the distinction of being the only
film in which Buster took sole writing and directing
credit. It was also his last two-reel silent comedy; during the production of this film, Joe Schenck told
Buster to start making feature films.

Above and opposite:
THE LOVE NEST
*(1923), Buster's last
silent two-reel comedy.*

BUSTER HAD MET NATALIE TALMADGE while working with Roscoe Arbuckle at the Comique Film Corporation in New York, where she worked first as a combination secretary and script girl for the unit and was eventually promoted to secretary-treasurer.

Natalie's two sisters, Norma and Constance, were movie stars. Norma was the eldest of the three. She came into stardom through Vitagraph and had established herself as one of the most popular dramatic actresses in films. Norma furthered her position of power within the film industry by marrying her producer, Joe Schenck, in 1916. Constance (who was called "Dutch") was the youngest. She had played the important role of the Mountain Girl in D. W. Griffith's *Intolerance* (1916), and had embarked on a series of light comedies that were very successful.

Prior to Natalie, Buster's girlfriend was Alice Lake, a former Keystone player who had joined Comique's repertory company. When Comique moved to California, Buster also had a relationship with Metro actress Viola Dana.

Natalie was among those who made the move from New York to California with the Comique

Above: Buster and Natalie Talmadge on their wedding day, May 31, 1921, at the home of Joe Schenck and Norma Talmadge in Bayside, Long Island. Norma Talmadge, Buster, Natalie, and Constance Talmadge. Photograph by Potter.

Right: Natalie clutches a rolling pin, and Buster's broken right ankle (which is still bandaged from his accident making the abandoned first version of THE ELECTRIC HOUSE*) is shackled by a ball and chain in this gag photograph taken shortly after their marriage.*

Buster with sons Bobby (left) and Jimmy (right), 1924.

company. It was in California that Buster and Natalie's romance began. Although not as beautiful as her two sisters, Natalie was nevertheless attractive, demure, and intelligent.

Natalie, however, soon missed New York and left Comique to return East. When Buster was inducted in the army and stationed at Camp Upton in Long Island, Natalie visited him. For the next two years their relationship existed entirely through correspondence, mostly Natalie sending news of herself and her family to Buster.

Buster was a lowly comic as far as the Talmadge family was concerned, and not that important in the motion-picture industry. He was not what Peg Talmadge, the mother and matriarch (Fred Talmadge, her husband, was an alcoholic who had abandoned the family), would really have liked Natalie to have had as a husband.

However, Peg Talmadge wanted her middle daughter married. Joe Schenck was instrumental in making Peg happy with the notion of a Natalie Talmadge-Buster Keaton marriage. Since Schenck produced the Norma and Constance Talmadge films as well as Buster's, Natalie's marriage to Buster would keep it all within the family. He also encouraged Buster with respect to Natalie.

In January 1921 Natalie wrote Buster from New York a letter that read in part, "I am alone now, the only one left living with mother. If you still care all you have to do is send for me."[9] Buster and Natalie were soon engaged, but with no wedding date set. He was at the time working on the later-abandoned first version of *The Electric House*, until his slapshoe became caught between the risers of the set's escalator and he broke his ankle. Unable to work with his right ankle in a cast, Buster traveled to New York to marry Natalie.

Buster and Natalie were married on May 31, 1921 (the same anniversary date as his parents) at Joe and Norma's home in Bayside, Long Island. Screenwriter Anita Loos was the bridesmaid, Constance Talmadge was matron of honor, and Ward Crane (who would play the rival in *Sherlock Jr.*) was Buster's best man. The guests were mainly the bride's family and friends. Among the wedding gifts were a Belgian police dog (Buster named him Captain) from Constance and a Rolls-Royce from Norma and Joe, which was delivered to them in Los Angeles. The newlyweds had no honeymoon. The day after the wedding they left New York on the *Twentieth Century Limited* for the five-day journey to Los Angeles.

The newlyweds had their first argument almost immediately. Natalie had hoped that she could convince Buster to move to New York and make his films at the Colony Studio. Buster refused. Arriving in Los Angeles, they could not agree on where they wanted to live. Buster had wanted to build a ranch in the San Fernando Valley, where they could have a working farm. Natalie preferred a home in Los Angeles. She won that argument.

Over the next several years, Buster and Natalie kept moving into more and more elaborate houses at Natalie's insistence. A frustrated actress, her way of competing with other movie stars was to live as luxuriously as they did. At one point during the marriage, Natalie's personal expenses for clothes and other items averaged nine hundred dollars a week. Natalie was in charge of the finances, and Buster's salary and bonuses were paid directly to her.

When Natalie became pregnant with their first child, Peg Talmadge left New York and moved in with Buster and Natalie. Constance, recently divorced, would eventually move in with them as well. The Talmadges were a close-knit family, and Buster soon felt that he had married not one woman but a whole family. Realizing he had more control at work than at home, he immersed himself in the making of his films.

Buster and Natalie's first child, Joseph Talmadge Keaton, was born June 2, 1922. He was named Joseph, as six earlier generations of first-born sons who preceded him had been. Buster was very proud to hand down the family tradition. However, Natalie preferred the name James and soon began calling their infant son Jimmy. She had the child christened James, which hurt Buster very much.

A second son, Robert Talmadge Keaton was born February 3, 1924. Both sons were baptized Catholics, for the Talmadges were a Catholic family. Buster himself was Protestant but was indifferent to how the children were baptized. He had no use for religion.

After Bobby's birth, Natalie decided she wanted no more children and forced Buster to move into the guest room, ceasing their physical relationship. Buster told her and his mother-in-law that he had no inten-

Buster at his Beverly Hills mansion, the Italian Villa, in November 1929. He once said, "It took a hell of a lot of pratfalls to build that dump."

MGMP-22904

Buster and Natalie return on the SS ***BREMEN*** *after a tour of Europe, September 22, 1930.*

tion of going without sex. He explained to both women that he would not support a mistress and that he would keep his extramarital affairs discreet, but he would find other partners. Natalie was content to look away.

The growing household necessitated a larger home. Buster designed a house and had it built for Natalie as a surprise, but when he showed her the house she found it too small. Buster sold it without ever having spent one night in it. He still tried to please her any way he could. The house that won Natalie's approval was a mansion designed by Gene Verge and built in Beverly Hills. Called the Italian Villa, the ten-thousand-square-foot two-story Mediterranean-style showplace was built in 1925 at a cost of three hundred thousand dollars. The palatial home, which had more than twenty rooms, including five bedrooms and servants' quarters, stood on three and a half acres. It had a beautiful swimming pool, tennis court, trout-stocked stream, and even an aviary.

They entertained lavishly at the Italian Villa. The barbecue parties they threw each Sunday from May to October were very popular among the Hollywood elite. Buster himself would prepare the barbecued steaks, chicken, and English lamb chops.

Despite the beautiful home and two wonderful children, it was inevitable that the marriage would end. When Buster lost control of his film work at M-G-M he drank heavily, and his affairs with actress Dorothy Sebastian and M-G-M stock contract player Kathleen Key were far from discreet. The honeymoon Buster and Natalie never had was taken in 1930 when the two traveled through Europe, but it was unsuccessful at bringing them closer together.

Natalie sued for divorce on July 25, 1932, citing infidelity; an affair with an extra aboard their ninety-eight-foot yacht (which was named *Natalie*) was used as grounds for the divorce. The court awarded her custody of Jimmy and Bobby, and Buster was ordered to pay alimony and child support. Buster was not confrontational. Although community property laws in California did not entitle her to more than half of everything, Buster allowed her to keep nearly all of the assets, including the Italian Villa, two of their three cars, the yacht, other property, and cash in the bank. She continued to take him to court after the divorce, although each time it had the opposite effect than what Natalie intended; the judge would lessen the amount Buster was to pay. She also made it very difficult for Buster to see Jimmy and Bobby after the

two boys left the Black-Foxe Military Institute, a private military school in Hollywood.

In 1934 Natalie obtained a court order that legally changed Jimmy and Bobby's surnames from Keaton to Talmadge, which devastated Buster. Natalie never remarried, and her bitterness toward Buster never diminished.

It was not until 1938, when Jimmy, having earned a driver's license, drove to Cheviot Hills with his younger brother that the relationship between Buster and his sons was able to be repaired in some way. The day Jimmy and Bobby came to see him was one of the happiest days of Buster's life.

With sons Jimmy (left) and Bobby (right), as grandfather Joe Keaton looks on, in Buster's M-G-M bungalow, c. 1930.

THREE AGES (1923)

THREE AGES WAS THE FIRST OF Buster's independent feature-length comedies. He had wanted to make features since 1920, when Joe Schenck gave him his own unit, but only after Chaplin and Lloyd had begun to make features was Buster allowed to do so. Marcus Loew, the head of Metro, told Schenck he wanted Buster to make features for Metro to release. The agreement called for Buster to make two features a year, one for spring release, and the other for autumn release. Schenck doubled Buster's salary to two thousand dollars a week (and later to twenty-five hundred dollars) and a twenty-five percent share of the net profits from the films.

Three Ages was a parody of *Intolerance*, D. W. Griffith's epic of love's struggle throughout the ages, which interwove four stories. Buster told his story in three: the Stone Age, the Roman Age, and the Modern Age. The three stories, in parallel episodes, were virtually three two-reelers, which minimized his risk—if the feature failed, he could convert the film into three two-reel comedies. The situation of rival suitors, Buster and Wallace Beery, trying to win the affection of leading lady Margaret Leahy, was repeated in all three episodes. Beery, who would become a great star in the 1930s, was a well-known character actor when Buster hired him for *Three Ages*. He had

KN20
62

worked for Essanay and Mack Sennett in the 1910s and had received praise as King Richard in *Douglas Fairbanks in Robin Hood* (1922).

Margaret Leahy was a blonde English girl who had won a "New British Film Star" competition, in which the prize was to appear in one of Buster's films as his leading lady. Leahy was pretty, but had neither the talent nor the temperament for acting. Buster had difficulties with her. Easy scenes had to be shot over and over again. However, he did not complain and tried to make the best of the situation. Buster had wanted Constance Talmadge for the leading lady in *Three Ages* (she had played the Mountain Girl in

Opposite: With Blanche Payson in the Stone Age episode of THREE AGES.

Above: In the Roman Age episode of THREE AGES, *Buster finds himself in the lion's den. An intertitle reads, "He vaguely remembered that somewhere—sometime— somehow—somebody made friends with a lion doing something to its paws."*

Above: This behind-the-scenes photograph from the Stone Age episode of THREE AGES *shows Buster pulling Blanche Payson's hair, as several crew members out of camera range on the right wait for Buster to be pushed off the rock by Payson and land safely in a firefighter's tarp.*

Right: Buster with his gagmen, all wearing his trademark porkpie hat, at the Keaton Studio during production of THREE AGES. *Joe Mitchell, Clyde Bruckman, Buster, Jean Havez, and Eddie Cline.*

Above: Buster breaks his fall from the top of a building by plunging through several canvas window awnings before grabbing onto a drainpipe in the Modern Age episode. His ability to perform such stunts earned him the nickname "The Little Iron Man" at the studio.

Right: Margaret Leahy, preparing for the Stone Age episode, is stretched out on a dolly with a handle concealed in her hair. Buster, in costume for the Modern Age episode, demonstrates to his stand-in how to pull her hair. Buster used a stand-in for insert shots involving his right hand to conceal the fact that he had lost the tip of his right index finger as a child.

Intolerance). Buster and Constance wanted to work together, but Schenck—who produced both their films—would not allow it. Talmadge was a star in her own right, and Schenck felt, as most producers did at that time, that each motion picture had one star and supporting players. To put two stars together in a film was considered a waste of talent.

The Stone Age sequence, which was filmed on location in Chatsworth, California, has Buster introduced atop the back of a brontosaurus. Buster had seen Winsor McCay's animated dinosaur short *Gertie* (1914) and wanted something like that for *Three Ages*. Max Fleischer, the creator of the popular *Out of the Inkwell* cartoons with Koko the Clown, created a small model of the dinosaur with a little Buster riding on its back and brought it to life using stop-motion animation.

Fred Gabourie designed some large sets for the Roman episode, but they were not as elaborate or as expensive as they look in the film. The Coliseum set was built up only to the first couple of tiers; the rest was a glass shot. Glass shots, a well-known technique in the 1920s before process screens, were elaborate backgrounds painted on glass and positioned precisely before the camera. The chariot race, with Buster and his dog team, was shot on the location of a

Buster experiences the Fall of Rome in this gag still from THREE AGES.

The THREE AGES love triangle, as seen in the Modern Age episode. Buster's rival for the hand of Margaret Leahy is Wallace Beery.

Hollywood exposition. The episode was filled with silly gags, the most memorable perhaps being Buster's encounter with a ridiculously fake lion.

During the filming of the Modern Age episode, a mishap occurred that was worked into the picture. The scene required Buster to leap from one building to another. A set was constructed on the Hill Street tunnel in downtown Los Angeles. With the street below, it gave the illusion that it was twelve stories up, but it was really a set with a thirty-five-foot drop. Buster used the lid of a skylight as a springboard to make an eighteen-foot jump from one rooftop to another. He misjudged the spring of the board and failed to make the leap, hitting the wall of the other side and falling into the net. He bruised his knees and was in bed for three days. When they ran the footage of the accident, Eddie Cline and the crew suggested changing the sequence in order to work the shot into the picture. They picked up days later with the fall, which cuts to Buster landing onto an awning (which breaks his fall), whereupon he swings from that to a rainspout into an open window and down a pole. He has landed in the local fire station. Bewildered, he finds himself upon the rear platform of a fire truck as it speeds off to a fire. According to

Buster, this proved to be the biggest laugh-getting sequence in the picture.

Even more so with the features than with the shorts, previews were an essential tool in the creation of Buster's films. A rough cut of the film would be screened so that Buster and his crew could gauge audience reaction and then go back to the editing room to help the high spots and reshoot scenes that did not work. They never previewed the films in Hollywood for fear that somebody connected with the studios would be in the audience and might steal a sequence or a gag, film it, and release it before Buster's picture went into distribution. Glendale, Long Beach, San Bernadino, Riverside, and Santa Ana were favorite preview locations. Two previews were the average for one of Buster's features. *Three Ages* was the exception. Margaret Leahy's inability to act forced Buster to preview the film eight times. He reshot her scenes over and over again to get a passable performance from her.

Three Ages was a commercial success, but it was a transitional film filled with the unbelievable slapstick that belonged to the period of Buster's shorts. He was now confident that his next feature, *Our Hospitality*, would be even better.

OUR HOSPITALITY IS ONE OF Buster's most perfectly constructed films. Like *The General* (1926), his best-known and most admired film, *Our Hospitality* is a period piece, set in the American South. Both films employ visual beauty and dramatic integrity as a backdrop to Buster's brilliant original comedy.

Directed by Buster and John G. (Jack) Blystone, *Our Hospitality* featured the Keaton family. Buster's wife, Natalie Talmadge, at first objected to Buster's taking her and their infant son on location to the picturesque country of Truckee and Lake Tahoe, but when Buster offered Natalie the part of leading lady in the picture, she retracted her objections. Their son Jimmy (billed as Buster Keaton, Jr.) is seen in the film's prologue, and Buster's father, Joe, plays the railroad engineer.

Below: Riding a replica of the Gentleman's Hobby-Horse, the first bicycle, in OUR HOSPITALITY.

Opposite: Buster assumes his classic pose astride a miniature horse.

The story, from an idea by Jean Havez, was loosely derived from the decidedly unhumorous real-life feud between the Hatfields and the McCoys, two large family clans whose hatred of each other was legendary. The film begins with a prologue of straight melodrama, in which the feud between the two families (renamed the Canfields and the McKays) is established. The main story, set twenty years later in 1831, has Buster playing twenty-one-year-old Willie McKay, a New York dandy who is summoned to the South to claim his family's estate. To film Willie McKay's journey to the South, Buster was inspired to use one of the first steam locomotives ever manufactured. Buster chose to reproduce an English locomotive, George Stephenson's *Rocket*, because it looked much funnier than its American counterpart.

Buster was scrupulous with every detail of the picture. The art direction is of exceptional quality, as are the costumes. The entire production was so carefully researched and staged that Buster's precise duplication of the Gentleman's Hobby-Horse, the first bicycle ever made, was later given to the Smithsonian in Washington at the institution's request.

The dramatic logic of the film's narrative, to which Buster gave a comic twist, was a departure from anything he had done previously. Buster later explained:

We were very conscious of our stories. We learned in a hurry that we couldn't make a feature-length picture the way we had done the two-reelers; we couldn't use impossible gags, what we call "cartoon" gags, like the

kind of things that happen to cartoon characters.
We lost all of that when we started making feature
pictures. They had to be believable, or your story
wouldn't hold up.[10]

Despite the meticulous planning and precise execution of the film, the production of *Our Hospitality*
was fraught with difficulties and laden with unantici-
pated problems. Joe Roberts, who played Joseph
Canfield, suffered a stroke while on location and was
hospitalized in Reno, Nevada. He recovered suffi-
ciently to continue in the film, although his weak-
ened condition is apparent in several scenes. Just a
month after the final retake, Roberts died.

Three weeks after shooting began on location,
Natalie Talmadge discovered she was pregnant with

Opposite: With cameramen Elgin Lessley
and Gordon Jennings just prior to filming
the leap over the waterfall for OUR
HOSPITALITY.

Above: This behind-the-scenes photograph
of Buster in the Truckee River was taken
moments before his hold-back wire broke,
propelling him down the river where he
nearly drowned.

Right: Buster makes the waterfall leap to rescue his girl in Our Hospitality. *The leap was influenced by the climactic swing across the skyscraper in Harold Lloyd's* Safety Last *(1923) and the ice floe sequence in D. W. Griffith's* Way Down East *(1920). He took in so much water executing the stunt that he had to be given medical attention.*

Opposite: The waterfall sequence was not filmed on location in Truckee, but on a set built over a large Hollywood studio swimming pool.

their second son, Bobby. To complete the film, Buster was forced to photograph Natalie in such a way as to camouflage her pregnancy.

One of the most outstanding sequences in *Our Hospitality* entails Willie McKay being pursued and ultimately falling into a river. McKay's sweetheart sets out to help, and she too falls in, so McKay has to help her. The scene, which was shot at the Truckee River (a favorite Keaton location), nearly killed Buster. He was splashing in the river with a hold-back wire tied around him. At one point, the wire broke, and Buster took off like a shot down the river. Ernie Orsatti and several other men working on the film ran after him along the riverbank, unable to help him. Finally, Buster was able to grab onto a branch of an overhanging tree, preventing himself from smashing into the rocks, but not before a whole school of little water snakes swam around him. What must have seemed to Buster like a million baby eels were flicking their tongues at him, and he did not know whether they were poisonous or not. All he could think of was finding something to hold onto before he was smashed to bits. Of course, all of that is in the film in what is perhaps its most thrilling scene. The finished sequence is one of Buster's marvels, a demonstration of his physical dexterity and skill as well as his filmmaking genius.

Although most of *Our Hospitality* was filmed on location, the amazing waterfall rescue sequence was actually photographed in Hollywood. Buster constructed the waterfall over a large studio swimming pool, with a miniature set to create the illusion of a distant valley below the falls. Buster performed all the stunt work for the rescue himself, which was physically demanding as well as dangerous, and he took in so much water hanging underneath the falls that medical assistance was required. As Buster later recalled, "I had to go down to the doctor right there and then. They pumped out my ears and nostrils and drained me, because when a full volume of water like that comes down and hits you and you're upside down—then you really get it."[11]

Despite all the difficulties, Buster remembered the production fondly. The summer stay in Tahoe with his family reminded him of his happy boyhood summers spent on Lake Muskegon, Michigan. Buster was proud of *Our Hospitality* (he always referred to the film as simply *Hospitality*) and considered it one of his best films.

S HERLOCK J R. IS A SHOWCASE OF
stage gags and illusions that Buster had learned in
vaudeville, translated with great ingenuity to the
screen. Demonstrating Buster's love for the movies
more than any other of his films, *Sherlock Jr.* was
also the most technically challenging picture he
ever made.

Buster plays a projectionist in a small-town movie
theater who dreams of becoming a detective. He is
rejected by his girl (Kathryn McGuire) after being
falsely accused of having stolen her father's pocket
watch, which was actually stolen and pawned by his
rival for the girl, played by Ward Crane. *Sherlock Jr.*
becomes a film within a film in a dream sequence
that occurs when Buster goes back to the theater's
projection booth and falls asleep once the evening

*Above and opposite: Buster is a film
projectionist who aspires to be a great
detective in* SHERLOCK JR.

film is running. Imagining he is a character in the movie he is projecting, he simply walks into the screen and becomes Sherlock Jr., the great detective. The film ends with Buster awakening to find his girl in the projection booth, having discovered his innocence of the crime.

Buster's entire reason for making the film was to create the situation of a motion-picture projectionist in a theater who falls asleep and visualizes himself becoming involved with the characters on the screen. The dream sequence was the excuse for all the film's impossible gags. Had Buster not had one of the best cameramen in motion pictures, Elgin Lessley, he would never have made *Sherlock Jr.* Lessley executed the special effects so perfectly that cinematographers and other film technicians of the time went to see

Sherlock Jr. repeatedly, amazed by its effects, to try to figure out how certain scenes in the film were done.

The picture on the screen within the screen was a theater set, lit in such a way as to look like a film being projected. The changing of scenes on the screen within the screen was achieved by making everyone freeze while the set was altered. Lessley had to film screen and theater separately for exterior shots, using surveyor's instruments. One of the exterior scenes involved Buster surrounded by two lions. Buster filmed the scene in a large circular cage at Universal, and this was the only time he did not get along with animals. He was in the cage alone, with Elgin Lessley outside the cage shooting through a hole. The two big lions started to follow him and, with bushes and other tropical foliage concealing the

cage, Buster became nervous because he was not quite sure where the gate to the cage was located, in case he needed to make a hasty exit. When he safely got out of the cage, Lessley announced that Buster had to repeat the shot for the foreign negative. In silent films, two cameramen were necessary because virtually everything was shot with two cameras, placed side by side. One made the negative for America, the other the negative for Europe and other countries abroad. Buster said, "Europe ain't going to see this scene!" Europe did eventually see the scene; Buster had a duplicate negative made from the domestic version of the film.

Many gags in *Sherlock Jr.* were not camera tricks at all. Buster photographed them in long takes to show these amazing feats just as they happened. The best

Opposite: This still depicts a sequence that does not appear in Sherlock Jr.; *it was either abandoned or cut from the film prior to release. The preoccupied ticket-office girl remains unidentified. However, she does appear elsewhere in the film as the girl who works the service counter of the confectionery shop.*

Above: Buster examines his celluloid world.

125

example of this comes when Buster, trapped by a dead end, dives straight through a peddler woman's tray and apparently disappears completely through her body (the peddler woman is actually Sherlock Jr.'s assistant, Gillette, in disguise). It was a reworking of one of Joe Keaton's stage tricks, which involved a small hinged trapdoor in the wall directly behind the tray lid and what looks like Gillette's chest. The bottom half of his body was actually lifted in a horizontal position; he wore a dress over his top half and the bottom half was faked with a costume hanging down containing mannequin dummy ankles and feet. After Buster dove through, Gillette's legs were lowered and the wall closed. The skirt of the dress was weighted with buckshot so it would not move. Gillette then walked away from the wall. It was a very dangerous

stunt. Buster restaged it for Donald O'Connor years later for *The Buster Keaton Story* (1957), and Donald did an admirable job executing this risky stunt.

Buster had two accidents while filming *Sherlock Jr.* The first accident, which was more serious, occurred when Buster was running along the top of a freight car and was struck by the flow of water from a water tower. He misjudged the force of the water, which hit him extremely hard. It tore his hands loose from the rope, and he was thrown to the track. His head hit directly on the rail. He finished the shot, which required him to get up and run away from two men who were chasing him. He had a headache for a few hours, took a few stiff drinks, went to bed, and was fine the next day. Eleven years later he had a complete physical examination with X rays. The doctor

K22-95

asked Buster, "When did you break your neck?"
Buster said, "I never broke my neck." The doctor
showed Buster the X-ray, which revealed a callous
that had grown over the fracture, near the top verte-
bra. Buster realized he must have broken his neck
went he hit the track making *Sherlock Jr.*!

The second accident, which was minor compared
to the first, happened in a scene in which Buster
calls a motorcycle cop and jumps on his handlebars.
The bike speeds off, hits a pothole in the street, and
the cop falls off without Buster realizing it. The cop
was actually Buster. Ernie Orsatti, a prop man who
later was an outfielder for the St. Louis Cardinals,
was Buster's size, so Buster dressed Ernie in his own
costume and wore the cop uniform to achieve the
stunt. When Buster went back to finish the scene
alone on the motorcycle, he had to sit on the handlebars, where he had control of the speed but no
brakes. At one point he passed a row of workmen
shoveling in a long ditch, and a shovel full of dirt
accidentally hit him in the face. Buster lost control,

*Above: Buster rides the handlebars of a
policeman's motorcycle. The motorcycle
cop is an unidentified player, and Steve
Murphy is in the background.*

*Opposite: Buster is about to become a part
of the action in the film on the screen in
the dream sequence from* SHERLOCK
JR. *Buster's father, Joe, is the man on the
film screen.*

*In a reworking of one of his father's
old stage tricks, Buster dives straight
through the body of his assistant,
Gillette (disguised as a peddler woman).*

went straight toward the cameras, and wound up flying off the bike and hitting the windshield of a car.
Miraculously, Buster did not sustain any injuries.

Roscoe Arbuckle started as director on *Sherlock Jr.*
Arbuckle, as a result of the Virginia Rappe scandal,
unjustly was not allowed to work as an actor but did
work as a director, using his father's first two names,
William Goodrich. He was still so bitter and hurt by
the ordeal that it was impacting his comedy judg-
ment, and Buster had to take him off the picture
after a few weeks.

It took five months to make *Sherlock Jr.* When first
previewed, the film was not well received, so Buster
recut the picture; a second preview was also unsatis-
factory. After a third preview he did some further cutting and released it. Buster had difficulty structuring
it as a feature. He shot more than 60,000 feet of film

Buster and leading lady Kathryn McGuire in the final scene of the dream sequence from SHERLOCK JR.

for *Sherlock Jr.*, but the final print was only 4,065 feet. Buster felt it worked better as a shorter film, playing like two two-reelers: the first two reels set up the situation, and the last two reels contain the comedy conclusion. As a result of the cuts, the film is about one reel (approximately ten to twelve minutes) shorter than most comedy feature films of the period.

At its core, *Sherlock Jr.* is a film about film. It contains self-reflective jokes about the nature of film, as well as about illusion and reality, and indicates the impact of the movies on audiences of that time, which was unlike that of any medium before or since. Keaton reflects on this phenomenon in the film's last scene, when he looks to the movie on the screen to show himself how to act with his girlfriend. *Sherlock Jr.* has influenced other filmmakers, most notably Woody Allen in *The Purple Rose of Cairo* (1985).

THE NAVIGATOR (1924)

Above: THE NAVIGATOR (1924) is virtually a comic duet with Buster and Kathryn McGuire as two idle rich people who find themselves the only passengers on a ship adrift at sea. The helpless pair cannot prepare even a simple breakfast without problems.

Opposite top: One of the most famous images of Buster is this beautifully composed still from THE NAVIGATOR.

Opposite bottom: A portrait of Buster from THE NAVIGATOR.

THE NAVIGATOR, AN ABANDONED ocean liner, is the stage upon which Buster creates a charming comic duet between a pair of wealthy society simpletons who unwittingly find themselves adrift on the high seas and are forced to take care of themselves and ultimately each other. Buster's most commercially successful film, *The Navigator* is second only to *The General* in its use of a grand and elaborate set piece as a backdrop to an intimate comedy of character.

Fred Gabourie, Buster's technical director, had promised Buster, after the difficulties with the filming of the launch sequence in *The Boat*, that he would someday find a boat that could be used to top the two-reeler. When Gabourie came across the *Buford*, a full-fledged ocean liner, that was on loan to director Frank Lloyd who was filming *The Sea Hawk* (1924), he knew he had found Buster the perfect prop. The *Buford* was so intriguing as a film prop that a story was written to make use of it.

The *Buford* was called "the Soviet Ark" and was used by the U.S. government to deport anarchists and radicals rounded up during the 1919 Red Scare. It was a five-hundred-foot ocean liner, and Buster leased it from the Alaskan-Siberian Navigation Company for twenty-five thousand dollars. It was repaired and repainted (with the name *Navigator* on the side), and the cast and crew lived on the ship for ten weeks, with much of the filming done near Avalon Bay, off Catalina Island.

Gabourie's find inspired Jean Havez to create a story of two idle people alone and adrift on an empty ship. Buster plays Rollo Treadway, introduced with the title, "Rollo Treadway—heir to the Treadway fortune—a living proof that every family tree must have its sap." Rollo decides to get married. His girl, Betsy

O'Brien (played by Kathryn McGuire), declines his marriage proposal, so Rollo (who has already arranged two steamship tickets to Honolulu) decides to go anyway. He ends up boarding the wrong ship— a ship belonging to Betsy's father that is set adrift by foreign spies. Betsy manages to get aboard as well, and by morning the two discover that they are the only passengers on a ship adrift at sea. The comedy grows from the complications of two helpless people (who have never done anything for themselves) having to adapt to the rough conditions.

Buster believed that the film's plot, which begins with a serious dramatic prologue involving spies and foreign agents, required a codirector for the dramatic sequences. Donald Crisp, who had established himself in D. W. Griffith's *Broken Blossoms* (1919) as a character actor and who went on to play fatherly roles in *How Green Was My Valley* (1941) and *Lassie, Come Home* (1943), was hired to direct the serious parts, but soon he became interested only in working on the comedy scenes with Buster. Buster was not happy with Crisp's work and reshot many of his dramatic scenes after Crisp left the production, as he felt they were overacted. The lasting contribution Crisp left to the film was his face. The angry face in the oil portrait that scares Rollo when it swings at his porthole is the face of Donald Crisp.

The underwater sequence, in which Rollo has to go overboard in a deep-sea-diving suit to stop the ship from sinking, was mired with unexpected difficulties. Buster refused to use a double and insisted on going down himself, even though diving was very dangerous. They first tried to shoot the scene in the Riverside municipal swimming pool. However, the weight of the extra water created when they built up the pool to accommodate the mock-up of the *Navigator*'s stern ruined the pool. The Keaton company had to pay to rebuild it.

They next tried waters off Catalina Island, but the water was not clear because it was fish-spawning season. The eventual location choice for the scene was Lake Tahoe in Nevada. It took four weeks to complete the underwater sequence. The water was crystal clear but extremely cold, and Buster could stay down for only thirty minutes at a time. The two cameramen worked in a specially constructed wooden box with a glass panel, submerged about twenty feet in

these "Coming Attractions runners") to promote the film. While underwater making repairs to the ship, Buster picks up a starfish, attaches it to his chest, and proceeds to direct fish traffic with the twelve hundred rubber fish the property department built. They were suspended on thin, strong strings moved by a large machine—mounted on four telegraph poles—above the water. Buster loved the sequence, but audiences did not laugh when they previewed the film. Buster concluded that this was because the scene interfered with the hero's job of saving the ship and the girl, and it interrupted the story. Removed from the story and shown in a trailer, the scene was a success.

The Navigator was received with unanimous praise and was Buster's most commercially successful film. It established his reputation as a major filmmaker, like Chaplin and Lloyd, and was one of Buster's two favorite films, along with *The General*.

the lake. Ice had to be packed around the cameramen to prevent the glass panel from fogging up.

Not all of the problems concerned the water. No one ever told Buster that one should never be lowered into the water on a rope ladder when wearing a deep-sea-diving suit, but instead a stationary ladder should always be used. Buster went into the water on the rope ladder, and his feet raised up to a point where he was flat on his back and his face was pressed against the glass face plate of the suit's helmet so that he could not breathe. If one looks closely at the scene in the film, the panic on his face is clearly evident. Finally, he let go of the rope and pulled on the line for the crew to let him go. Buster dangled in the water for a while to get his breathing back. His crew had no idea exactly what was happening.

A favorite sequence of Buster's had to be cut from the picture but was used in the trailer (Buster called

Above: With Donald Crisp, preparing to film Buster descending the ladder into the water. Crisp would leave the production prior to filming the underwater scenes in Lake Tahoe.

Right: Buster in his diving suit, complete with hat.

Opposite: Cast and crew of THE NAVIGATOR *lived aboard the ship for ten weeks in waters off Catalina Island, visible in the background.*

Buster plays Jimmie Shannon, who is too timid to propose to his sweetheart (Ruth Dwyer), in SEVEN CHANCES. *This prologue sequence was photographed in two-strip Technicolor.*

TODAY CONSIDERED ONE OF BUSTER'S best pictures, *Seven Chances* was a film Buster did not like until very late in his life. His dislike for the film began when the story was forced upon him by Joe Schenck, who bought *Seven Chances*, a play written by Roi Cooper Megrue (based on a short story by Gouverneur Morris), for twenty-five thousand dollars without consulting Buster. Buster had seen the play on Broadway in 1916. It was not a commercial success; in fact, it was one of theater producer David Belasco's failures. Moreover, it was an unbelievable farce, and Buster as a rule wanted believable stories for his feature pictures. What made matters worse was that John McDermott, a director and screen-writer, had sold the story to Schenck as part of a deal in which Schenck promised McDermott he would direct the film. Buster had recently borrowed a lot of money from Schenck and owed him several favors, so he reluctantly went along with the idea of McDermott as his new director.

McDermott started casting, hired extra writers, and ordered sets to be built, intending to faithfully adapt the farce to the screen. The bills were coming in, and he was spending large sums of money. After two weeks, Buster and Lou Anger confronted McDermott, and he left the production. To heighten what Buster considered an unpromising story, Buster photographed the prologue of the film in two-strip Technicolor—a novelty in 1925—and hired Snitz Edwards, the Jewish comedian and veteran Broadway character actor, for the important comedy role of the attorney. Edwards's memorable performances in Rex Ingram's *The Prisoner of Zenda* (1922), *Souls for Sale* (1923), and Douglas Fairbanks's *The Thief of Bagdad* (1924) had made him an appealing casting choice. Buster liked his work so much that he used Edwards again in *Battling Butler*, *The General* (in a scene that was cut just prior to the film's release), and *College*.

In *Seven Chances* Buster plays Jimmie Shannon, who learns at noon on his twenty-seventh birthday that he must be married by seven o'clock that evening in order to inherit a fortune. Bungling a marriage proposal, he is rejected by his longtime sweetheart. By the time she reconsiders, Jimmie is already making the rounds at his country club, where his impromptu proposals to seven different women (his seven chances) are rejected. In desperation, Jimmie's business partner places an appeal for a bride in the local newspaper, pleading that Jimmie needs a bride to meet him at the church at five o'clock. The advertisement receives an overwhelming response. The climax of the film finds Buster chased by five hundred would-be brides in full wedding regalia, and ends with one of Buster's most astounding acrobatic and cinematic feats—racing down a hill while bombarded by an avalanche of enormous boulders.

The rockslide climax was not in the original play or film scenario. The original climax of the film was just an elaborate chase, ending with Buster running down the side of a hill, the brides following behind. When the film was previewed for the second time, Buster thought he had a bad picture and that there was nothing he could do about it. However, Buster and his team heard laughter just as the scene began to fade out. They did not know what had caused the laughter, so they ran the film again at the studio the next day. At the screening they discovered that Buster had dislodged a rock, and it in turn had loosened two others coming down the side of the hill. As the rocks started to roll after him, the preview audience sat up in their seats. They found the sequence funny and were expecting more.

To build on this moment, Buster had Fred Gabourie fabricate fifteen hundred papier-mâché rocks that ranged from grapefruit size to boulders eight feet in diameter. They found a new location, on the Ridge Route in the High Sierras. The mountain was steeper than a forty-five-degree angle to accommodate the rolling boulders. They reshot the sequence with the brides chasing Buster and incorporated the boulders. The scene was carefully worked out; much thought went into where the different-sized rocks would be placed and where they would roll down the incline. The improvisation came in dodging the rocks once they were let loose. Buster felt that the scene saved the film.

The rock chase may have saved the film, but it was a quiet moment of photographic virtuosity that Buster liked best. It was the scene where he drives from his country club to his sweetheart's house and back again to the country club. He gets into a 1922 Mercer Raceabout, starts the engine, releases the brake, and sits back to drive, but the car does not move from its spot: only the background changes, dissolving from one location to another. The effect was achieved by Elgin Lessley with the use of surveyor's instruments. Buster loved this simple scene. He also loved the Mercer Raceabout, so much so that he bought two of them: one was for the film

The arrival of five hundred would-be brides.

Buster is chased by the five hundred would-be brides through the city streets.

and the other went to his sister-in-law Constance Talmadge.

Seven Chances was a success because the team worked over the material to make a stage farce into a Buster Keaton film; the second half of the picture—eluding brides and boulder rocks—was created by Buster and his writers, and it is the comedy in its second half for which the film is remembered. The film was in fact the last in which the team of Clyde Bruckman, Jean Havez, and Joseph Mitchell worked together. Bruckman went to work for Harold Lloyd, who was making *For Heaven's Sake* (1926); Havez died in 1925; and Mitchell went to write stories for Universal.

Despite its commercial success, Buster never felt satisfied with the film. When Raymond Rohauer wanted to pay off various copyright holders so that he could reissue the film, Buster told him not to bother. He felt it was his worst picture. When Raymond pursued it anyway, Buster was disgusted that Raymond wasted his money on the film. *Seven Chances* was revived at the third New York Film Festival in September 1965; the film had not been seen in over thirty-five years. To Buster's surprise, and contrary to his long-held impression, the film proved to be—and remains—a spectacular crowd-pleaser.

GO WEST (1925)

Go West is unique in Buster's work as the only film in which he combined comedy and pathos in a manner similar to Charlie Chaplin's trademark style of filmmaking in films such as *The Gold Rush* (1925). At once sentimental and a clever parody of sentimentality, *Go West* has fewer gags and more dramatic scenes than Buster's other films. It is his most romantic film with his most unusual "hero-ine," a beautiful little Jersey cow named Brown Eyes.

Buster had a great affinity for animals, and in Brown Eyes he found both an affectionate and obedi-

Below: Buster plays a wistful tramplike character in Go West, *a flattering parody of Chaplin.*

Opposite: In the opening sequence, Buster hauls all his possessions to the general store, where he sells them for $1.65.

K25-156

ent animal that he trained himself in ten days. He started working with her by using a little rope around her neck, walking her everywhere and feeding her tidbits. This way he befriended her. By the time they started shooting the film, he just took black sewing thread and tied one end around her neck and the other end to his little finger. Everywhere he went she stayed right with him and never broke the thread. It got to the point where she was with him all the time.

Go West was partly made on location at George "Tap" Duncan's Valley Ranch, about fifty miles north of Kingman, Arizona. Buster and his crew were on the location for about three weeks in the summer of 1925. The desert locale was so hot that they had to pack ice around the cameras to prevent the emulsion of the film from melting. However, the desert heat did not give them as much of a problem as when Brown Eyes went into heat! She became disobedient, and Buster and the crew had to wait two weeks until she recovered from it.

In the film, Buster plays a lonely drifter named Friendless (the names "Friendless" and "Brown Eyes" were taken from characters in D. W. Griffith's *Intolerance*). The film's opening sequence, in which Friendless sells all his possessions to a general store for $1.65, only to have to give back most of it when he realizes he forgot to withhold personal items such as his mother's picture, wonderfully establishes his character and the semi-humorous, sentimental tone to the film. With his remaining coins, Friendless buys a loaf of bread and a sausage. He rides the boxcars, first journeying to New York but soon following the advice popularized by journalist and political leader Horace Greeley to "Go west, young man. Go west."

He arrives in Arizona, where he gets a job as a ranch hand. In a scene reminiscent of *Androcles and the Lion*, Friendless sees the ostracized Brown Eyes limping, and he comes to her aid, removing a rock wedged in her hoof. As a result of this kind act, Friendless has now made his first friend. The pathos comes from these two unloved and inept characters finding each other. Buster's character is devoted to his only companion and does everything he can to keep his beloved cow from being sent to the stockyard.

Buster planned a magnificent visual climax to conclude the film, but it did not work according to plan. In the film, Friendless unleashes steer at the train depot, causing bovine chaos through Los Angeles as he leads them to the stockyard. Some of these scenes were actually photographed in downtown Los Angeles, where he had three hundred head of steer on location, but much of the city sequence was actually filmed on a street set at the studio. What Buster intended, but was unable to create, was an actual stampede chase scene, leading the cattle to the stockyard like the Pied Piper. Friendless goes into a costume shop and sees a red devil's suit, knowing that steer do not like red and will chase it. Buster donned the costume thinking he would get a funny sequence, but the steer would not chase him. He had to have cattlemen push them to go as fast as they would go. That hurt the film, as it was to be the big finish. In the end, Buster's cameramen had to trick it from all angles—along with undercranking the cameras—to create the illusion of a stampede. Though the finished sequence remained a disappointment to Buster, failing to meet his initial expectations, it is exceptionally well made. Buster—when he wanted or had to be—was a highly skilled film illusionist.

Working without his usual team of gag writers Jean Havez, Clyde Bruckman, and Joseph Mitchell for the first time, Buster brought in Lex Neal, an old friend from his childhood summers spent in Bluffton, Michigan, and Raymond Cannon to help with gags. After the cattle chase, they decided to end the film with a delightful scene. Friendless has singlehandedly delivered all the ranch owner's cattle to the stockyard. In gratitude, the ranch owner tells him in an intertitle, "My home

and anything I have is yours for the asking." "I want her," responds Friendless, pointing in the direction of the ranch owner's pretty daughter. Friendless then walks right past the girl to his beloved Brown Eyes immediately beside her. The film ends with the four of them driving off in the ranch owner's car, Friendless and Brown Eyes happily side by side in the back seat.

The film is most memorable for its little moments. When Buster plays cards in the bunkhouse with a couple of cowboys, he points out that one player is cheating. The dishonest card player points a gun at him and remarks, "When you say that— SMILE." Buster, of course, is unable to smile, and he does the famous Lillian Gish gesture from *Broken Blossoms* of pushing the corners of his mouth up with two fingers.

Buster believed that this scene would draw big laughs from audiences appreciating the threefold parody of his own character's deadpan expression, the reference to Lillian Gish in *Broken Blossoms*, and Westerns in general ("When you say that—SMILE" was a famous line from the popular western *The Virginian*). But in previews, he was disappointed because it did not get the response he had expected. Audiences just felt sorry for him. However, Buster liked the scene so much he kept it in the finished film.

A character comedy more than a gag comedy, *Go West* is a very successful film on that basis and therefore the (perhaps misguided) inspiration for *Battling Butler*.

Opposite top: Buster as Friendless.

Opposite bottom: "When you say that—SMILE," demands the ranch foreman (Ray Thompson) after Buster has accused him of cheating at cards.

Below: Buster accompanies his beloved cow, Brown Eyes.

ONE OF BUSTER'S FAVORITE FILMS, *Battling Butler* was also one of his most commercially successful motion pictures, second only to *The Navigator*. Buster's pride in the film was based on its tremendous popularity and his physical mastery in the climactic boxing bout. Modern audiences do not respond the same way to *Battling Butler* as they did in 1926, and it is today perhaps the least known of his silent features. The comedy is not as strong as in his other features, and the climactic fight seems to be out of key with the rest of the film.

The film was based on a stage play, *Battling Buttler*, an English musical comedy that had been a success on Broadway in 1923. What attracted Buster was the boxing aspect of the original stage show. Buster and his team of gagmen—Paul Gerard Smith, Al Boasberg, Charles H. Smith, and Lex Neal—discarded all the songs and dances, eliminated one "t" from the name in the play's title, and reworked the script to fashion it into a Keaton film.

Battling Butler is the story of pampered playboy Alfred Butler, a character similar to the roles Buster had played in *The Saphead* and *The Navigator*. Alfred is sent off by his father to the mountains in the hope that a hunting and fishing trip will make a man out of him. "Roughing it" in the mountains in the company of his valet (wonderfully played by Snitz Edwards), Alfred discovers that he shares the same

Alfred "Battling" Butler (Francis MacDonald) and his wife (Mary O'Brien, with black eye), encounter the other Alfred Butler with his wife (Sally O'Neil) in BATTLING BUTLER.

name as a famous boxer, Alfred "Battling" Butler, the world lightweight champion contender. Alfred pretends to be the boxer in order to impress the mountain girl (played by Sally O'Neil) with whom he has instantly fallen in love. After their marriage, he attempts to pass himself off as the famous boxer and trains to fight the real Battling Butler's upcoming championship bout with the Alabama Murderer.

The unexpected climax of the film is dramatic rather than comic. The film begins like *The Navigator*, introducing the pampered hero in much the same manner as his earlier film, but instead of the usual strong comedy audiences had grown to expect from him, the picture develops into a light comedy and ends with a dramatic climax. Abandoning the climax from the original play, in which the hero at the last minute does not have to fight, Buster added his own climax, as he felt that he could not lead an audience to expect all through the film that his character is going to fight in the ring and then not do it. So he staged a fight in the dressing room in which his character takes on the real Battling Butler, who has just won the title in the ring against the Alabama Murderer.

The fight is dramatic, and Buster's character is brutally hit by the real "Battling" Butler. When the prizefighter hits Alfred's beloved valet, Alfred becomes uncontrollable and furiously punches out the champion. A dramatic fight scene was new to film comedy, and Buster was pleased with the finished result.

Buster's Alfred Butler character, who can take any amount of pain and still win at the end, is like Buster himself. This similarity perhaps explains why Buster liked the film so much. The dramatic fight was the

With Mickey Walker, welterweight champion of the world, on the set of BATTLING BUTLER. *Walker was a friend of Buster's and advised him on the film's climactic fight.*

big scene in the film, and since he was the director, he staged it exactly the way he wanted it. Buster was part masochist; he did not seem to mind the bruises and strained muscles that were everyday occurrences in the boxing sequences.

The best comedy scenes are early in the film, and one of Buster's favorite moments was the duck-shooting sequence, in which Alfred is no match for the little duck that repeatedly descends underwater and reappears on the other side of Alfred's small canoe. Alfred eventually capsizes the boat trying to get the duck. Thirty-one years later Buster reworked this duck-hunting routine for the film made for the 1957 summer-stock production of *Merton of the Movies*.

Battling Butler was the last Keaton film to be released by Joe Schenck under his distribution agreement with Metro-Goldwyn-Mayer. Now Buster's films would be released by United Artists where Schenck was president. The film's commercial success allowed Buster the freedom to make next his most expensive and ambitious film, *The General*.

THE GENERAL IS INDISPUTABLY Buster's finest film and one of the most visually stunning films ever made. Set against the backdrop of the American Civil War, *The General* tells the story of the theft of a train engine and a lone engineer's efforts to save it and his beloved. The film was based on an actual Civil War incident, and Buster's attention to detail in the film—from the period vistas that rival Mathew Brady's original photographs of the era, to the loving re-creation of the steam locomotive, the *General*, itself—is astounding. Within the precise rendition of the 1860s American landscape, Buster manages to weave a rich tapestry of comic situations employing all of the essential elements of his humor, including mechanical mishaps set against grand venues and ceaseless troubles encountered by an unlikely hero, in this case locomotive engineer Johnnie Gray. *The General* is, without question, Buster's masterpiece.

Above: Reading during a break in production of THE GENERAL. Photograph by Byron Houck.

Opposite: As engineer Johnnie Gray in front of his beloved locomotive in THE GENERAL. This photograph reveals the parallel tracks of the Oregon Pacific & Eastern Railroad. Many of the film's scenes were shot on the one-half mile of double track, with the cameras mounted on a moving train on the northern track and Buster in his replica of the original GENERAL engine maintaining a similar pace on the parallel track to the south. Photograph by Byron Houck.

Clyde Bruckman had brought to Buster's attention William Pittenger's book *Daring and Suffering: A History of the Great Railway Adventure* (republished as *The Great Locomotive Chase*, the edition Bruckman and Buster had seen), in which the author, a Northern soldier in the Civil War, recounted an 1862 raid in which he had taken part: a group of Union soldiers infiltrated Confederate territory near Marietta, Georgia, and hijacked a locomotive (the *General*) with the intention of crippling transportation and communication by destroying track, burning bridges, and cutting telegraph lines while driving the train north. Pittenger's account was told from the Northern point of view. Buster switched it to the Southern point of view for the film, as he felt, "You can always make villains out of the Northerners, but you cannot make a villain out of the South."[13] He reworked the material with Bruckman, creating a love interest as well as the battle scene that climaxes the film. He also emphasized the locomotive chase, knowing that a train would be the perfect prop for him.

Motivated by his usual desire for authenticity, Buster originally wanted to shoot the film in the authentic terrain of Chattanooga, Tennessee, and Atlanta, Georgia. However, Oregon was eventually chosen, as it was able to provide the appropriate locomotives, track, and period atmosphere. Shooting began in June 1926 in Cottage Grove, Oregon, after Buster's crew had re-created the town of Marietta, Georgia, using engravings from Pittenger's book as their guide. Buster told his crew, "It's got to be so authentic it hurts."[14]

Buster plays Johnnie Gray, a railroad engineer who, as an intertitle explains, has two loves in his life—his engine, which is named the *General*, and his girlfriend, Annabelle Lee. When Northern raiders kidnap his engine and Annabelle, he commandeers another engine, the *Texas*, and sets off in pursuit.

Marion Mack was cast as Annabelle Lee. Her character is subjected to more rough treatment than Buster's typical love interest, but she is also more intelligent than his usual leading lady. She starts out as simple and silly, but she develops into Johnnie Gray's partner in rescuing the *General*. She even learns to handle the engine reasonably well. Buster's character is also much more complex than usual; the character he plays is not the helpless incompetent of many of his earlier feature pictures. Johnnie Gray is a capable railroad engineer galvanized into action to save his locomotive, and his girl.

In addition to its character development, the structure of the film is also impressive. The film is perfectly designed as an elaborate double chase—from South to North and from North to South, as Johnnie Gray sets out to retrieve the *General* and

The cannon used in THE GENERAL *was a reproduction of an actual Civil War railroad gun. Buster was knocked unconscious when he stood too close to it when firing a cannonball. This celebrated scene with the cannon is actually a reworking of a gag from* THE NAVIGATOR, *in which Buster used a miniature cannon. Photograph by Byron Houck.*

On the cowcatcher. Photograph by Byron Houck.

then is chased by Northern troops as he takes the locomotive back to Confederate lines. The majesty of the film's great set pieces lies not only in how well executed they are, but also in that they are photographed in long shots; the authenticity of the image is clearly apparent and is never fabricated through editing. The comedy derived from these set pieces is in the "reaction" shots, usually coming from Buster, responding to what has just happened.

The most spectacular scene in the film comes when the locomotive, the *Texas*, collapses from a burning railroad trestle into the river thirty-five feet below. An old engine, with the name *Yonah*, was remodeled into a replica of the *Texas* that could be wrecked. Gabourie and his crew built a full-size railroad trestle over the Row River at Culp Creek in

Oregon and sank the engine in the river just for the shot. The destruction of the train was the most expensive single shot of the entire silent-film era, costing forty-two thousand dollars. People came from all over Oregon to watch the truly spectacular destruction of the locomotive on July 23, 1926. The subsequent battle sequence was also on a grand scale, and Buster hired four hundred members of the Oregon National Guard to play the Union and Confederate armies. Each man had a blue uniform and a gray uniform, and they would change back and forth. The National Guard came in handy when a fire, started by sparks from one of the engines, set the pine forest location ablaze. The cast, crew, and National Guard were sent out to fight it. The fire was extinguished, but the thick smoke prevented further filming. They

K27-153.

Opposite top: Buster overhears Union battle plans as he hides underneath a table at the enemy's camp. Joe Keaton, Tom Nawn, Jim Farley, Glen Cavender, and Mike Donlin. Photograph by Byron Houck.

Opposite bottom: Buster is exposed as a spy in a cut sequence from THE GENERAL. *Snitz Edwards is on the left and Glen Cavender is holding the gun. Photograph by Byron Houck.*

Left: With leading lady Marion Mack. Photograph by Byron Houck.

had to wait for a rain to come in and clear out the smoke, so they stopped location shooting in Oregon and returned to Los Angeles to film interior scenes. When a rainstorm cleared the smoke, they went back to Oregon for nearly two weeks in September and finished the picture.

The destruction of the locomotive engine, the forest fire, and the resulting delay drove up the budget of *The General* considerably. Finally completed, the film had cost seven hundred fifty thousand dollars, more than any other Keaton feature and an enormous sum for any film at that time. Joe Schenck was terrified that the film was going to break the company.

Buster, however, believed that the expenses were justified, as he was convinced he had a film that would surpass his greatest commercial success, *The Navigator*. To his surprise, *The General* was badly received and was not a box-office success. It was

considered too slow in its pace, with not enough laughs. The battle scene had critics like Robert E. Sherwood upset that Buster had shown men being killed in a comedy.[15] Audiences and critics of the time, expecting a slapstick Keaton comedy, did not know what to make of the film, which was almost as dramatic as it was comic. Rediscovered in the 1950s, *The General* is regarded as one of the greatest films ever made.

The General was Buster's personal favorite of all his films, largely because he did everything himself—he wrote, directed, and starred in the film. He was proud of the film's dramatic structure, its epic scale, and its authenticity. When Buster was asked why he believed *The General* looked more authentic than *Gone with the Wind* (1939), he modestly replied, "Well, they went to a novel for their story. We went to history."[16]

The destruction of the TEXAS *in* THE GENERAL *was photographed by six cameras and was the most expensive shot of the entire silent-film era. Photograph by Byron Houck.*

Buster poses on the wreckage of the YONAH *(the name of the engine that was used as a replica of the original locomotive,* TEXAS*). It remained a tourist attraction until 1941 when it was removed for scrap due to demands for metal during World War II. Photograph by Byron Houck.*

THE HIGH PRODUCTION COSTS and disappointing box-office returns of *The General* prompted Joe Schenck to insist that Buster's next picture be less expensive and more conventional in subject matter. *College* was influenced by one of Harold Lloyd's greatest successes, *The Freshman* (1925), which began a trend in Hollywood of films set on the college campus. Buster's individual touches are found in the film's plentiful gags, which counteract the derivative plot.

In *College*, Buster plays Ronald, a high-school bookworm and a momma's boy who, because of his dislike for athletics, becomes unpopular with his classmates. At Clayton College, where he is working his way through school, Ronald resolves to become a great athlete in order to win back the affection of classmate Mary Haynes from star athlete Jeff Brown.

Despite all his sporting equipment, uniforms, and a series of "How To" athletic guides, Ronald's efforts on the baseball field and athletic track end in disaster. In baseball, the only way he can get to first base is by being hit in the rear end by a fastball. He forces two men out when he decides to run around all the bases, passing by his fellow base runners before sliding into the home

Buster gets behind the camera for the filming of the crew race in COLLEGE.

plate. In the track-and-field events, his sprinting is so bad two young boys who have wandered into the athletic field easily overtake him. In hurdling, he manages to knock down every hurdle except the last one. Surveying all the toppled hurdles, he pushes over the last hurdle to make his failure complete. In the broad jump he ends up having his head buried in the sand and his feet kicking in the air. The sympathetic college Dean (played by Snitz Edwards) arranges for Ronald to be coxswain on the varsity crew team in an important race. Ronald singlehandedly destroys the first racing shell, *Damfino* (the name of the vessel in *The Boat*), when he leaps into it and goes straight through the bottom, causing it to sink. The replacement boat is the more secure *Old Iron Bottom*. Knowing that he must succeed as coxswain to win back the affection of Mary, Ronald the incompetent is transformed to Ronald the hero when the racing shell's rudder tears loose halfway through the race: he ingeniously fastens the rudder to himself, sits on the end of the stern, and steers the team to victory.

The film culminates with a race to the rescue. Ronald, immediately after winning the race, has to save Mary, who is being held against her will in her

Ronald is greeted by the college dean (Snitz Edwards), while Jeff Brown (Harold Goodwin, at far right) and his other roommates are less than enthusiastic about his arrival.

dormitory room by Jeff Brown. In a brilliant sequence, Ronald finally succeeds at everything he has failed at earlier on the athletic field: he sprints like the fastest runner across campus, hurdles over a series of hedges, broad jumps over an ornamental pond, and uses a clothesline support like a pole and vaults into Mary's dorm-room window to save her.

The film has an uncharacteristically bleak conclusion for a Keaton film. Ronald and Mary are shown going into a church and coming out married, which is where a conventional comedy would have ended. *College* has a coda: a series of quick dissolves, first showing the couple as parents surrounded by their children, then as a crotchety old couple, and then as twin gravestones side by side in the cemetery, similar to the headstone that reads "The End" at the conclusion of *Cops*. This coda is out of key with the rest of the film, which is entirely optimistic, and some view-

ers have interpreted this ending as a commentary on Buster's unhappy marriage to Natalie Talmadge.

When Schenck transferred away Lou Anger, Buster's studio manager, to United Artists in an effort to improve exhibition markets for the company, Buster lost a loyal collaborator who never challenged his authority. Although Buster chose Harry Brand, his publicity man, to replace Anger, he was never happy with his choice. Brand was more eager to please Schenck than Buster and was constantly looking for ways to cut costs. An example of one of their clashes was when Brand took Snitz Edwards off salary without Buster's permission; Buster had wanted to keep him around a few extra days for whatever reason.

153

A disaster on the baseball field, Ronald forces his team into a triple play. Buster enjoyed filming COLLEGE
because it gave him a chance to play baseball, his favorite sport. The scene was filmed at Bovard Athletic Field, once on
the University of Southern California campus. The USC Administration building appears in the background.

Buster was never a confrontational person, and therefore did not argue with Brand and what he perceived as Brand's interference. He just stopped work and played baseball with the crew for three days to show Brand who was boss.

It was Harry Brand who suggested that Buster hire James W. Horne, the film's credited director. Horne had not made many films (he would later go on to direct many Laurel and Hardy comedies), and Buster did not think he was a good director. In fact, Buster directed most of the film and had Horne standing by to direct an occasional scene in which Buster did not appear. Buster did not hold the credited writers, Carl

Harbaugh (who plays the crew coach in the film) and Bryan Foy, in high regard either. However, they were on salary, and he gave them the writing credit even though Buster created most of the film's story and gags.

Credits did not mean much to Buster, although he was angered by the "Supervised by Harry Brand" credit in the main titles of *College*, which he thought belittling toward himself. Furthermore, he was upset that it was done without his permission. He saw the film at the Senator Theater in San Francisco while filming *Steamboat Bill, Jr.* and was surprised, as he had edited the film and checked the sample print just prior to the film's release. Buster later found out that

Ronald disguises himself as a black waiter in an "All Colored Help" restaurant in one of his hapless part-time jobs.

it was inserted quietly by Brand after Buster had approved the finished version, and with Schenck's permission.

College marks the one occasion in all his independently made silent films that Buster used a stunt double. For the film's climax, where Ronald must pole vault into a second-story window, he hired Lee Barnes. Barnes had won the Gold Medal for pole vaulting at the 1924 Olympic Games. When Buster met him, he was attending the University of Southern California. Buster was unable to perform the vault, and since he did not want to spend over a month in training to do the stunt himself, he hired Barnes to do it for him.

Harold Goodwin, who plays the terrible Jeff Brown, first worked with Buster in *College*. He was in real life a very nice man who would become a life-long friend and collaborator of Buster's. Buster had seen him in Sydney Chaplin's popular film *The Better 'Ole* (1926), and Hal would later appear with Buster in *The Cameraman*, in several Educational shorts, and on television. Hal later became a real estate broker, and he ended up living a mile from Buster's ranch in Woodland Hills.

Despite creative and monetary restrictions, Buster liked *College*. The film's rich and plentiful gags—particularly those of Buster trying to become an athlete—are its primary attractions.

STEAMBOAT BILL, JR., BUSTER'S last independently produced feature, is one of his most enjoyable films. It was made on a tight budget, and Buster put most of the production's resources into making its climactic scene a spectacular one. The result, a full cyclone and the chaos that ensues, creates the most memorable and inventive climax in all of Buster's films.

Buster's character is Willie Canfield, Jr., the city-raised son of Mississippi riverboat captain "Steamboat Bill" Canfield (played by Ernest Torrence). Steamboat Bill's rival is the richest man in town, J. J. King, who would like to put Canfield's ramshackle boat, the *Stonewall Jackson,* out of business. The small and foppishly dressed Willie must prove himself worthy in the eyes of his big and burly father. Junior eventually accomplishes this task by rescuing his father, King, and his sweetheart (King's daughter) in Buster's most chaotic and acrobatic film climax, in which he is challenged by, among other torments, a cyclone, a flood, and houses tearing apart at the seams.

Charles (Chuck) Riesner brought the rough idea of the film to Buster and was loaned out from Warner Brothers to direct the picture. Riesner had known Buster from vaudeville (he always called him "Little Buster"), in which he worked for many years as a performer before entering films as a writer, actor, and director. He was a collaborator on most of Chaplin's First National films and associate director on *The Gold Rush.* Chuck Riesner had also directed several films starring Chaplin's elder half-brother, Sydney, prior to *Steamboat Bill, Jr.,* including the very successful *The Better 'Ole.* Buster and Chuck worked well together, and the two remained friends throughout the years.

The film was shot almost entirely on location on the west bank of the Sacramento River opposite Sacramento where a three-block-long town front street was constructed, in the summer of 1927. As with *College,* Schenck insisted that Buster keep costs down, and Harry Brand was once again the credited production supervisor. However, it was Brand who was responsible for driving up the film's budget considerably. Buster originally intended to climax the film with an extended flood sequence on the river. Brand objected to this idea when he saw the massive sets that were to be submerged into the river, thinking it would escalate the film's budget. He also felt that the flood was an inappropriate subject for a comedy, for the Mississippi River had actually flooded its banks in 1927, causing fatalities and major damage. Schenck agreed with Brand, and Buster was forced to substitute the cyclone for the flood, a change that Schenck and Brand thought would be not only considerably cheaper but less offensive to those who had suffered through the Mississippi flood. As all of the film's sets and gags had been designed around the flood climax, Buster and Riesner had to rework the comedy material, and Fred Gabourie had to rebuild the sets.

The cyclone sequence is only half of the film's climax, and Buster was able to sneak back in part of the flood scene and the river rescue that he had originally wanted. Buster always tried to work in at least one scene involving water when he made his own silent features, as his staff had a superstitious belief that having Buster immersed in water ensured a successful film.

Although it was not part of the original plot, the cyclone was carefully planned, and great care was taken in its execution. Six airplane propellers with

Attired in "work clothes" on his father's boat in STEAMBOAT BILL, JR.

37

Buster as Willie Canfield, with Ernest Torrence as his father, "Steamboat Bill" Canfield, in STEAMBOAT BILL, JR. *Buster enjoyed working with Torrence, who was a popular character actor in the 1920s.*

Opposite: Undaunted by a rapidly developing cyclone, Buster delivers a loaf of bread laden with tools to his incarcerated father in a scene from STEAMBOAT BILL, JR.

big Liberty motors were used to create the wind effect. Only one such propeller was used for the moment when Buster attempts to walk against the wind; that is how powerful they were. Cables and a 120-foot crane set on a barge were used to tear buildings apart, and Fred Gabourie devised a lightweight facade—which was connected with cables linked to a cantilever—to create the moment when the front of the hospital blows away, leaving only the floor and a bewildered Buster on a hospital bed.

The cyclone scene is spectacular on a visual level, but it is even more fascinating when one realizes that several situations in the sequence are drawn from Buster's own childhood. Joe Keaton often told the

story of the young Buster being swept away in a cyclone to be found unharmed a block away, just as Willie is uprooted in the film. The sequence showing Junior in an abandoned theater recalls Buster's days with The Three Keatons. One comedy bit has a dazed and confused Buster mistaking a painted backdrop of a lakefront for the real thing as he tries to dive right into the canvas, only to slide down the drop. The routine is similar to his parody of swimming-and-diving star Annette Kellerman's Original Aboriginal Australian Splash, which he had performed in vaudeville. Another scene that echoes Buster's years on the stage is the moment when Willie encounters the ventriloquist's dummy. As a seven-year-old boy in vaudeville Buster was fascinated with a ventriloquist's dummy named Red Top; he even wanted to kidnap it as his playmate. The ventriloquist, named Trovollo, who owned Red Top discovered Buster's plan to abduct his dummy after an evening show and sneaked back into the theater just before Buster arrived. As Buster reached for Red Top

in the dark and empty theater, Trovollo, hiding behind Red Top, brought the dummy to life. Red Top shot up and yelled, "Don't touch me, boy, or I'll tell your old man!" Scared out of his wits, Buster ran out of the theater as fast as he could. In the film, Willie is frightened by a ventriloquist's dummy, which appears momentarily to come to life on its own.

The most famous moment in all of Buster's films is the shot from *Steamboat Bill, Jr.* in which the front of a two-story building collapses over him; miraculously, he passes unharmed through an open window. He and Arbuckle had staged a similar scene in *Back*

Stage, and Buster used the gag again in *One Week* and *The Blacksmith*. For *Steamboat Bill, Jr.*, the gag was much more elaborate than anything Buster had done before. Although he and his team planned to make it as safe as possible, the stunt was, in fact, very dangerous. No camera tricks or editing were used; it is all one continuous shot. Buster later described how the shot was achieved:

First I had them build the framework of this building and make sure that the hinges were all firm and solid. It was a building with a tall V-shaped roof, so that we could make this window up in the roof exceptionally high. An average second-story window would be about twelve feet, but we're up about eighteen feet. Then they lay this framework down on the ground and build the window around me. We built the window so that I had a clearance of two inches on each shoulder, and the top missed my head by two inches and the bottom of my heels by two inches. We mark that

Buster strums along with musicians on location in Sacramento for STEAMBOAT BILL, JR *while members of the crew enjoy the fun. In the silent-film era, musicians often performed during filming to help actors achieve a certain mood, emotion, or tempo. Director Chuck Riesner is seen wearing a fedora. Marion Byron (whom everyone called "Peanuts") is directly behind Buster with her arm around Buster's sister, Louise, who doubled for Byron in the water scenes, as Byron could not swim.*

Buster poses with the 120-foot crane used to tear buildings apart for the famous cyclone climax.

ground out and drive big nails where my two heels are going to be. Then they put the house back up into position while they finish building it. They put the front on, painted it, and made the jagged edge where it tore away from the main building; and then we went in and fixed the interiors so that you're looking at a house that the front has blown off. Then we put up our wind machines with the big Liberty motors. We had six of them and they are pretty powerful: they could lift a truck right off the road. Now we had to make sure that we were getting our foreground and background wind effect, but that no current ever hit the front of that building when it started to fall, because if the wind warps her she's not going to fall where we want her, and I'm standing right out in front. But it's a one-take scene and we got it that way. You don't do those things twice.[17]

The front of the building was on a base plate and on hinges. It weighed several thousand pounds and could easily have killed Buster. Chuck Riesner could not watch the stunt being filmed. He and a Christian Science practitioner were praying for Buster's safety on another part of the outdoor set. The shot went as planned, and Buster was unharmed. In his later years, Buster would say that had he not felt so helpless and frustrated about his marriage and career—to the point that he did not care what happened to himself—he would never have risked the falling wall. He was, however, pleased with the results. No other Keaton moment better shows Buster's talents for civil engineering.

*These photographs record the most famous scene in S*TEAMBOAT *B*ILL*, J*R*., arguably the most dangerous comedy stunt ever filmed. The distance between a brilliant sight gag and tragedy was a matter of a few inches.*

Buster's character emerges unscathed, and the film ends happily, but Buster himself was not as fortunate in real life. It was while filming the falling wall sequence that Buster was told that *Steamboat Bill, Jr.* was to be the last of his independent films and the last film to be produced at his own studio. His previous United Artists releases, *The General* and *College*, were not box-office successes (in part owing to inadequate distribution by United Artists). Schenck had decided to abandon independent production entirely in order to focus on running United Artists. He arranged for Buster to sign with Metro-Goldwyn-Mayer; his brother, Nicholas, was president of M-G-M's parent company, Loew's, Incorporated.

Buster was assured he would be given the very best treatment at M-G-M.

Buster, however, knew better. As the wall falling over him was filmed on Sunday morning, Labor Day weekend, 1927, Buster was well aware that he would be losing creative control over the making of his films. In addition, his marriage to Natalie was rapidly deteriorating. Buster was at the height of his creative powers in 1927, but his failing marriage, the loss of creative control over his films, and the advent of sound motion pictures all occurring simultaneously seemed to conspire against him. He began to drink heavily, leading to the alcoholism that would precipitate his creative decline.

BUSTER ALWAYS MAINTAINED THAT signing with Metro-Goldwyn-Mayer was the worst mistake of his life, and that he should have heeded the warnings of Charlie Chaplin and Harold Lloyd, who both advised him against joining the company. Although M-G-M was at that time the most prestigious film studio in Hollywood, its highly structured operations were not conducive to Buster's unfettered style of filmmaking. Buster, however, had no choice; the days of the small independent companies were drawing to an end, and he did not have the financial resources to produce his own films.

Buster signed a two-year contract with M-G-M on January 28, 1928, at a salary of three thousand dollars per week. All but the last of his M-G-M starring films would be released as Buster Keaton Productions, a contractual vanity concession for Buster that included M-G-M agreeing to pay his old production company twenty-five percent of the net profits (of which Buster received twenty-five percent). Although Nicholas Schenck was the president of M-G-M's parent company, Loew's, Incorporated, it was Louis B. Mayer as vice-president and general manager, and Irving Thalberg as vice-president and head of production who ran the studio. Buster was M-G-M's first comic star, and the studio did not know what to do with him. He was contractually promised to be consulted on story and direction; however, the decision of the producer was final. Buster's films were mainly produced by Lawrence Weingarten, Thalberg's brother-in-law.

Buster's arrival at M-G-M was documented with many publicity stills, including this comic photograph taken in December 1927. Pictured with Buster is studio guard R. J. Owens.

THE FIRST FILM BUSTER MADE FOR
M-G-M was *The Cameraman*, which was his last
truly great film and one of his personal favorites. It
was based on his own story idea, and he was able to
reassemble much of his old crew, including gagman
Clyde Bruckman, cinematographer Elgin Lessley,
and technical director Fred Gabourie.

Edward M. Sedgwick was the credited director on
nearly all of Buster's M-G-M features. Like Buster,
Sedgwick was a former vaudevillian who performed
in a family act similar to The Three Keatons. The
Five Sedgwicks featured Ed, his parents, and sisters
Josie and Eileen. He entered films as an actor in 1913
and in 1921 began directing. Buster and Ed developed
a close friendship (they both loved baseball) and
worked well together on the direction of the films.

In a scene from THE CAMERAMAN
*(1928), Buster shows off his second-hand
newsreel camera to Sidney Bracy and
Marceline Day.*

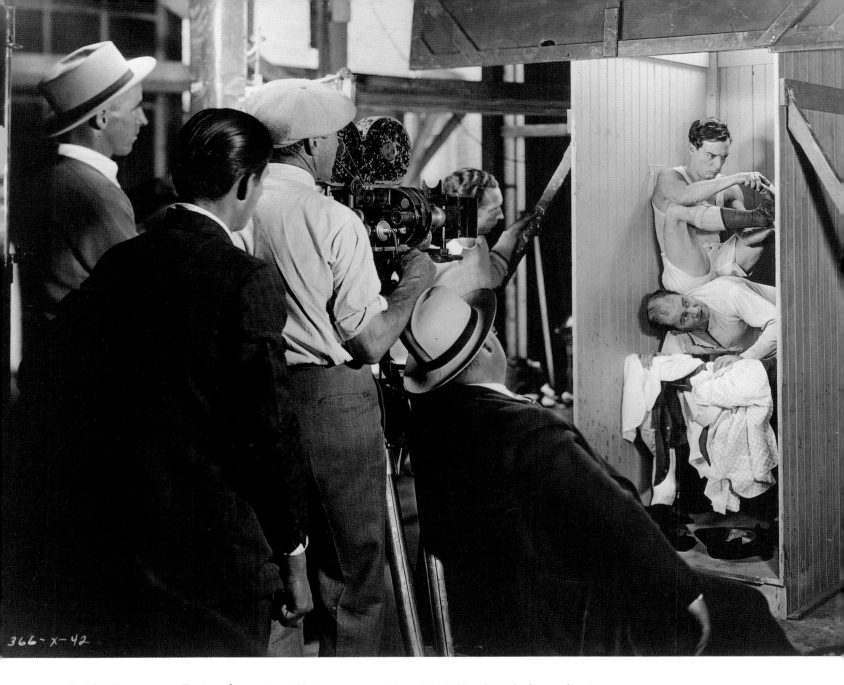

366-X-42

In *The Cameraman* Buster plays a street tintype photographer who trades in his tintype for a newsreel camera in order to win the affection of Sally (Marceline Day), who works as script girl and secretary at the M-G-M Newsreel company. With his antiquated, second-hand camera, Buster sets out to photograph news events on the streets of New York City, hoping to get a job with the newsreel company. His efforts to date Sally and as a newsreel cameraman are dashed at every turn by rival cameraman Stagg (Harold Goodwin). With assistance from a little organ-grinder's monkey (whom he unintentionally acquires), Buster proves himself to Sally and provides the newsreel company with exciting footage of a Chinese gang fight and a yacht club regatta, which brings about a happy ending.

Above: With Ed Brophy in the famous changing-room sequence. Edward Sedgwick is seated next to the cameramen.

Below: With Josephine the monkey between takes of THE CAMERAMAN.

The Cameraman was made from a prepared script, although he persuaded the studio to allow him to improvise on a few occasions. Two of the film's best scenes—Buster pantomiming a baseball game alone in an empty Yankee Stadium and Buster trying to open his piggy bank—were not in the script.

Filming began in May 1928 and was completed at the end of June. Buster had planned to make the film entirely on location in New York City. This soon proved to be impossible since he was continually recognized, and the crowds that gathered interfered with the filming. Except for the baseball pantomime and a few street scenes photographed early one Sunday morning, the film was made at the M-G-M studio in Culver City or at nearby locations.

The scene Buster liked best was the changing-room scene. In the film, Buster takes Sally on a date to a swimming pool (filmed at the Municipal Plunge in Venice, California). He tries to change his clothes in a cramped cubicle with an unfriendly fellow bather (Ed Brophy, Buster's unit manager). The two men become entangled in each other's clothes as each struggles to change into his swimsuit. A classic sequence, it later served as the inspiration for the famous scene in the Marx Brothers comedy *A Night at the Opera* (1935) in which a large group crowds into Groucho's stateroom, creating the requisite Marx Brothers chaos.

The Cameraman shows Buster's love of the film medium. He had fun creating the technical mistakes (as when his character double exposes his news film, creating such images as a battleship sailing down Fifth Avenue) and making use of actual newsreel film. The film opens with footage of fighting from World War I. Footage of Gertrude Ederle receiving the key to the city of New York from Mayor Jimmy Walker (not long after she swam the English Channel) is used to set the film's first scene. The film ends with news footage of Charles Lindbergh's 1927 New York parade after returning from his famous solo flight across the Atlantic.

The Cameraman was both a critical and box-office success. The comedy was well integrated into the story, and the screen relationship between Buster and Marceline Day had an emotional depth unseen in any of Buster's previous films. It proved to be such a model for the studio that for many years *The Cameraman* was used at M-G-M as a training film to illustrate what the company considered a perfectly constructed comedy.

Marceline Day only notices Buster as they are surrounded by some of the spirited swimmers who compete for her attention in the swimming-pool sequence.

TALKING FILMS HAD TAKEN OVER the film industry by the time *Spite Marriage* went into production in November 1928. Buster had wanted to make the film with sound, using a minimum of dialogue and sound effects, but M-G-M refused, as they wanted to use the few sound stages they had available for musicals and dramas rather than comedies. However, the film was released with a synchronized musical score and sound effects.

Buster plays Elmer, a trouser presser in a tailor's shop, who borrows his customer's fine clothes in order to impress the stage actress Trilby Drew (Dorothy Sebastian). He attends every performance of the Civil War melodrama in which she appears, and one night he gets the chance to act in the play as an extra. Elmer ruins the performance, but Trilby takes notice of Elmer and asks him to marry her. He fails to realize that she only wants to marry him in

order to spite her rakish beau, leading man Lionel Delmore (Edward Earle). On their wedding night, Trilby gets drunk and passes out on the floor of their hotel room, where Elmer struggles with the onerous task of putting her into bed. She abandons Elmer the next morning, leaving him disconsolate. The film's complicated second half has Elmer entangled with a group of bootleggers. He manages to reunite with and save Trilby aboard an abandoned yacht on the high seas, which wins him her love, and the film ends with the couple happily reconciled.

As with *The Cameraman*, Buster worked from a prepared script from his own story idea. Two of the main writers on *The Cameraman*, Richard Schayer and Lew Lipton, worked on the film with Ernest Pagano and Bob Hopkins. However, Buster's key

Above: With leading lady Dorothy Sebastian on the set of SPITE MARRIAGE *(1929).*

Opposite: With Dorothy Sebastian in the putting-the-bride-to-bed sequence, the film's most memorable moment.

Above: The cast and crew of SPITE
MARRIAGE *on location in December
1928. Actress Lelia Hymans is seated on
the far left and actor Edward Earle is to
the right of her (wearing the top hat).
Writer Ernest Pagano is seated in front of
Earle. Director Ed Sedgwick is seated in
the center, and Ernie Orsatti (outfielder
for the St. Louis Cardinals, who had just
returned from the World Series to work
again for Buster) is between Sedgwick
and Buster. Norman MacNeil, the musi-
cian on the set (holding an accordion),
is behind Buster.*

*Opposite: In his M-G-M bungalow in
October 1928, Buster works out gags for*
SPITE MARRIAGE *with the help of
the radio. He used popular tunes to help
him time each scene properly and coins,
which he placed on a piece of paper to
block scenes, as people.*

collaborators—Bruckman, Lessley, and Gabourie—
had departed or were assigned to other projects
before *Spite Marriage* began production. Buster was
beginning to feel restricted by M-G-M's insistence on
a carefully prepared script and by the often complicated or inappropriate gags that the studio suggested he
incorporate into the films. He was losing more control
at the studio, and the unhappiness of his marriage to
Natalie was resulting in his drinking more heavily. He
was also beginning to lose faith in his own ideas.

Spite Marriage spurred a series of battles between
Buster and the film's producer Larry Weingarten.
Buster fought against the complicated gangster plot
of the second half of the film, preferring to eliminate
it in favor of a simpler story, but to no avail.
Weingarten and Irving Thalberg were adamant about

HGMP·8653

their own ideas for Buster's films. Weingarten did not like the putting-the-bride-to-bed scene, feeling that kind of low comedy did not belong in the film. Buster had to argue the scene's merit innumerable times with Weingarten in order to keep it in. When *Spite Marriage* was released, Buster was vindicated; the sequence became the film's most memorable moment, and he used variations of it later in the films *Parlor, Bedroom and Bath* (1931), *The Passionate Plumber* (1932), *Speak Easily* (1932), *What—No Beer?* (1933), *Nothing but Pleasure* (1940), *Taming of the Snood* (1940), and Red Skelton's *I Dood It* (1943); onstage for the Cirque Medrano in 1952; and for television. The routine was also reprised by director William Wyler in *Roman Holiday* (1953) with Gregory Peck and Audrey Hepburn.

Buster's heroine in *Spite Marriage* was Dorothy Sebastian, who proved to be one of his best leading ladies. A talented actress, her characterization of Trilby Drew is more believable than most of the women in Buster's earlier films. During the making of *Spite Marriage*, Buster and Dorothy began an affair that would last two years. Buster enjoyed her ability to have a good time. They both shared a liking for practical jokes, bridge, dancing, and drinking (although she had a low tolerance for alcohol, and her propensity for passing out after a few drinks earned her the nickname "Slambastian"). She appears briefly in *Free and Easy* (1930), and the two worked together again in the Educational comedy *Allez Oop* (1934).

BUSTER'S FIRST APPEARANCE in a talking picture was in M-G-M's promotional all-star feature *The Hollywood Revue of 1929*. Constructed as a vaudeville revue to showcase the studio's talent and directed by Chuck Riesner, nearly every M-G-M star appeared in the film, including Buster, who performs his "Princess Rajah" routine, which he originated in the army during World War I and later adapted in the Arbuckle short *Back Stage*. Buster's silent performance was one of the film's highlights, along with the film's two-strip Technicolor finale in which all the stars, dressed in matching raincoats and hats, join the chorus of "Singin' in the Rain," a song revived and made famous in the 1952 M-G-M musical of the same name starring Gene Kelly.

Below: With George K. Arthur in the "Singin' in the Rain" finale to THE HOLLYWOOD REVUE OF 1929.

Opposite: In THE HOLLYWOOD REVUE OF 1929, *Buster performs the "Princess Rajah" dance that he developed in World War I.*

MGMP-18349

421-149

It took M-G-M a year to find a subject they considered suitable for Buster's first starring sound feature film. *Free and Easy* was filled with the production values—songs, dances, and costumes—that audiences wanted from the early talkies but with little of the famous Keaton style of comedy.

Ed Sedgwick, Cecil B. DeMille, Buster, Joe Farnum, and Fred Niblo in **Free and Easy** (1930). Niblo, best known for directing **Ben-Hur** (1925), appeared as a monologist on the same bill as The Three Keatons in Richmond, Virginia, in 1902.

Buster plays Elmer J. Butts, a garage owner from Gopher City, Kansas, who, as a member of Gopher City's Chamber of Commerce, assumes the role of manager to the newly crowned "Miss Gopher City," the aspiring actress Elvira Plunkett (Anita Page), when he accompanies her and her mother (Trixie Friganza) to Hollywood. While en route to Hollywood by train, Elvira meets movie star Larry Mitchell (Robert Montgomery), who invites her to the premiere of his new film at Grauman's Chinese

Theater and to visit the M-G-M studio. Elmer, who secretly loves Elvira, tags along, but as her manager he manages only to mess things up. His bumbling is eventually put to use in roles as a comedy actor, along with Elvira's mother. Elvira does not find stardom in Hollywood, but instead a marriage proposal from Larry Mitchell, which she accepts. The film's final scene has Buster dressed as Pagliacci staring sadly at Elvira with the knowledge that she does not love him. As Larry Mitchell sings "It Must Be You" for the cameras, Elvira looks at her fiancé lovingly. In a medium close-up, a heartbroken Elmer slowly closes his eyes as the film fades out.

Free and Easy provides fascinating glimpses of early Hollywood and the filmmaking process. The scenes at the Chinese Theater, with appearances by Jackie Coogan, William Haines, and William Collier, Sr., fully re-create film premieres of the period. The scenes at the film studio provide Buster an opportunity to create havoc on film sets (which was an old and tired comedy contrivance by 1930), with film directors Fred Niblo and Cecil B. DeMille and actors Karl Dane, Dorothy Sebastian, and Lionel Barrymore appearing as themselves. Wallace Beery also appeared in the film, but his sequence was cut prior to release.

To have a major star like Wallace Beery cut out of a film completely was not unusual for M-G-M, a studio sometimes called "Re-take Valley." Large parts of films were often remade if the management of the company thought they could be improved. With *Free and Easy* Buster also began the practice of making foreign-language versions of the films. Having made one film he disliked, he would remake it two or three times over for the Spanish, French, or German versions. Buster acted with different cast members for each foreign version, speaking his lines from cue cards written out phonetically, for which he was paid

Trixie Friganza and Buster in FREE AND EASY.

twelve thousand five hundred dollars per extra film. He was the only M-G-M star who made the foreign versions. Different actors replaced the stars in all the rest of the studio's foreign versions except Greta Garbo's German-language version of *Anna Christie* (1930).

Buster's first starring effort in a talking film, however, demonstrates the studio's tragic lack of understanding of his talents. Instead of scenes involving physical comedy, Buster is made to sing and dance (he even sings the film's title song in a musical-comedy number). The dialogue was written by a staff of writers who were joke happy, looking for funny things to say, but who did not focus on the action. This was what Buster fought against at the studio. His character is also much different from that in his

silent films. The studio tried to make him into a sad clown, but Buster had never appealed for sympathy in his own films. As the reins were much tighter when the studio converted to sound, Buster was unable to improvise or make suggestions once a script was presented to him. Wonderful scenes of physical comedy improvised on location in silent films were replaced by rigid scripts acted out in interior settings. Stuck for the most part on sound stages, Buster managed only an occasional unscripted pratfall, which seem awful when accompanied by natural sounds. It was a hopeless situation for Buster: some of the most commercially successful features of his career were those over which he had little control and which remain his worst in terms of artistry.

BUSTER'S SECOND ALL-TALKING starring feature, *Doughboys*, went into production in May 1930. Based in part on several of Buster's own experiences in the army, the script (by Richard Schayer, Al Boasberg, and Sidney Lazurus) has Buster playing millionaire playboy Elmer J. Stuyvesant, a character similar to his roles in *The Saphead*, *The Navigator*, and *Battling Butler*. It is the period of World War I. While Elmer waits for Mary (Sally Eilers), the girl he has been trying unsuccessfully to impress, outside the store where she works, his chauffeur, stirred by a recruiter's speech about fighting the enemy, abandons Elmer and his manservant Gustave (Arnold Korff). In need of a new chauffeur, Elmer unintentionally enlists in the army by mistaking a nearby recruiting station for an employment agency.

The film becomes a typical military comedy, with scenes in boot camp, complete with a belligerent drill sergeant (Ed Brophy), and in the trenches. Military life is made tolerable for Elmer by the presence of the ukulele-strumming recruit Nescopeck (Cliff Edwards) and Mary, who has joined the army's entertainment division. "Over There" in France, Elmer endures life in a trench for a short time before the war is over. The film ends with Elmer and Mary as husband and wife, with Nescopeck and Elmer's other army friends as business partners in the manufacture of gold-plated ukuleles.

Cliff "Ukulele Ike" Edwards, a character actor famous for his trademark instrument, was responsible for the ukulele and the film's delightful musical interlude in which Buster, Edwards, and director Ed

Sedgwick (who appears in the film as Guggleheimer, the camp cook) scat sing while aboard ship bound for France. Edwards appeared with Buster in his next two films, and they became good friends, both delighting in singing old vaudeville songs and playing the ukulele.

The comic highlight of *Doughboys* is the stage revue performed for the entertainment of the troops in which Buster's character, dressed as a woman, is thrown around the stage as the female partner to an Apache dancer. For this scene, Buster drew on his own wartime experience, as he had put on similar shows for the troops in France while waiting to come home.

Opposite: Buster as a World War I soldier in DOUGHBOYS *(1930).*

Right: King Vidor visits Ed Sedgwick and Buster on the M-G-M back lot during the production of DOUGHBOYS. *Vidor had directed M-G-M's great silent war film,* THE BIG PARADE *(1925), and was an old friend of Sedgwick's from when they both lived in Texas.*

lothario in a plan devised by Jeffery Haywood (Reginald Denny), whose girlfriend will not marry him until her elder sister Angelica (Dorothy Christy) marries first. The problem is that Angelica is only attracted to Casanova types, and the ruse plotted by Jeffery escalates out of control when Reginald manages to become involved with several women during the course of one evening at the Seaside Hotel.

Although certain scenes of *Parlor, Bedroom and Bath* play as filmed theater and contain the running around and fast talk Buster disliked, the film also has many scenes in Buster's old silent manner. The

LARRY WEINGARTEN HAD SEEN A 1930 revival of *Parlor, Bedroom and Bath*, a 1917 stage farce by Charles W. Bell and Mack Swan, and decided it would be a good vehicle for Buster. (It had been adapted for the screen originally by Metro in 1920 and starred Eugene Pallette.) Buster was in Europe on a three-month vacation with Natalie when the decision was made to remake the property, and he was annoyed that the decision had been made without consulting him. Moreover, Buster disliked the fast tempo and hysterical behavior inherent in farce. He maintained that farce was always based on simple misunderstanding or mistaken identity, which in a legitimate story would be quickly resolved.

In *Parlor, Bedroom and Bath* Buster plays Reginald Irving, a shy sign tacker, who poses as a

best of them is a reworking of the comic situation from *One Week*, this time involving the Austin Bantam roadster Buster is driving that breaks down on the railroad tracks as a train approaches. This scene demonstrates what Buster had always advocated at M-G-M: that a sound film does not require continuous talk, and that it could still have several minutes of action played out in silence. Buster believed dialogue should be used when necessary, but he did not want his screen character to talk for talk's sake. However, at M-G-M in 1930 more than a moment of silence was virtually unthinkable.

The film also enjoys a good supporting cast, including light comedian Reginald Denny and Charlotte Greenwood, a gangly character actress who was very agile and could perform some amazing

539-62

splits. The scene in which Greenwood's character, Polly Hathaway, instructs Buster in lovemaking is one of the film's best moments.

An added attraction to *Parlor, Bedroom and Bath* is that Buster's own Italian Villa was used for the film's opening scenes, which give an excellent view of the beautiful grounds and swimming pool of the Beverly Hills mansion as it looked in 1930.

Opposite: Charlotte Greenwood, Buster, and Dorothy Christy in PARLOR, BEDROOM AND BATH *(1931).*

Above: A train destroys the American Austin Bantam roadster, but Buster and Joan Peters emerge unharmed. Buster was able to drive the car for about a week before it was destroyed for the film.

A gag photograph of Buster taken on the set of SIDEWALKS OF NEW YORK in May 1931. The newspaper headline had nothing to do with Buster, but it made for a great photograph.

BUSTER CONSIDERED *Sidewalks of New York* to be the worst picture he made for M-G-M. Making the film was also a miserable experience. Ed Sedgwick, with whom Buster had developed an excellent working relationship, was committed to another film, so producer Larry Weingarten assigned two young men, Jules White and Zion Myers, to direct. White and Myers had worked at the studio on a series of comedy shorts that featured dogs playing all the roles, called Dogville comedies. Buster could not help but feel insulted when their promotion—after having directed dog films—was to direct him. Inexperienced at directing actors in a feature film, White and Myers alternated telling Buster how to walk, talk, stand, and fall. They acted more like animal trainers than film directors.

Buster was also unhappy with the film's plot. Buster plays uptown millionaire Homer Van Dine Harmon, who converts one of his Lower East Side tenements into an athletic club in order to reform a gang of local kids, most specifically Clipper (Norman Phillips, Jr.), one of the neighborhood gang leaders whose pretty elder sister Margie (Anita Page) Homer has fallen instantly in love with and wishes to impress.

The film's best moments are Homer's attempts to put on wrestling, boxing, and amateur theatrical shows as entertainment for the local gang. The boxing scene, in which Homer takes on a local fighter in the ring, had the potential to be one of Buster's best sequences. Owing to his lack of control over the direction, the scene does not come close to the work Buster did in *Battling Butler* in terms of dramatic realism, nor does it exploit the comedy potential of a boxing-match situation, as Chaplin was to achieve fully in *City Lights* (1931)—arguably his greatest film—made as a silent film and released earlier in the same year as *Sidewalks of New York*.

Convinced the film would be a flop, Buster was dismayed when *Sidewalks of New York* grossed more than any of his other films. His credibility at M-G-M was being eroded by the success of the films that he predicted would be failures. When Buster asked Thalberg for his own unit at M-G-M to make the type of films he wanted, Thalberg declined. The M-G-M management believed they were providing him the story material and other support Buster needed to make successful films. Moreover, given his increasing alcohol problem, they were unsure of Buster's reliability in managing the production of important films (budgeted at two hundred seventy-five thousand dollars each).

With Anita Page in SIDEWALKS OF NEW YORK *(1931).*

Buster takes out his growing frustration toward M-G-M on Jimmy Durante as Mona Maris looks on between takes of *THE PASSIONATE PLUMBER* (1932).

ALTHOUGH BUSTER MADE IT KNOWN during the production of *Parlor, Bedroom and Bath* that he thought farce comedy was inappropriate material for him, his next film, *The Passionate Plumber*, was also based on a farce, *Her Cardboard Lover*, by Jacques Deval. M-G-M had made it previously as a Marion Davies vehicle entitled *The Cardboard Lover* (1928), and it was to be made again by the studio as *Her Cardboard Lover* (1942) with Norma Shearer. The film was shot with the frantic speed of a farce; principal photography was completed in just nineteen days. Buster was not fond of his role—which had been played on the stage by Leslie Howard—and despite dialogue by Ralph Spence (who was known to doctor a bad film into a good one with his clever title writing and dialogue) and a

Jimmy Durante, Buster, and Gilbert Roland in the pistol-dueling scene from THE PASSIONATE PLUMBER.

good cast, he felt the finished film was only fair.

Buster plays Elmer Tuttle, an American plumber working in Paris who is summoned to the home of wealthy socialite Patricia Alden (Irene Purcell) to repair a leak in her bathroom. There he manages to be mistaken for her lover by her boyfriend, Tony Lagorce (Gilbert Roland). Elmer later agrees to help Patricia resist the philandering Tony's advances by becoming her ever-present bodyguard. In the finale Tony is exposed as a two-timer in the presence of both Patricia and his other lover, Nina (Mona Maris), and Patricia declares her undying love and appreciation to Elmer.

The Passionate Plumber was the first of three films in which Buster worked with Jimmy Durante, a New York nightclub and vaudeville comedian who was known for his trademark large nose, mispronunciations, and malapropisms. Although Durante played the supporting role of McKracken the chauffeur, Buster sensed that M-G-M intended to build up Durante's career at his expense. Buster felt that he and Durante lacked comic chemistry and that his fight against excessive talk was lost with Durante, who was impossible to direct because no one could keep him quiet. He seemed to talk through every scene. However, Buster liked Durante as a friend, and the two remained on good terms throughout the years.

Buster greatly enjoyed working with his friend Gilbert Roland, the Mexican-born actor with whom he had traveled around Europe the previous year. At the start of his long career, Roland played romantic leads like Tony, and he had a real-life affair with Norma Talmadge. Buster was also happy to have Ed Sedgwick back as director for this film and his two remaining M-G-M starring features.

The most memorable scene in *The Passionate Plumber* is the pistol-dueling scene between Buster and Roland, with Durante acting as Buster's second. It was one of Buster's favorite routines, and he would repeat it later in subsequent film, stage, and television appearances. It is the highlight of the film and among the cleverest sequences he created for the M-G-M films.

Buster, Thelma Todd, and Jimmy Durante enjoy a game of cards during production of **SPEAK EASILY** *(1932).*

SPEAK EASILY, WHICH WAS BASED on a Clarence Budington Kelland story called "Footlights," had a legitimate story that Buster thought appropriate for a sound comedy. It was the best film Buster made with Jimmy Durante, who plays a character similar to the real Durante.

Buster is Timolean Zanders Post, a sheltered classics professor who yearns for adventure but is too conservative and sensible to do anything about it. His valet, in an effort to prompt Post into action, presents him with a bogus letter stating he is heir to seven hundred fifty thousand dollars. The ruse empowers him to seek out the adventure he craves.

Post finds his adventure with Jimmy (Jimmy Durante) and the Midnight Maid Company, a group of amateur players who perform an awful musical revue. Impressed with their show, Post pays their outstanding bills and takes them to New York, where he finances their Broadway debut.

The show is totally revamped in New York by an experienced stage director (Sidney Toler) and vamped by new dancer Eleanor Espree (Thelma Todd). In a variation of scenes from *Spite Marriage* and *Free and Easy*, Post's accidental onstage intrusions destroy the intended performance on opening night, with the audience roaring with laughter. The audience believes that the mistakes are deliberate. The professor, having discovered his inheritance is fake, is able to pay off his debts by selling a half interest in his hit show to an enthusiastic investor.

Buster's performance in *Speak Easily* is his finest in the sound features he made at M-G-M, an amazing accomplishment considering his personal problems and his drinking, which was escalating out of control during that time. Filming began in early May 1932, and by the time it was completed in mid-June, Buster's frequent absences from the set due to drinking binges and hangovers caused the studio to lose eleven shooting days, which reportedly cost M-G-M

thirty-three thousand dollars. The production cost was four hundred twenty thousand dollars, making it Buster's most expensive M-G-M film. Although *Speak Easily* is uneven in quality, Buster received good reviews, and the picture was a commercial success.

Buster consults with director Ed Sedgwick (seated in the orchestra with the back of his head just visible) prior to filming a scene with Sidney Toler and Jimmy Durante in SPEAK EASILY.

655-8

With Jimmy Durante in a scene from WHAT—NO BEER? *(1933).*

WHAT-NO BEER?, BUSTER'S LAST starring feature film for M-G-M, was an embarrassment to him. Drinking more than a bottle of whiskey a day, and in no condition to work, he was in terrible physical condition when the film went into production in December 1932. Natalie had been given an interlocutory decree of divorce in August of the previous year, as well as custody of Jimmy and Bobby. The effects on Buster show on the screen; his voice is congested and his body is sluggish, his movements slow. Moreover, the script was terrible. Durante, who shares equal billing with Buster, talks incessantly. Buster, ill and depressed, takes a back seat to Durante.

Buster plays taxidermist Elmer J. Butts who, in partnership with Jimmy (Jimmy Durante), purchases an abandoned brewery after the repeal of Prohibition. The two entrepreneurs have trouble with the law (Prohibition had not yet been officially repealed) and with local gangsters, but by the end they are shown as the happy millionaire owners of a beer garden.

Buster contributed gag material to only one scene in the film: Elmer dodging barrels of beer rolling down a hill is a reworking of the boulder rockslide chase from *Seven Chances*.

Buster was just another M-G-M employee with *What—No Beer?* His contract renewal of July 9, 1930 had been very similar to his lucrative original con-

tract. However, with his 1932 contract he was obliged to have twenty percent of his three-thousand-dollar weekly salary taken out each week until the thirty-three thousand dollars in losses the studio incurred from his absences during *Speak Easily* had been repaid. Moreover, his new contract no longer required M-G-M to make him the star; he was, in fact, co-star in *What—No Beer?* with Durante, and the profit-sharing arrangement between M-G-M and Buster Keaton Productions was not included.

M-G-M sent Buster to various alcohol rehabilitation clinics during this period. However, Buster's drinking continued, and his erratic behavior caused further absences that resulted in nearly two weeks of lost shooting time. Shortly after *What—No Beer?* was completed in January 1933, Louis B. Mayer sent Buster a letter of termination. Mayer had always disliked Buster, the reason for which has never been fully explained. With Thalberg on a leave of absence from the studio after suffering a massive heart attack, Mayer took it upon himself to get rid of Buster. Keaton would eventually return to M-G-M as a gagman and supporting actor. Although he would go on to make three more starring features (all made outside the United States between 1934 and 1946), with his termination letter of February 2, 1933, Buster's days as a major motion-picture star were over.

NONE OF THE MAJOR STUDIOS wanted to hire Buster following his termination from M-G-M; he had been labeled within the industry as an unreliable alcoholic. Buster considered the period from 1933 to 1935 to be the two worst years of his life.

Buster had met Mae Scriven, a professional nurse, when she and a physician were hired to accompany him to an alcohol rehabilitation clinic in Arrowhead Springs prior to the production of *What—No Beer?* She continued to provide care when he returned home and kept him sober and able to work. However, Buster's drinking and erratic behavior returned. He decided to go to Mexico for the New Year's holiday, and Mae went with him. On January 8, 1933, they were married by a judge in Ensenada, Mexico. Buster could not remember the wedding; he was drunk at the time.

His marriage to the twenty-eight-year-old Scriven received worldwide publicity because a full year had not elapsed since the interlocutory decree of divorce from Natalie became final. With all the publicity surrounding the marriage, Buster felt obligated to officially marry Mae. They were quietly married again in Ventura, California, on October 17, 1933, after his divorce from Natalie became final.

Buster's marriage to Mae lasted less than three years and meant nothing to him. He needed someone to look after him, and Mae had wanted to be the wife of a movie star.

Buster and Mae lived in the six-room house he had purchased at 3151 Queensbury Drive in Cheviot Hills when he was still working for M-G-M. Mae continued to help him get his drinking under control, but periods of sobriety were quickly followed by drinking binges. Buster also suffered from delirium tremens. Eventually, Mae decided to go back to work, not as a nurse, but as a hairstylist. She persuaded Buster to finance a beauty shop, which had a sign that looked like "Buster Keaton's Beauty Shop" (the word "Mrs." was in tiny lettering). He later insisted that she change the sign.

During this period Buster made two features, *Le Roi des Champs-Elysées* in France and *The Invader* in England. Buster thought that neither film was good, both having been made by producers who did not have enough money to finance a quality production.

Le Roi des Champs-Elysées was the better of the two films. Buster had received an offer from producer Seymour Nebenzal of the Paris-based Nero Films to make a feature film in Paris for the salary of fifteen thousand dollars. The salary did not include traveling expenses, so Buster and Mae sold three hundred fifty dollars worth of war savings bonds to book a passage to Europe via freighter in June 1934.

In the film Buster plays dual roles: Buster Garnier, a mild-mannered man employed by a large company to dress as a millionaire and hand out leaflets that look like bank notes; and Jim Balafre, an escaped American gangster who is an exact double of Buster. Fast-paced and filled with Keaton touches, the film has Buster being mistaken for the look-alike gangster. Buster is excellent in the dual roles; however, the film comedy is not particularly inspired, and the fun of the first scenes is not maintained through the rest of the film. If *Le Roi des Champs-Elysées* had had more of the qualities that René Clair was achieving at that time—visual film with minimal dialogue, carefully choreographed action, and sound limited to effects and the occasional song—Buster might have had a whole new career in France.

With Mae and Elmer, the first of many Saint Bernard dogs Buster would own throughout his life (all of which he would name "Elmer," the name of the character he played in several films).

Le Roi des Champs-Elysées is notable for Buster's smile at the film's fade-out. Buster had fought throughout his career against ending a film this way, but director Max Nosseck insisted. Although it is a startling and unexpected sight to see Buster smile, this image does not provide an effective ending.

Filming was completed in just twelve days. Nero Films was hoping to profit from Buster's European popularity, which had remained strong. Unfortunately, the film received only limited distribution, and it was never released in the United States.

After completing *Le Roi des Champs-Elysées*, Buster was offered twelve thousand dollars to play the starring role in a film in London produced by Sam Spiegel. Spiegel, who would later produce films such as *On the Waterfront* (1954), *The Bridge on the River Kwai* (1957), and *Lawrence of Arabia* (1962), had never produced a film when he offered Buster the contract. He also had very little money.

The Invader was based on Buster's own story idea, and he contributed most of the film's gags. Buster plays Leander Proudfoot, a rich American who sails his yacht, the *Invader* (which was the name of Joe Schenck's yacht), to a little Spanish town. In a local cantina he finds love and trouble in the form of a cabaret dancer named Lupita (Lupita Tovar).

That the film was underfinanced is clearly evident on the screen. Buster did the film only for the money, and his drinking added to the financial problems of the production. The film was not released until 1936 and was a failure in both Great Britain and in the United States, where it was released under the title *An Old Spanish Custom*.

Upon their return to the United States, Buster was forced to declare personal bankruptcy and was sued by the Internal Revenue Service for twenty-eight thousand dollars in back taxes. His drinking continued, and his relationship with Mae quickly deteriorated. The marriage ended over the July 4th weekend in 1935 during a trip to Santa Barbara when Mae discovered Buster in bed with Leah Sewell, a friend of Buster's sister Louise, who was also a guest at their hotel. Sewell was a wealthy Los Angeles socialite who, along with her husband Barton Sewell, had gained notoriety for their sexual adventures when they were involved in a wife-swapping divorce suit. When Buster's affair with Sewell continued beyond the weekend at

Buster as gangster Jim Le Balafre reveals his distinctive tattoo to prove his identity in LE ROI DES CHAMPS-ELYSÉES *(1934).*

THE INVADER (1936).

Santa Barbara, Mae packed up half of everything at the Cheviot Hills house. She literally took half of everything: two sets of silver flatware were divided in half, for example. She did not take one complete set. Soon after, she filed for divorce.

The most disturbing aspect of the divorce to Buster was that when Mae left she took Elmer, his Saint Bernard. He hired a private detective to find Elmer, but the search proved futile. The divorce from Mae became final on October 14, 1936, and she later resurfaced when she unsuccessfully tried to sue Paramount Pictures for five million dollars for libel over *The Buster Keaton Story*.

Buster's drinking came to a crisis in October 1935, when his physician, Jack Shuman, decided he needed immediate hospitalization. He was put in a strait-jacket and taken to the U.S. Veterans General Hospital in West Los Angeles, where he was placed in the psychiatric ward. When he was released more than a week later, he went home and had two double Manhattans at the clubhouse of the nearby Cheviot Hills Country Club. Buster resolved they would be his last two drinks, and he remained sober for the next five years.

37.

SINCE BUSTER WAS NOT RECEIVING any offers from major Hollywood studios, his friend Ernest Pagano (who had been a writer on *Spite Marriage*) persuaded him to join Educational Films Corporation of America in 1934 where he was guaranteed six pictures a year at five thousand dollars per film. Buster made sixteen two-reel comedy shorts for the company before it dissolved in 1937.

Educational, which began as a distributor of travelogues and instructional films, enjoyed a unique position as a relatively prestigious distributor of short comedies in the 1920s. However, the lack of adaptability of the company's comedians to sound films, the popularity of animated cartoon shorts, and the cost of sound production had reduced its position by 1934 when Buster joined it. The Educational shorts were made in three to five days (Buster had spent four to six weeks on his own silent two-reelers), and

Buster's participation in these comedies no doubt further lowered his reputation within the film industry. Most of the Educationals were made at the General Service Studio in Hollywood and were directed by Charles Lamont, with whom Buster collaborated on the gags.

Grand Slam Opera (1936) was the only film Buster liked of the entire Educational series. It was also the best sound short he ever made. A parody of the "Major Bowes Amateur Hour" radio show (called "Colonel Crow Amateur Night" in the film), *Grand Slam Opera* was made just after he stopped drinking; his performance and the comedy material are at a very high level. Buster is credited with the film's story, along with Lamont, who directed. Buster plays Elmer, who leaves his hometown of Gopher City, Arizona, by train to seek fame in New York. As his train is about to leave, he stands on its observation platform as the people of the town serenade him with "So Long, Elmer" to the music of "So Long, Mary" by George M. Cohan. Buster paid the three-hundred-dollar licensing fee out of his own pocket to secure the rights to the Cohan song rather than have the film go over budget.

In another memorable parody, Buster has fun with the famous "Fancy Free" number from the film *Top Hat* (1935) when he tries to dance like Fred Astaire in his hotel room in preparation for his appearance on

With Hal Goodwin in GRAND SLAM OPERA *(1936).*

the talent show. He turns on the phonograph and begins to tap dance on the floor, on top of a night stand, and along the fireplace mantel, and ends with a disastrous leap onto his bed.

Managing to get on Colonel Crow's amateur hour, Elmer juggles—a visual talent that a radio audience would fail to appreciate. When the radio show's musical conductor (Hal Goodwin) cuts Elmer's performance short and kicks him, Elmer retaliates by hitting him with a broom as the orchestra plays "The Anvil Chorus" from Verdi's *Il Trovatore,* the various hits in perfect synchronization with the music (which was the most popular vaudeville routine Buster and his

father performed as The Three Keatons). Elmer ruins the broadcast and, defeated, leaves the city to go back home. However, he hears on the radio that he has won the contest after all, and they are looking for him. Returning to New York, he wins the prize and the girl with whom he is smitten (Diana Lewis).

Members of Buster's family joined him in two Educational comedies. *Palooka from Paducah* (1935), had Joe, Myra, and sister Louise in the cast. The appearance of Buster with his parents in this film was the last professional teaming of The Three Keatons. Myra, Louise, and brother Harry "Jingles" joined Buster in *Love Nest on Wheels* (1937).

Joe Keaton would never work for anyone but his "Bussy," as he affectionately called Buster. By the time of the Educational comedies, Joe and Myra had separated, but they remained friends and never divorced. The whole family remained very close. Joe used to come to dinner every Sunday when I was married to Buster. At that time Joe had achieved sobriety and had a darling lady friend whom everyone adored. He lived his last years in a theatrical boarding hotel in downtown Los Angeles near Pershing Square until he was hit by a car at a crosswalk, an accident that led to a hospital stay, from which point his health deteriorated and he never recovered. He died in 1946 at the age of seventy-eight. Myra lived with Buster and me in the house on 1043 Victoria Avenue in Los Angeles until she died in 1955. She was a very independent lady. Standing just four feet ten inches tall and weighing about seventy pounds, she rolled her own cigarettes and drank straight bourbon. She enjoyed playing pinochle, and she and Buster were staunch pinochle partners. Harry "Jingles" and Louise, who had lived with us until then, moved out on their own. Until Myra's death, Buster supported the entire family, which is why he recruited them for some of the Educational shorts when his finances were particularly low.

Buster next worked for Columbia in a series of two-reel comedies, which he did only for the money. He was paid twenty-five hundred dollars per film, half of what Educational had paid him. Buster called these films "cheaters," as they were made as quickly and as cheaply as possible. Columbia distributed the shorts free to the exhibitors who played Columbia features, so Columbia chief Harry Cohn saw them as a low priority. Buster asked Cohn if he would put a little more time and money into them, arguing that he could turn out a quality short that Cohn could sell instead of give away as part of a package. Cohn, however, was not interested. Most of the Columbia shorts were filmed in three days. Buster made ten two-reelers for the company, and he disliked them all except the first, *Pest from the West* (1939), which is a remake of *The Invader* as a comedy short instead of a feature. Although most of the shorts were directed by Jules White (with whom Buster worked reluctantly on *Sidewalks of New York*), *Pest from the West* was directed by Mack Sennett veteran Del Lord, and Clyde Bruckman worked with Buster on the screenplay. Buster tried to make the first one special, and he succeeded. Although the subsequent Columbia shorts have their moments, none of them were of the same caliber as the first.

The one good aspect of the Columbia shorts is that they received wide distribution—greater than that of the Educational shorts—and, as a result, people in the film industry could see that Buster was working and in fine form. Consequently, he soon began to get offers from other studios for supporting roles in major feature films. In 1940 Buster stopped making "cheaters" at Columbia. As Buster said, "I just got to the point where I couldn't stomach turning out even one more crummy two-reeler."[18]

P EST FROM THE W EST (1939), *Buster's first and best two-reel comedy for Columbia.*

AFTER EDUCATIONAL FOLDED IN 1937, and before he made two-reel shorts for Columbia, Buster joined the writing staff of Metro-Goldwyn-Mayer as a gag writer and comedy consultant. He worked in this capacity on and off until 1950.

Buster worked with almost everybody at M-G-M. He was one of many writers who had a hand in the Marx Brothers' films *At the Circus* (1939) and *Go West* (1940). He admired their talent but was irritated with their work habits. They did not care about rehearsing or any preplanning. They would just improvise when it was time to shoot a scene. The same was true with Abbott and Costello, with whom he worked on *Abbott and Costello in Hollywood* (1945). The difference between Buster and the M-G-M comedians was that Buster's heart and soul went into his work. When Buster was making a film, he and his team would work morning and night to make sure it was as perfect as it could be. He checked on the scenery, oversaw the cast and the locations, directed the film, saw the rushes, edited the film, and attended the previews. M-G-M never allowed Buster to do much beyond gag writing and occasional supporting roles during this period, although he did direct three one-reel shorts for the company in 1938: *Life in Sometown U.S.A.* (1938), *Hollywood Handicap* (1938), and *Streamlined Swing* (1938).

Buster worked best with Red Skelton, who admired Buster and was eager to take any gag suggestions Buster may have had for him. Buster reworked several of his old films for Skelton: *Spite Marriage* became Skelton's film *I Dood It* (1943), *The General* became *A Southern Yankee* (1948), and *The Cameraman* was reworked as *Watch the Birdie* (1951).

Buster shared an office with Ed Sedgwick in the writer's building, where he built all kinds of Rube

With Alice Faye in a scene from HOLLYWOOD CAVALCADE *(1939). Despite his expert pie-throwing technique, Buster never threw pies in his own comedies. This film is responsible for the myth that Buster's silent films were filled with pie fights.*

Goldberg-like gadgets. The most elaborate of these contraptions, called "The Nutcracker," moved nuts through a complicated mechanical maze before they were crushed by a pile driver. The office was called "The Boar's Nest," and since it was near the studio commissary, everybody would stop in and visit.

Away from M-G-M Buster was busy with all sorts

Buster addresses the audience in THE VILLAIN STILL PURSUED HER *(1940), a whimsically exaggerated film version of a mid-nineteenth-century stage melodrama.*

The Cirque Medrano was a one-ring circus that sat fifteen hundred people. Buster's appearance there marked the reopening of the circus after having been closed all through the war years. The first act had traditional circus and animal acts. The second act was called the floorshow, in which Buster did a dueling sketch that was originally performed in *The Passionate Plumber*. Revered by the Medrano clowns and a big success with audiences, Buster was surprised that the French still remembered him from his early films. They would line up for autographs and treated him as a great star, which made him feel wonderful because American audiences had all but forgotten him by this time.

of acting projects in the late 1930s and 1940s, including supporting roles in films such as *Hollywood Cavalcade* (1939), *The Villain Still Pursued Her* (1940), and *San Diego, I Love You* (1944). He also acted in East Coast summer-stock productions of *The Gorilla* in 1941 and *Three Men on a Horse* in 1949. Buster had so much fun performing before an audience again that he dismissed his initial reservations about appearing in a European circus and agreed to an offer to perform at the Cirque Medrano in Paris in September 1947.

We returned to the Medrano for another four-week engagement in 1952 and again in 1954. For the return engagement in 1952 Buster did a New Year's Eve sketch, which was taken from the scene in *Spite Marriage* in which Buster puts the drunk woman to bed. I performed this sketch with him. Buster and I make our entrance covered in streamers and carrying small props indicating that we have just come from a New Year's Eve party. We are both exhausted,

Buster plays a municipal bus driver (with passengers Jon Hall and Louise Allbritton) in SAN DIEGO, I LOVE YOU *(1944), one of his most memorable supporting roles.*

As Erwin Trowbridge in a summer-stock production of THREE MEN ON A HORSE at the Berkshire Playhouse, Stockbridge, Massachusetts, in June 1949. Frank Buxton, Kendall Clark, Buster, Janet Fox, and Eddie Hyans. Photograph by Shapiro.

Buster and Ed Wynn re-create a scene from Buster's first film, THE BUTCHER BOY, for THE ED WYNN SHOW, which originally aired December 22, 1949. This was Buster's first appearance on television. Photograph by Pierce Grant.

and I am very drunk. Buster takes off his coat and his hat and is occupied with a chest of drawers upstage. Meanwhile, I take the stole from around my neck and wad it up like a pillow, falling asleep on the floor. Buster comes downstage around the foot of the bed and stumbles over me, and the rest of the sketch is Buster's effort to put me to bed. The whole act ran about fifteen minutes. Although I was still working as a dancer at M-G-M, I had no previous acting experience. Working with Buster required precision—he was very precise and mathematical with his work—but I was really no more than a breathing prop in the sketch. I worked well enough that I became his permanent woman partner, onstage as well as offstage.

Television brought Buster back into prominence. He embraced the new medium at a time when most of Hollywood was avoiding it. Buster's first appearance on television was the initial broadcast of *The Ed Wynn Show* in December 1949, which was the first important broadcast to originate from the West Coast. He re-created his first scene in films, buying a pail of molasses as in *The Butcher Boy*. He was such a success that he was offered his own television show almost immediately. *The Buster Keaton Show* ran for about seventeen weeks on KTTV in Los Angeles. Buster loved working in front of a live audience, but it soon became very difficult to prepare comedy material fast enough, even though he was working

with his old gagman Clyde Bruckman. It was a local show—it could not be sold outside Los Angeles because of the poor picture quality of kinescopes—and was very low budget. The following year brought another program called *The Buster Keaton Show* (which was called *Life with Buster Keaton* in syndication). He did thirteen half-hour episodes on film, which could be distributed all over, but the hitch was there was no live audience, which had been what made television enjoyable for Buster. Moreover, the demands of early television were such that he was

expected to film an entire episode in just one day. Even with the help of Eddie Cline, Clyde Bruckman, and Hal Goodwin, it proved impossible, and he would not renew to do more. He started doing guest appearances on television. The Buster Keaton revival began with the television shows, guest appearances, and even commercials. Young people and children who had never heard of him or seen his work were discovering him for the first time.

Buster's appearances on television interested producers who saw that Buster was still able to do the things he had done thirty years before, eager to work, and available. Just before his first work in television, M-G-M had finally given Buster a nice supporting role in *In the Good Old Summertime* (1949) with Judy Garland and Van Johnson. The same year, Billy Wilder hired Buster to play in *Sunset Boulevard* (1950). He had a wonderful time because all he did was play bridge with old friends Gloria Swanson, Anna Q. Nilsson, and H. B. Warner for one day.

The most exciting project for Buster during this period came along when Charlie Chaplin cast him for his film *Limelight* (1952). Buster considered

Chaplin to be the greatest motion-picture comedian and the greatest of all comedy directors.

In the film, Chaplin and Buster perform a British music hall comedy act. In the sketch they play two slightly crazed musicians: Buster the bespectacled pianist who is constantly fumbling his sheet music, and Chaplin the violinist whose legs keep shrinking up inside his trousers. After dismantling the piano and ruining a violin, they perform a comedy musical duet that ends when Chaplin—in a musical frenzy—falls off the stage into the bass drum in the orchestra pit.

Buster worked on the film for three weeks, from just before Christmas 1951 through the second week of January 1952. There was an outline prepared by Chaplin, but

Above: Buster polishes a Studebaker for promotional purposes about the time of the first The Buster Keaton Show, *1950. Although his television show was sponsored by California Studebaker dealers, he always drove a Cadillac. Photograph by Otto Rothschild.*

Left: Buster and me performing the sketch of putting the woman to bed for Toast of the Town, *which aired on November 5, 1950.*

the comedy was mostly improvised on the set. Buster had a wonderful time working with Chaplin.

Raymond Rohauer, Buster's business partner, began the rumor that Chaplin cut out Buster's best scenes in the film. It was an effort on Raymond's part to try and build up Buster and diminish Chaplin. Buster did not think it was true. He greatly enjoyed working with Chaplin on *Limelight*, which is considered historic in its teaming of the two great comic geniuses of film.

A favorite memory for both Buster and myself was the time we spent in 1957 in an East Coast touring production of *Merton of the Movies*, the 1922 play by George S. Kaufman and Marc Connelly, which Buster had always liked. The first stop on the tour was Spring Lake, New Jersey, where the production was not very good. Buster and the other key actors of the play, including James Karen and Jane Dulo, reworked the script, which was done with the permission of Marc Connelly.

Above: Buster and me at the Cirque Medrano in Paris in 1952, moments before going into the ring to perform the New Year's Eve sketch, which is the scene of putting the woman to bed from SPITE MARRIAGE. Photograph by Pierre J. Dannès.

Top right: Buster and me in the Cirque Medrano skit. Photograph by Pierre J. Dannès.

One of the things added to the production that was not in the original play was a scene in Act II in which the characters in the play are watching the rushes from a movie they are making. We used my 16mm camera to film the "rushes," all featuring Buster as the movie-struck Merton Gill. These rushes were such a success that we continued to photograph more material during the play's tour to make the rushes a little longer. The finished film lasted about ten minutes and showed Buster duck hunting, including a funny sequence with Buster emerging from the water and aiming his gun at a duck. He shoots at the duck and water comes out of the gun barrel. The best part of the sequence was totally unplanned: the duck then swam over and bit the end of the gun. It always received a tremendous laugh from the audience.

By the time the tour ended at the Huntington Hartford Theater in Hollywood, it was a wonderful show. Buster loved doing the play, and Jim Karen and

Jane Dulo became two of our closest friends. *Merton of the Movies* was one of the highlights of his later years.

Buster really enjoyed hearing the laughter of an audience when performing live onstage. In 1960 Buster went on the first national touring company production of the 1959 Broadway musical *Once Upon a Mattress*. Dody Goodman was Princess Fred and Buster played King Sextimus the Silent. It was a perfect role for Buster, as there was no dialogue for him until the end of the show, so he was able to do everything in pantomime. I was even in the tour, playing Lady Maybelle, one of the ladies in waiting. When the tour reached the "Bible Belt," it was arranged that I was the only one of the ladies in waiting who would be goosed or pinched by the lecherous King Sextimus. That way, if any conservative ladies complained, they could be reassured that the woman being subjected to this behavior was his real-life wife. The tour started in Chicago and stayed three to six weeks in places such as San Francisco, Los Angeles, Denver, St. Louis, Detroit, several stops in Ohio, Louisville, Pittsburgh, and Boston. After the national tour ended, Buster and I appeared in the bus-and-truck tour of the show with Imogene Coca as Princess Fred in Columbus and Washington, D.C., and concluding with a brief engagement in a summer-stock production at Melody Fair in North Tonawanda, New York, in the summer of 1961. Buster enjoyed the entire year he was in the show.

Opposite: With Charlie Chaplin in the dressing-room scene from LIMELIGHT *(1952).*

Right: Buster and Chaplin perform a bit of business that was not used in the final cut of LIMELIGHT. *Photograph by W. Eugene Smith. Posthumous reproduction print from the original negative. Copyright the Heirs of W. Eugene Smith.*

Below: Buster and Chaplin perform a comedy musical duet in LIMELIGHT. *Photograph by W. Eugene Smith. Posthumous reproduction print from the original negative. Copyright the Heirs of W. Eugene Smith.*

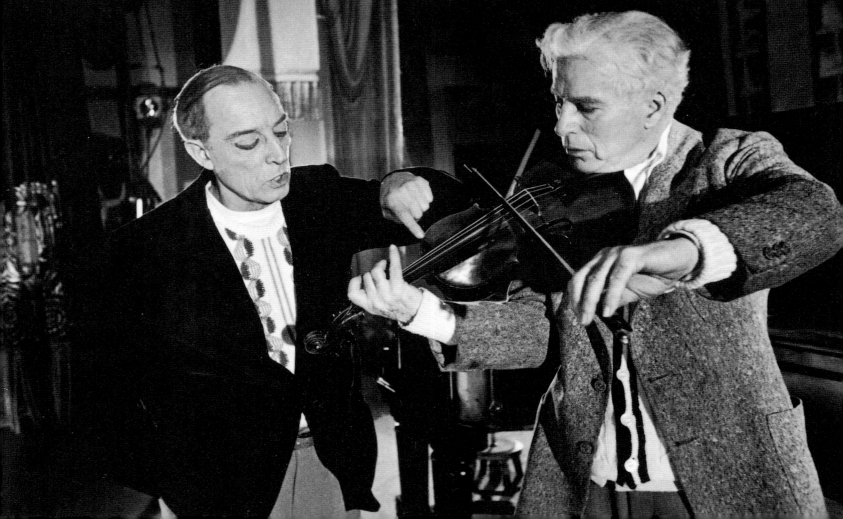

Buster experiments with a time-machine helmet in an episode of The Twilight Zone *called "Once Upon a Time," which was filmed in September 1961 and originally aired nationally on December 15.*

Buster in the summer-stock production of Merton of the Movies, *1957*

With Donald O'Connor on the set of The Buster Keaton Story *(1957).*

Less enjoyable was Samuel Beckett's *Film*, an experimental twenty-minute black-and-white short film virtually without sound, which was made in New York in the summer of 1964. *Film* was Samuel Beckett's first and only motion picture, and he came to New York to supervise the production. It was directed by the prominent stage director, Alan Schneider, who had worked with James Karen in Edward Albee's *Who's Afraid of Virginia Woolf?* in London. Despite their many accomplishments, neither Beckett nor Schneider had any knowledge of making films.

Above: On the set of the uncompleted feature film Ten Girls Ago, *1962. Photograph by John Sebert.*

Right: With Sid Caesar during production of It's a Mad, Mad, Mad, Mad World *(1962).*

Below: Buster and me on the set of Route 66. *He appeared in an episode called "Journey to Nineveh," which was filmed in June 1962 and originally aired nationally on September 28.*

Nor did they have any knowledge of Buster's films. Buster was evidently their third choice (Irish actor Jack MacGowran and Zero Mostel were unavailable). It was James Karen who persuaded Schneider to hire Buster. Jim also arranged three days of screenings of some of Buster's silent films at the Museum of Modern Art for the benefit of Beckett and Schneider. Jim and his wife, Susan Reed, appeared with Buster in *Film*, and we stayed with them at their home in Nyack during the three-week production.

Buster had no idea what *Film* was about. His character was called "O," and his back was to the camera for most of the film. Since he was already contractually obligated to the project, and because they were not interested in any suggestions he might make, Buster showed up, wore the clothes, and did exactly what Schneider and Beckett told him to do.

The exterior shots of Buster running in a heavy overcoat were filmed near the Brooklyn Bridge, where the temperature was in the nineties with high humidity. He did take after take and never complained, but Buster was glad when shooting was completed. People who understand *Film* may think highly of it. Buster was not one of them.

Buster appeared in four beach party films— *Pajama Party* (1964), *Beach Blanket Bingo* (1965), *How to Stuff a Wild Bikini* (1965), and *Sergeant Deadhead* (1965)—between August 1964 and January 1965. They were made by the B-movie assembly line known as American International Pictures and usually shot in two weeks in Malibu or on some public beach. The films were silly and made for teenagers, but Buster enjoyed doing them. They paid well, and it was easy work for him. Because Buster liked to work, he sometimes accepted projects that were beneath his talents. However, it was his appearances on television, in commercials, and even in the beach party films that exposed Buster to younger audiences and created an interest in his silent pictures.

Buster had a ball making *The Railrodder*. It was directed by Gerald Potterton, who had asked Buster to go to Canada to make the short film for the

Above: Buster with Ed Sullivan in an appearance on THE ED SULLIVAN SHOW, *which aired on December 22, 1963.*

Left: As Chief Rotten Eagle in PAJAMA PARTY *(1964).*

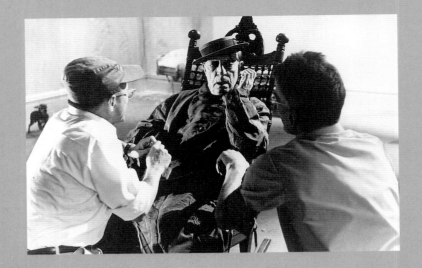

Left: With director Alan Schneider and playwright Samuel Beckett on the set of FILM *(1965). Photograph by Boris Kaufman.*

Below: Buster and me at the evening gala show of FILM *at the Venice Film Festival in September 1965 where he received a standing ovation. "This is the first time I've ever been invited to a film festival," he said at the time, fighting back tears, "but I hope it won't be the last."*

Bottom: Don Rickles (left) and Harvey Lembeck (right) with Buster during production of BEACH BLANKET BINGO *(1965). Standing in the doorway behind them is director William Asher and his wife, actress Elizabeth Montgomery.*

National Film Board of Canada. Buster agreed, and for six weeks in the autumn of 1964 we traveled more than four thousand miles across Canada from Halifax, Nova Scotia, to Vancouver, British Columbia. The plot of the film is simple: Buster stumbles upon a "speeder" (a small, motorized rail car) and drives it across the country.

At one point in the film, there is a scene where Buster's little speeder travels across a very high trestle bridge. At that moment, the large map Buster has been reading blows up into his face, completely enveloping him. It is a great gag—but very dangerous. Gerry Potterton and Buster argued about it for over an hour. Gerry did not want Buster to put himself in danger, but Buster was stubborn and would not give in. Finally, they did the gag the way Buster

wanted it, and it is one of the best scenes in the film. Buster never had an ego, but in moments like this, he just knew what he was doing—it was as simple as that.

Although *The Railrodder* would not be Buster's last film, it proved to be his last film in the classic silent style of filmmaking. Indeed, *The Railrodder*, completed at the twilight of Buster's career, plays much like one of his early two-reelers. It is also fitting that Buster's last film in the silent style focused on the railroad, a subject he held most dear and the centerpiece of his most acclaimed film. Buster maintained a fascination with complex machinery throughout his life, and both intricate machines and the elaborate

With the clapboard during production of THE RAILRODDER (1965). Photograph by Sam Tata.

Buster scans the horizon on location for THE RAILRODDER. Photograph by Sam Tata.

Below: The final scene of WAR ITALIAN STYLE *(1967). Released after Buster's death, it is his last screen image. Pictured from the back are Ciccio Ingrassia and Franco Franchi.*

Bottom: With Lucille Ball in the television comedy special A SALUTE TO STAN LAUREL, *which was taped in July 1965 and originally aired nationally on November 23.*

Right: Buster gets some additional makeup between takes of A FUNNY THING HAPPENED ON THE WAY TO THE FORUM *(1966).*

comedic situations that flow from their inevitable entropy were central themes of his work. The great irony of Buster Keaton's art, of course, was that his stoic expression always remained constant despite his chaotic surroundings.

Only three months after *The Railrodder* was released, Buster Keaton, who began his career as a knockabout child prop and completed it on the harrowing high rail, was finally at peace. Yet, as long as the films of Buster Keaton endure and new generations continue to embrace his genius, the great Keaton, once and forever silent, shall never be stilled.

Buster's trademark hat was worn in his very first film, *The Butcher Boy*. The hat was very similar to the hat he had used on the stage. In silent films, every film comedian had a signature hat. Derbies were the most popular, with both Charlie Chaplin and Roscoe Arbuckle wearing them, and Harold Lloyd adopted the straw hat. Buster set out to create his own hat, which would set him apart from the other comedians as well as endure rough treatment and still keep its shape.

Buster bought gray fedora hats in his size, which was 6⅞. He preferred the fedoras manufactured by Stetson, but used other brands when Stetsons were not available. He then ripped out the inside lining and folded in the crown, as seen in the series of photographs above.

The second step was to cut the brim down to size (a normal fedora has too wide a brim) to about two inches.

The third step was to flatten and stiffen the brim. This was done with three heaping teaspoons of granulated sugar in one cup of warm water. With a small paint brush, he wet the top and bottom of the brim with the sugar water. The last step was to use a steam iron to flatten out the brim. The hat was placed right side up on a hard surface and let to dry to further stiffen and flatten the brim.

Buster had difficulty keeping the brim flat. He never tipped his hat or removed it by holding the brim. He always held the hat from the crown, as the brim was delicate.

Buster went through half a dozen hats per film in the silent era. Later, he could make two hats last a whole year, unless he was working on a project in which there were scenes involving water. If he played around with water, Buster could go through as many as twelve hats a year. The felt disintegrates if it becomes too wet, and the hats just fall apart and cannot be reused. Buster trained me to make most of his hats for him not long after we were married.

My favorite memory of Buster making his hat is when we were in Germany in 1962 to promote the screenings of *The General.* He needed a new hat. Buster went to a little hat shop next to our hotel in Frankfurt and pointed out the hat he wanted to the little elderly man who ran the shop. Buster pantomimed everything, as he did not speak German and the shopkeeper did not speak English. Buster tried on the fedora and liked it. He then pantomimed scissors, and the shopkeeper handed Buster a pair of sheers. Buster proceeded to tear the entire hat lining out, fold down the crown, and cut the brim. The old man looked like he was about to have a stroke because Buster had not yet paid for the hat. When Buster finished and placed the hat on his head to test it, the old man recognized who Buster was and what was taking place in his hat shop.

Buster making a porkpie hat, c. 1963.

MY DEVOTION TO BUSTER KEATON goes back more than forty years, to the first showings of *The General* and *The Navigator* at London's National Film Theatre in the 1950s. When, by a series of unlikely circumstances, I found myself in Hollywood in 1964, one of the first people I set out to see was Keaton.

I expected a star to live in one of those huge mock-Tudor or Castilian buildings in Beverly Hills—the sort of place he owned in the 1920s. Confronted by a simple wooden bungalow in the San Fernando Valley, I thought I had gone to the wrong house. But you could not argue with the name: "The Keatons."

I expected Buster Keaton to be a morose, bitter man. I expected to find him sitting glumly in a corner, talking in monosyllables about the people who had ruined his career. I was prepared for a difficult encounter and was already making allowances for "great artist . . . hard life." The reality could scarcely have been more different.

Eleanor Keaton opened the door; she was a strikingly attractive woman who reminded me of Lucille Ball. Before I could enter, the gap was filled by a colossal Saint Bernard. Grinning, Eleanor tried to keep the door open, drag the dog in, and shake hands, all at once. From the next room came thundering hooves and gunshots from a television set. "Buster!" called Eleanor. The noise stopped, abruptly. "The studio put Buster on standby today," she explained. "If I'd had some place to call you, I'd have canceled the visit. But they aren't shooting today after all."

Buster Keaton emerged from the next room. He was short and stocky, he looked younger in actuality than most recent photographs one saw of him—and he laughed. That was the last thing I expected from the deadpan comedian. But several times during the interview, a suddenly remembered incident would be accompanied by a spontaneous, infectious laugh. As for his voice, it sounded like an anchor chain going out.

The Saint Bernard—Elmer—nuzzled him hopefully. "This dog sits on the couch to watch television," he said. Aware that a demonstration was required, the dog trundled over to a couch and heaved his back legs on to the seat, leaving his front paws on the ground. He then stared, deadpan, at the Keatons' Christmas tree, substituting that for the television set. Keaton grinned. "Come on," he said. "We can talk better next door." The dog raced us inside and, as I set up my tape recorder, it panted noisily into the microphone.

On a lower level than the rest of the house, the room was decorated with photographs, certificates, and awards. A billiard table occupied one side; Keaton's "saloon" was on the other. It had swinging bar doors, and the best beer in town, but it was only the size of a telephone kiosk. Two cowboy hats, one presented by the Cattlemen's Association of Fort Worth, Texas, the other from Oklahoma, hung in the far corner of the room, next to a fireman's hat, signifying that Keaton had been made a member of the Fire Department of Buffalo, New York. An Oscar stood on a table—"to Buster Keaton for his unique talents which brought immortal comedies to the screen"—next to a "George," one of the Eastman House awards, of which Keaton seemed especially proud. I was taken aback by the smiling photograph of Roscoe Arbuckle that dominated one wall—I was affected by the propaganda that still surrounded the Arbuckle case, and which made one think him guilty. An original lithograph of the train the *General* dominated the other wall. Underneath was a hilarious shot of three Busters sitting in the poses of the three wise monkeys. There was a picture of his father, Joe Keaton, with the locomotive he drove in *Our Hospitality* and, surprisingly, one of Natalie Talmadge, Keaton's first wife, with their two boys. A more recent photograph showed Buster Keaton with Harold Lloyd and Jacques Tati. A stunt check for $7.50 commemorated a stunt Keaton did for Lew Cody in 1928 for *The Baby Cyclone*.

I have just listened again to the tape I recorded on that occasion, and while I am embarrassed by my wide-eyed naiveté, it did have the effect of engaging Keaton's interest. I got many of the standard answers—familiar from other interviews—but I also got a lot that was fresh. He was full of enthusiasm and charm, and Eleanor chimed in occasionally with additional information. The most touching moment occurred when she prompted him to tell a story about a lion on *Sherlock Jr.*

Keaton chuckled. "I'm in the cage out at Universal, where they had all the animals at that time. It's a big round cage, about sixty to eighty feet in diameter, full of tropical foliage. With a whip and a chair and a gun, the trainer gets the two lions in position and I go to mine. My cameraman is outside the cage, shooting through a hole. The trainer says, 'Don't run, don't make a fast move, and don't go in a corner.' Well, there is no corner in a round cage!" Buster laughed, pushed the table out of the way and began to demonstrate. It was a perfect re-creation of the scene in *Sherlock Jr.*, with Keaton doing his wonderful walk across the room, whistling nonchalantly. I was so accustomed to seeing him in silent films that I was astonished to hear the whistle.

"I start to walk away from one lion—and lookit, there's another one, there! I got about this far and I glanced back and both of them were *that* far behind me, walking with me!" Keaton was helpless with

laughter. "And I don't know these lions personally, see. They're both strangers to me. Then the cameraman says, 'We've got to do the shot again for the foreign negative.' I said, 'Europe ain't gonna see this scene!'" More laughter, and Keaton returned to his seat.

"Years later, Will Rogers used that gag—'Europe ain't gonna see this scene.' We made a dupe negative out of *that* baby. I've worked with lions since, and some nice ones."

It was the only time I met Buster Keaton. He died just over a year later, in February 1966. I included the interview in my first book, *The Parade's Gone By . . . .* In 1986, David Gill and I were able to make a three-part documentary for Thames Television that we called *Buster Keaton: A Hard Act to Follow* (1987). Eleanor proved the most important contributor.

Born in Hollywood, California, in 1918, Eleanor was years younger than Buster. She was so strong and self-reliant, she always struck me as a character from the Old West. She had a refreshingly unsentimental outlook on life and a wonderfully dry sense of humor. After two unhappy marriages Buster found in Eleanor the perfect wife—and she later proved to be the perfect widow. She would do anything to advance the cause of Keaton. (Her car had the license plate KEATON 1.) She helped us in countless ways when we were making the documentary, aside from giving us the most marvelous interview. She remembered so much of what Buster had told her that we were quite shocked, after the program went out, to hear a constant stream of fresh reminiscences that we would have loved to have had in the film. Our reaction amused her so much that she suggested making a fresh documentary entitled *What Eleanor Forgot to Tell Us*.

When one embarks on a biographical documentary, one is liable to uncover some unpleasant facts about the subject. After we had finished the Keaton film, however, we realized that we had found no one who had a single unkind word to say about the man—and this was a fellow who went through a rough period of alcoholism. All those who knew him seemed to have loved him.

And what admiration they had for Keaton the filmmaker! When I present programs to people unfamiliar with silent films, I always include Keaton's short comedy *One Week*. And I show it complete, for it is ruinous to leave anything out. The picture is the perfect comedy. Inspired by *Home Made*, a documentary about portable housing produced by the Ford Motor Company (he got ideas from the strangest places), he was able to come up with an elaborate comedy. He was then age twenty-four, like Orson Welles when he began *Citizen Kane* (1941), and this is a sort of *Citizen Kane* of the two-reeler. Keaton starred, directed (with his long-time collaborator Eddie Cline), did all his own stunts (one landed him in the hospital), helped to work out the gags, and assisted with the special effects. This was a fellow who had barely attended grade school, let alone film school. Yet he combined the talents of an artist, a dramatist, a clown, and a civil engineer. Put this eighty-year-old film in front of an audience and just listen to the laughter. The film's only drawback is that it overshadows everything else you show with it.

The director was a figure of little importance in comedy films in those days. The comedian was the whole show, and was expected to come up with the gags—with the help of gagmen. This was so well understood that sometimes Keaton did not bother to take directing credit for a picture, and gave it to one of the gagmen. But his ability as a director was perhaps his most remarkable talent. He was so good that he should have been given dramatic pictures to make from time to time.

Although nearly eighty percent of all silent films have been lost, Buster Keaton's independent silent-film legacy survives complete. Thanks largely to Raymond Rohauer, the films are in worldwide distribution: in cinemas, in screenings with live orchestral accompaniment, at film societies and festivals, and on television and home video. It seems likely that each new generation will rediscover Buster Keaton.

Notes

INTRODUCTION

1. *The Dramatic Mirror*, March 16, 1901, article contained on page three of Myra Keaton's scrapbook of theatrical clippings. As most of the clippings in the scrapbook are unattributed, page notations cited are the scrapbook page number. Additional citation information is given when possible. Myra Keaton's scrapbook was donated by Eleanor Keaton to the Academy Foundation, where it is part of the Buster Keaton Collection at the Margaret Herrick Library of the Academy of Motion Picture Arts and Sciences, along with her other Buster Keaton-related photographs, papers, and artifacts.
2. This unbelievably low figure originates from Buster Keaton and is probably a myth; it is less than what Biograph paid motion-picture extras per week in 1910. Buster Keaton with Charles Samuels, *My Wonderful World of Slapstick* (Garden City, N.Y.: Doubleday & Company, Inc., 1960), 94.
3. Arbuckle made a few films for the Selig Polyscope Company starting in 1909 and later worked four weeks in Nestor Comedies released by Universal prior to joining Keystone.
4. Keaton had already starred in one feature, *The Saphead* (1920), when he was loaned out to Metro Pictures by Joe Schenck prior to starting his own series of shorts. Based on the popular play *The New Henrietta*, the film was not directed by Keaton and therefore displays little of Keaton's ingenuity or style beyond that as an actor.

BUSTER KEATON REMEMBERED

1. A close reading of Myra Keaton's scrapbook reveals that the story of how Buster received his famous nickname evolved over the years. In one account, Buster's nickname was conferred on him by "George Pardey, an old-time legitimate comedian." *The Dramatic Mirror*, January 23, 1904, in Myra Keaton scrapbook, 32.
2. Keaton with Samuels, 13.

3. Buster Keaton, interview by Bob and Joan Franklin, Columbia University Oral History Research Office, 1958, transcript p. 4.
4. Rudi Blesh, *Keaton* (New York: The Macmillan Company, 1966), 71.
5. *Variety*, 15 February 1921.
6. Buster Keaton, interview by Fletcher Markle, *Telescope*, Canadian Broadcasting Corporation television program, 1964.
7. Buster Keaton, interview by Bob and Joan Franklin, Columbia University Oral History Research Office, 1958, transcript pp. 11–12.
8. Chaplin later used Truckee, California, for filming selected exterior location scenes for *The Gold Rush* (1925). *The Frozen North* and *The Gold Rush* share similar snow-inspired comedy moments.
9. Keaton with Samuels, 165.
10. John Gillett and James Blue, "Keaton at Venice," *Sight and Sound* 35, no. 1 (January 1966), 27.
11. Ibid., 28.
12. Although *The General* had its New York premiere on February 5, 1927, and Los Angeles premiere March 11, 1927, it was registered for copyright on December 22, 1926, and the world premiere of the film was held in Tokyo on December 31, 1926. Since publication date (in the case of motion pictures, release date) is the official date for any work, 1926 is used throughout the text as the date for the film.
13. Gillett and Blue, 29.
14. Blesh, 271.
15. Robert Sherwood, *Life*, 24 February 1927, 26.
16. David Robinson, *Buster Keaton* (London: Secker & Warburg, 1969), 143.
17. Gillett and Blue, 29.
18. Keaton with Samuels, 259.

Bibliography

BOOKS

Benayoun, Robert. *The Look of Buster Keaton*. Edited and translated by Randall Conrad. New York: St. Martin's Press, 1983.

Bengston, John. *Silent Echoes: Discovering Early Hollywood Through the Films of Buster Keaton*. Santa Monica, Calif.: Santa Monica Press, 2000.

Blesh, Rudi. *Keaton*. New York: The Macmillan Company, 1966.

Brownlow, Kevin. *The Parade's Gone By . . .* New York: Alfred A. Knopf, 1968.

Brownlow, Kevin. "The D. W. Griffith of Comedy." In *Projections 4½*, edited by John Boorman and Walter Donohue. London: Faber and Faber, Ltd., 1995.

Brundidge, Harry T. *Twinkle, Twinkle Movie Star!* New York: Dutton, 1930.

Coursodon, Jean-Pierre. *Buster Keaton*. Paris: Seghers, 1973.

Dardis, Tom. *Keaton: The Man Who Wouldn't Lie Down*. New York: Charles Scribner's Sons, 1979.

Edmonds, Andy. *Frame Up!: The Untold Story of Fatty Arbuckle*. New York: William Morrow, 1991.

Gilliatt, Penelope. "Buster Keaton." In *Unholy Fools*. New York: Viking Press, 1973.

Horton, Andrew, ed. *Buster Keaton's Sherlock, Jr.* Cambridge: Cambridge University Press, 1997.

Keaton, Buster, with Charles Samuels. *My Wonderful World of Slapstick*. Garden City, N.Y.: Doubleday, 1960.

Keaton, Buster. "What Are the Six Ages of Comedy?" In *The Truth About the Movies by the Stars*, edited by Laurence A. Hughes. Hollywood: Hollywood Publishers, 1924.

Kerr, Walter. "Last Call for a Clown." *Harper's Bazaar* (May 1952). Reprinted in *Pieces at Eight*. New York: Simon and Schuster, 1957, 195–202.

——. *The Silent Clowns*. New York: Alfred A. Knopf, 1975.

Kline, Jim. *The Complete Films of Buster Keaton*. New York: Citadel Press, 1993.

Knopf, Robert. *The Theater and Cinema of Buster Keaton*. Princeton: Princeton University Press, 1999.

Lebel, J. P. *Buster Keaton*. 1964. Translated by P. D. Stovin. London: A. Zwemmer Ltd.; New York: A. S. Barnes & Co., 1967.

Macleod, David. *The Sound of Buster Keaton*. London: Buster Books, 1995.

Mast, Gerald. *The Comic Mind: Comedy and the Movies*. Indianapolis: The Bobbs-Merrill Company, 1973.

McCaffery, Donald W. *Four Great Comedians: Chaplin, Lloyd, Keaton, Langdon*. London: A. Zwemmer Ltd.; New York: A. S. Barnes & Co., 1968.

Meade, Marion. *Buster Keaton: Cut to the Chase*. New York: Harper Collins, 1995.

Moews, Daniel. *Keaton: The Silent Features Close Up*. Berkeley: University of California Press, 1977.

Oldham, Gabriella. *Keaton's Silent Shorts: Beyond the Laughter*. Carbondale and Edwardsville, Ill.: Southern Illinois University Press, 1996.

Rapf, Joanna E., and Gary L. Green. *Buster Keaton: A Bio-Bibliography*. Westport, Conn.: Greenwood Press, 1995.

Reed, Rex. "Buster Keaton." In *Do You Sleep in the Nude?* New York: New American Library, 1968.

Robinson, David. *Buster Keaton*. London: Secker & Warburg, 1969.

Schneider, Alan. "On Directing *Film*." In *Film*, by Samuel Beckett. New York: Grove Press, 1969.

Scott, Oliver Lindsey, ed. *Buster Keaton: The Little Iron Man*. Christchurch, New Zealand: Buster Books, 1995.

Terkel, Studs. "*Buster Keaton*." In *The Spectator*. New York: The New Press, 1999.

Wead, George, and George Lellis. *The Film Career of Buster Keaton*. Pleasantville, N.Y.: Redgrave Publishing Co., 1977.

Yallop, David A. *The Day the Laughter Stopped*. New York: St. Martin's Press, 1976.

PERIODICALS

Agee, James. "Comedy's Greatest Era." *Life*, 3 September 1949, 70–88.

Bishop, Christopher. "The Great Stone Face." *Film Quarterly* 12, no. 1 (fall 1958): 10–15.

——. "An Interview with Buster Keaton." *Film Quarterly* 12, no. 1 (fall 1958): 15–22.

Brownlow, Kevin. "Buster Keaton." *Film* 42 (spring 1965): 6–10.

Feinstein, Herbert. "Buster Keaton: An Interview." *Massachusetts Review* 4, no. 2 (1963): 392–407.

Gillett, John, and James Blue. "Keaton at Venice." *Sight and Sound* 35, no. 1 (January 1966): 26–30.

Gilliat, Penelope. "An Interview with Buster Keaton." *London Observer Weekend Review*, 24 May 1964, 31.

Houston, Penelope. "The Great Blank Page." *Sight and Sound* 37, no. 2 (spring 1968): 63–7.

Keaton, Buster. "Why I Never Smile." *Ladies Home Journal* (June 1926): 173–74.

Keaton, Joe. "The Cyclone Baby." *Photoplay* (May 1927): 98, 125–26.

Ludlam, Helen. "Yo Ho Ho and a Buster Keaton Location." *Screenland* (March 1929): 42–43, 110–111.

McCaffery, Donald. "The Mutual Approval of Keaton and Lloyd." *Cinema Journal* 6 (1967): 8–15.

Robinson, David. "Rediscovery: Buster." *Sight and Sound* 29, no. 1 (1959–60): 41–43.

INTERVIEWS

Keaton, Buster. Interview by Kevin Brownlow, 1964.

——. Interview by Herbert Feinstein. Pacifica Foundation, 1960.

——. Interview by Bob and Joan Franklin. Columbia University Oral History Research Office, 1958.

——. Interview by Arthur Friedman, 1956.

——. Interview by Fletcher Markle. *Telescope*. Canadian Broadcasting Corporation television program. 1964.

——. Interview by Dean Miller. WNBC Channel 4 television (New York), 1961.

——. Interview by George Pratt, 1958.

——. Interview by Studs Terkel, 1960.

MISCELLANEOUS

Buster Keaton contracts with Comique Film Corporation, Buster Keaton Productions, and Joseph M. Schenck, 1920–27.

Buster Keaton date books, 1908–15, 1917–18.

Buster Keaton Metro-Goldwyn-Mayer contract and production files, 1928–33.

Buster Keaton military personnel records and discharge papers.

Buster Keaton produced and unproduced film and television scripts, 1945–65.

Eleanor Keaton date books, 1956–66.

Myra Keaton scrapbook.

The Keaton Chronicle (quarterly publication of The Damfinos: The International Buster Keaton Society). 8, no. 1 (winter 1993) –8, no. 4 (fall 2000).

Robinson, David. "Buster Keaton: A Hard Act to Follow." London: Thames Television/Channel 4, 1987.

Filmography

The Butcher Boy (1917)
Released: April 23, 1917. Distributed by: Paramount Pictures. Produced by: Comique Film Corporation. Length: 2 reels. Story: Joe Roach. Scenario Editor: Herbert Warren. Scenario: Roscoe Arbuckle. Photography: Frank D. Williams. Producer: Joseph M. Schenck. Director: Roscoe Arbuckle. Cast: Roscoe Arbuckle, Buster Keaton, Al St. John, Josephine Stevens, Arthur Earle, Agnes Neilson, Joe Bordeau, Luke the Dog

A Reckless Romeo (1917)
Released: May 21, 1917. Distributed by: Paramount Pictures. Produced by: Comique Film Corporation. Length: 2 reels. Story: Joe Roach. Scenario Editor: Herbert Warren. Scenario: Roscoe Arbuckle. Photography: Frank D. Williams. Producer: Joseph M. Schenck. Director: Roscoe Arbuckle. Cast: Roscoe Arbuckle, Buster Keaton, Al St. John, Alice Lake, Corinne Parquet, Agnes Neilson

The Rough House (1917)
Released: June 25, 1917. Distributed by: Paramount Pictures. Produced by: Comique Film Corporation. Length: 2 reels. Story: Joe Roach. Scenario Editor: Herbert Warren. Scenario: Roscoe Arbuckle. Photography: Frank D. Williams. Producer: Joseph M. Schenck. Director: Roscoe Arbuckle. Cast: Roscoe Arbuckle, Buster Keaton, Al St. John, Alice Lake, Agnes Neilson, Glen Cavender

His Wedding Night (1917)
Released: August 20, 1917. Distributed by: Paramount Pictures. Produced by: Comique Film Corporation. Length: 2 reels. Story: Joe Roach. Scenario Editor: Herbert Warren. Scenario: Roscoe Arbuckle. Photography: George Peters. Producer: Joseph M. Schenck. Director: Roscoe Arbuckle. Cast: Roscoe Arbuckle, Buster Keaton, Al St. John, Alice Mann, Arthur Earle, Jimmy Bryant, Jospehine Stevens

Oh, Doctor! (1917)
Released: September 30, 1917. Distributed by: Paramount Pictures. Produced by: Comique Film Corporation. Length: 2 reels. Scenario: Jean Havez and Roscoe Arbuckle. Scenario Editor: Herbert Warren. Photography: George Peters. Producer: Joseph M. Schenck. Director: Roscoe Arbuckle. Cast: Roscoe Arbuckle, Buster Keaton, Al St. John, Alice Mann

Coney Island (1917)
Released: October 29, 1917. Distributed by: Paramount Pictures. Produced by: Comique Film Corporation. Length: 2 reels. Scenario Editor: Herbert Warren. Scenario: Roscoe Arbuckle. Photography: George Peters. Producer: Joseph M. Schenck. Director: Roscoe Arbuckle. Cast: Roscoe Arbuckle, Buster Keaton, Al St. John, Alice Mann, Agnes Neilson, James Bryant, Joe Bordeau

A Country Hero (1917)
Released: December 10, 1917. Distributed by: Paramount Pictures. Produced by: Comique Film Corporation. Length: 2 reels. Scenario Editor: Herbert Warren. Scenario: Roscoe Arbuckle. Photography: George Peters. Producer: Joseph M. Schenck. Director: Roscoe Arbuckle. Cast: Roscoe Arbuckle, Buster Keaton, Al St. John, Alice Lake, Joe Keaton, Stanley Pembroke

Out West (1918)
Released: January 20, 1918. Distributed by: Paramount Pictures. Produced by: Comique Film Corporation. Length: 2 reels. Scenario Editor: Herbert Warren. Scenario: Natalie Talmadge and Roscoe Arbuckle. Photography: George Peters. Producer: Joseph M. Schenck. Director: Roscoe Arbuckle. Cast: Roscoe Arbuckle, Buster Keaton, Al St. John, Alice Lake, Joe Keaton

The Bell Boy (1918)
Released: March 18, 1918. Distributed by: Paramount Pictures. Produced by: Comique Film Corporation. Length: 2 reels. Scenario Editor: Herbert Warren. Scenario: Roscoe Arbuckle. Photography: George Peters. Producer: Joseph M. Schenck. Director: Roscoe Arbuckle. Cast: Roscoe Arbuckle, Buster Keaton, Al St. John, Alice Lake, Joe Keaton, Charles Dudley

Moonshine (1918)
Released: May 13, 1918. Distributed by: Paramount Pictures. Produced by: Comique Film Corporation. Length: 2 reels. Scenario Editor: Herbert Warren. Scenario: Roscoe Arbuckle. Photography: George Peters. Producer: Joseph M. Schenck. Director: Roscoe Arbuckle. Cast: Roscoe Arbuckle, Buster Keaton, Al St. John, Charles Dudley, Alice Lake, Joe Bordeau

Good Night, Nurse! (1918)
Released: July 8, 1918. Distributed by: Paramount Pictures. Produced by: Comique Film Corporation. Length: 2 reels. Scenario Editor: Herbert Warren. Scenario: Roscoe Arbuckle. Photography: George Peters. Producer: Joseph M. Schenck. Director: Roscoe Arbuckle. Cast: Roscoe Arbuckle, Buster Keaton, Al St. John, Alice Lake, Kate Price, Joe Keaton

The Cook (1918)
Released: September 15, 1918. Distributed by: Paramount Pictures. Produced by: Comique Film Corporation. Length: 2 reels. Scenario Editor: Herbert Warren. Scenario: Roscoe Arbuckle. Photography: George Peters. Producer: Joseph M. Schenck. Director: Roscoe Arbuckle. Cast: Roscoe Arbuckle, Buster Keaton, Al St. John, Alice Lake, John Rand, Glen Cavender, Luke the Dog

Back Stage (1919)
Released: September 7, 1919. Distributed by: Paramount Pictures. Produced by: Comique Film Corporation. Length: 2 reels. Scenario: Jean Havez and Roscoe Arbuckle. Photography: Elgin Lessley. Producer: Joseph M. Schenck. Director: Roscoe Arbuckle. Cast: Roscoe Arbuckle, Buster Keaton, Al St. John, Molly Malone, Buddy Post, John Coogan

The Hayseed (1919)
Released: October 26, 1919. Distributed by: Paramount Pictures. Produced by: Comique Film Corporation. Length: 2 reels. Scenario: Jean Havez and Roscoe Arbuckle. Photography: Elgin Lessley. Producer: Joseph M. Schenck. Director: Roscoe Arbuckle. Cast: Roscoe Arbuckle, Buster Keaton, John Coogan, Molly Malone, Kitty Bradbury, Luke the Dog

The Garage (1920)
Released: January 11, 1920. Distributed by: Paramount Pictures. Produced by: Comique Film Corporation. Length: 2 reels. Scenario: Jean Havez and Roscoe Arbuckle. Photography: Elgin Lessley. Producer: Joseph M. Schenck. Director: Roscoe Arbuckle. Cast: Roscoe Arbuckle, Buster Keaton, Molly Malone, Harry McCoy, Daniel Crimmins, Luke the Dog

METRO FEATURE

The Saphead (1920)
Released: October 18, 1920. Distributed by: Metro Pictures. Presented by John L. Golden and Winchell Smith in conjunction with Marcus Loew. Length: 7 reels. Scenario: June Mathis. Based on *The New Henrietta* by Winchell Smith and Victor Mapes, adapted from *The Henrietta*, a play by Bronson Howard. Photography: Harold Wenstrom. Producer: Winchell Smith. Director: Herbert Blache. Cast: Buster Keaton, William H. Crane, Irving Cummings, Jack Livingston, Odette Tyler, Carol Holloway, Beulah Booker, Edward Jobson, Edward Connely, Edward Alexander

THE KEATON SILENT SHORTS

One Week (1920)
Released: September 1, 1920. Distributed by: Metro Pictures. Presented by: Comique Film Corporation. Length: 2 reels. Scenario: Buster Keaton and Eddie Cline. Photography: Elgin Lessley. Producer: Joseph M. Schenck. Directors: Buster Keaton and Eddie Cline. Cast: Buster Keaton, Sybil Seely, Joe Roberts

Convict 13 (1920)
Released: October 27, 1920. Distributed by: Metro Pictures. Presented by: Comique Film Corporation. Length: 2 reels. Scenario: Buster Keaton and Eddie Cline. Photography: Elgin Lessley. Producer: Joseph M. Schenck. Directors: Buster Keaton and Eddie Cline. Cast: Buster Keaton, Sybil Seely, Joe Roberts, Eddie Cline, Joe Keaton

The Scarecrow (1920)
Released: December 22, 1920. Distributed by: Metro Pictures. Presented by: Comique Film Corporation. Length: 2 reels. Scenario: Buster Keaton and Eddie Cline. Photography: Elgin Lessley. Producer: Joseph M. Schenck. Directors: Buster Keaton and Eddie Cline. Cast: Buster Keaton, Sybil Seely, Joe Keaton, Joe Roberts, Eddie Cline, Luke the Dog

Neighbors (1921)
Released: January 3, 1921. Distributed by: Metro Pictures. Presented by: Comique Film Corporation. Length: 2 reels. Scenario: Buster Keaton and Eddie Cline. Photography: Elgin Lessley. Producer: Joseph M. Schenck. Directors: Buster Keaton and Eddie Cline. Cast: Buster Keaton, Virginia Fox, Joe Keaton, Joe Roberts, Eddie Cline, James Duffy, The Flying Escalantes

The Haunted House (1921)
Released: February 10, 1921. Distributed by: Metro Pictures. Presented by: Comique Film Corporation. Length: 2 reels. Scenario: Buster Keaton and Eddie Cline. Photography: Elgin Lessley. Producer: Joseph M. Schenck. Directors: Buster Keaton and Eddie Cline. Cast: Buster Keaton, Virginia Fox, Joe Keaton, Joe Roberts, Eddie Cline

Hard Luck (1921)
Released: March 16, 1921. Distributed by: Metro Pictures. Presented by: Comique Film Corporation. Length: 2 reels. Scenario: Buster Keaton and Eddie Cline. Photography: Elgin Lessley. Producer: Joseph M. Schenck. Directors: Buster Keaton and Eddie Cline. Cast: Buster Keaton, Virginia Fox, Joe Roberts, Bull Montana

The High Sign (1921)
Released: April 12, 1921. Distributed by: Metro Pictures. Presented by: Comique Film Corporation. Length: 2 reels. Scenario: Buster Keaton and Eddie Cline. Photography: Elgin Lessley. Producer: Joseph M. Schenck. Directors: Buster Keaton and Eddie Cline. Cast: Buster Keaton, Bartine Burkett, Al St. John

The Goat (1921)
Released: May 18, 1921. Distributed by: Metro Pictures. Presented by: Comique Film Corporation. Length: 2 reels. Scenario: Buster Keaton and Mal St. Clair. Photography: Elgin Lessley. Producer: Joseph M. Schenck. Directors: Buster Keaton and Mal St. Clair. Cast: Buster Keaton, Virginia Fox, Joe Roberts, Mal St. Clair, Kitty Bradbury, Eddie Cline, Jean Havez

The Playhouse (1921)
Released: October 6, 1921. Distributed by: First National. Presented by: Comique Film Corporation. Length: 2 reels. Scenario: Buster Keaton and Eddie Cline. Photography: Elgin Lessley. Producer: Joseph M. Schenck. Technical Director: Fred Gabourie. Directors: Buster Keaton and Eddie Cline. Cast: Buster Keaton, Virginia Fox, Joe Roberts

The Boat (1921)
Released: November 1921. Distributed by: First National. Presented by: Comique Film Corporation. Length: 2 reels. Scenario: Buster Keaton and Eddie Cline. Photography: Elgin Lessley. Producer: Joseph M. Schenck. Technical Director: Fred Gabourie. Directors: Buster Keaton and Eddie Cline. Cast: Buster Keaton, Sybil Seely, Eddie Cline

The Paleface (1922)
Released: January 1922. Distributed by: First National. Presented by: Comique Film Corporation. Length: 2 reels. Scenario: Buster Keaton and Eddie Cline. Photography: Elgin

Lessley. Producer: Joseph M. Schenck. Technical Director: Fred Gabourie. Directors: Buster Keaton and Eddie Cline. Cast: Buster Keaton, Virginia Fox, Joe Roberts

Cops (1922)
Released: March 1922. Distributed by: First National. Presented by: Comique Film Corporation. Length: 2 reels. Scenario: Buster Keaton and Eddie Cline. Photography: Elgin Lessley. Producer: Joseph M. Schenck. Technical Director: Fred Gabourie. Directors: Buster Keaton and Eddie Cline. Cast: Buster Keaton, Virginia Fox, Joe Roberts, Steve Murphy, Eddie Cline

My Wife's Relations (1922)
Released: May 1922. Distributed by: First National. Presented by: Comique Film Corporation. Length: 2 reels. Scenario: Buster Keaton and Eddie Cline. Photography: Elgin Lessley. Producer: Joseph M. Schenck. Technical Director: Fred Gabourie. Directors: Buster Keaton and Eddie Cline. Cast: Buster Keaton, Kate Price, Joe Roberts, Monte Collins, Tom Wilson, Harry Madison, Wheezer Dell

The Blacksmith (1922)
Released: July 21, 1922. Distributed by: First National. Presented by: Comique Film Corporation. Length: 2 reels. Scenario: Buster Keaton and Mal St. Clair. Photography: Elgin Lessley. Producer: Joseph M. Schenck. Technical Director: Fred Gabourie. Directors: Buster Keaton and Mal St. Clair. Cast: Buster Keaton, Joe Roberts, Virginia Fox

The Frozen North (1922)
Released: August 1922. Distributed by: First National. Presented by: Buster Keaton Productions. Length: 2 reels. Scenario: Buster Keaton and Eddie Cline. Photography: Elgin Lessley. Producer: Joseph M. Schenck. Technical Director: Fred Gabourie. Directors: Buster Keaton and Eddie Cline. Cast: Buster Keaton, Joe Roberts, Sybil Seely, Bonnie Hill, Freeman Wood, Eddie Cline, Robert Parker

Daydreams (1922)
Released: September 1922. Distributed by: First National. Presented by: Buster Keaton Productions. Length: 2 reels. Scenario: Buster Keaton and Eddie Cline. Photography: Elgin Lessley. Producer: Joseph M. Schenck. Technical Director: Fred Gabourie. Directors: Buster Keaton and Eddie Cline. Cast: Buster Keaton, Renée Adorée, Joe Keaton, Joe Roberts, Eddie Cline

The Electric House (1922)
Released: October 1922. Distributed by: Associated First National. Presented by: Buster Keaton Productions. Length: 2 reels. Scenario: Buster Keaton and Eddie Cline. Photography: Elgin Lessley. Producer: Joseph M. Schenck. Technical Director: Fred Gabourie. Directors: Buster Keaton and Eddie Cline. Cast: Buster Keaton, Joe Roberts, Virginia Fox

The Balloonatic (1923)
Released: January 22, 1923. Distributed by: Associated First National. Presented by: Buster Keaton Productions. Length: 2 reels. Scenario: Buster Keaton and Eddie Cline. Photography: Elgin Lessley. Producer: Joseph M. Schenck. Technical

Director: Fred Gabourie. Directors: Buster Keaton and Eddie Cline. Cast: Buster Keaton, Phyllis Haver

The Love Nest (1923)
Released: March 1923. Distributed by: Associated First National. Presented by: Buster Keaton Productions. Length: 2 reels. Scenario: Buster Keaton. Photography: Elgin Lessley. Producer: Joseph M. Schenck. Technical Director: Fred Gabourie. Director: Buster Keaton. Cast: Buster Keaton, Joe Roberts, Virginia Fox

THE KEATON SILENT FEATURES

Three Ages (1923)
Released: September 24, 1923. Distributed by: Metro Pictures. Produced by Buster Keaton Productions. Length: 6 reels. Scenario: Clyde Bruckman, Joseph A. Mitchell, Jean Havez. Photography: William McGann, Elgin Lessley. Technical Director: Fred Gabourie. Producer: Joseph M. Schenck. Directors: Buster Keaton and Eddie Cline. Cast: Buster Keaton, Margaret Leahy, Joe Roberts, Lillian Lawrence, Wallace Beery, Blanche Payson

Our Hospitality (1923)
Released: November 19, 1923. Distributed by: Metro Pictures. Produced by Buster Keaton Productions. Length: 7 reels. Scenario: Jean Havez, Clyde Bruckman, Joseph Mitchell. Lighting: Denver Harmon. Costumes: Walter Israel. Photography: Elgin Lessley, Gordon Jennings. Art Direction: Fred Gabourie. Producer: Joseph M. Schenck. Directors: Buster Keaton and Jack Blystone. Cast: Buster Keaton, Joe Roberts, Ralph Bushman (later Francis X. Bushman, Jr.), Craig Ward, Monte Collins, Joe Keaton, Kitty Bradbury, Natalie Talmadge, Buster Keaton, Jr. (later James Talmadge)

Sherlock Jr. (1924)
Released: April 21, 1924. Distributed by: Metro Pictures Corporation. Produced by Buster Keaton Productions. Length: 5 reels. Scenario: Jean Havez, Joseph Mitchell, Clyde Bruckman. Electrician: Denver Harmon. Costumes: Clare West. Photography: Elgin Lessley, Byron Houck. Art Direction: Fred Gabourie. Producer: Joseph M. Schenck. Director: Buster Keaton. Cast: Buster Keaton, Kathryn McGuire, Joe Keaton, Ward Crane, Erwin Connelly

The Navigator (1924)
Released: October 13, 1924. Distributed by: Metro-Goldwyn Distribution Corporation. Produced by Buster Keaton Productions. Length: 6 reels. Scenario: Clyde Bruckman, Joseph Mitchell, Jean Havez. Electrician: Denver Harmon. Photography: Elgin Lessley, Byron Houck. Technical Director: Fred Gabourie. Producer: Joseph M. Schenck. Directors: Donald Crisp and Buster Keaton. Cast: Buster Keaton, Kathryn McGuire, Frederick Vroom, Clarence Burton, H. M. Clugston, Noble Johnson

Seven Chances (1925)
Released: March 16, 1925. Distributed by: Metro-Goldwyn-Mayer. Produced by Buster Keaton Productions. Length: 6 reels. Scenario: Clyde Bruckman, Jean Havez, Joseph

Mitchell, adapted from Roi Cooper Megrue's play originally produced by David Belasco. Electrician: Denver Harmon. Photography: Elgin Lessley, Byron Houck. Art Director: Fred Gabourie. Producer: Joseph M. Schenck. Director: Buster Keaton. Cast: Buster Keaton, T. Roy Barnes, Snitz Edwards, Ruth Dwyer, Frankie Raymond, Erwin Connelly, Jules Cowles

Go West (1925)
Released: November 1, 1925. Distributed by: Metro-Goldwyn-Mayer. Produced by Buster Keaton Productions. Length: 7 reels. Scenario: Buster Keaton, Raymond Cannon. Electrical Effects: Denver Harmon. Photography: Elgin Lessley, Bert Haines. Art Director: Fred Gabourie. Producer: Joseph M. Schenck. Director: Buster Keaton, assisted by Lex Neal. Cast: Buster Keaton, Howard Truesdale, Kathleen Myers, Ray Thompson, Brown Eyes (cow)

Battling Butler (1926)
Released: September 19, 1926. Distributed by: Metro-Goldwyn-Mayer. Produced by Buster Keaton Productions. Length: 7 reels. Scenario: Paul Gerard Smith, Al Boasberg, Charles H. Smith, and Lex Neal, adapted from the play by Stanley Brightman, Austin Melford, Philip Brabham, Walter L. Rosemont, and Douglas Furber. Electrical Effects: Ed Levy. Photography: J. D. Jennings, Bert Haines. Art Director: Fred Gabourie. Producer: Joseph M. Schenck. Director: Buster Keaton. Cast: Buster Keaton, Snitz Edwards, Sally O'Neal, Walter James, Bud Fine, Francis McDonald, Mary O'Brien, Tom Wilson, Eddie Borden

The General (1926)
Released: February 5, 1927 (the world premiere was held in Tokyo, Japan, on December 31, 1926). Distributed by: United Artists Corporation. Produced by Buster Keaton Productions. Length: 8 reels. Scenario: Buster Keaton, Clyde Bruckman, Al Boasberg, Charles Smith, from the book The Great Locomotive Chase by William Pittinger. Lighting Effects: Denver Harmon. Photography: Dev Jennings, Bert Haines. Technical Director: Fred Gabourie. Producer: Joseph M. Schenck. Directors: Buster Keaton and Clyde Bruckman. Cast: Buster Keaton, Marion Mack, Glen Cavender, Jim Farley, Frederick Vroom, Charles Smith, Frank Barnes, Joe Keaton, Mike Donlin, Tom Nawn

College (1927)
Released: November 1927. Distributed by: United Artists Corporation. Produced by Buster Keaton Productions. Length: 6 reels. Scenario: Carl Harbaugh, Bryan Foy. Lighting Effects: Jack Lewis. Editor: Sherm Kell. Photography: Dev Jennings, Bert Haines. Technical Director: Fred Gabourie. Supervisor: Harry Brand. Producer: Joseph M. Schenck. Director: James W. Horne. Cast: Buster Keaton, Ann Cornwall, Florence Turner, Harold Goodwin, Snitz Edwards, Flora Bramley, Carl Harbaugh, Sam Crawford

Steamboat Bill, Jr. (1928)
Released: May 12, 1928. Distributed by: United Artists Corporation. Produced by Buster Keaton Productions. Length: 7 reels. Scenario: Carl Harbaugh. Photography: Dev Jennings, Bert Haines. Technical Director: Fred Gabourie.

Supervisor: Harry Brand. Assistant Director: Sandy Roth. Producer: Joseph M. Schenck. Director: Charles F. Riesner. Cast: Buster Keaton, Ernest Torrence, Tom Lewis, Tom McGuire, Marion Byron

METRO-GOLDWYN-MAYER FEATURES

The Cameraman (1928)
Released: September 22, 1928. A Buster Keaton Production. Produced and Distributed by: Metro-Goldwyn-Mayer. Length: 8 reels. Story: Clyde Bruckman, Lew Lipton. Continuity: Richard Schayer. Titles: Joe Farnham. Settings: Fred Gabourie. Wardrobe: David Cox. Editor: Hugh Wynn. Photography: Elgin Lessley and Reggie Lanning. Producer: Lawrence Weingarten. Director: Edward Sedgwick. Cast: Buster Keaton, Marceline Day, Harold Goodwin, Sidney Bracy, Harry Gribbon, Edward Brophy, Josephine (monkey)

Spite Marriage (1929)
Released: April 6, 1929. A Buster Keaton Production. Produced and Distributed by: Metro-Goldwyn-Mayer. Length: 9 reels. Story: Lew Lipton. Adaptation: Ernest S. Pagano. Continuity: Richard Schayer. Titles: Robert Hopkins. Art Director: Cedric Gibbons. Wardrobe: David Cox. Editor: Frank Sullivan. Photography: Reggie Lanning, Frank Dugas. Producer: Lawrence Weingarten. Director: Edward Sedgwick. Cast: Buster Keaton, Dorothy Sebastian, Edward Earle, Lelia Hyams, William Bechtel, John Bryon

The Hollywood Revue of 1929 (1929)
Released: November 23, 1929. A Buster Keaton Production. Produced and Distributed by: Metro-Goldwyn-Mayer. Dialogue: Al Boasberg, Robert E. Hopkins. Art Director: Cedric Gibbons, Richard Day. Wardrobe: David Cox. Editor: William S. Gray, Cameron K. Wood. Recording Engineer: Douglas Shearer. Sound Technician: Russell Franks. Dances and Ensembles: Sammy Lee, George Cunningham. Music: Gus Edwards. Lyrics: Joe Goodwin. Photography: John Arnold, Irving G. Reis, Maximillian Fabian, John M. Nickolaus. Producer: Harry Rapf. Director: Charles F. Riesner. Cast: Marion Davies, John Gilbert, Norma Shearer, William Haines, Joan Crawford, Buster Keaton, Bessie Love, Conrad Nagel, Lionel Barrymore, Marie Dressler, Jack Benny, Stan Laurel, Oliver Hardy

Free and Easy (1930)
Released: March 22, 1930. A Buster Keaton Production. Produced and Distributed by: Metro-Goldwyn-Mayer. Scenario: Richard Schayer. Adaptation: Paul Dickey. Dialogue: Al Boasberg. Words and Music: Roy Turk, Fred E. Ahlert. Dances staged by: Sammy Lee. Recording Director: Douglas Shearer. Art Director: Cedric Gibbons. Wardrobe: David Cox. Photography: Leonard Smith. Editor: William LeVanway. Producer: Lawrence Weingarten. Director: Edward Sedgwick. Cast: Buster Keaton, Anita Page, Robert Montgomery, Trixie Friganza, Fred Niblo, Edgar Dearing, Gwen Lee, John Miljan, Lionel Barrymore, William Haines, William Collier, Sr., Dorothy Sebastian, Karl Dane, David Burton, Jackie Coogan, Cecil B. DeMille

Doughboys (1930)
Released: August 30, 1930. A Buster Keaton Production. Produced and Distributed by: Metro-Goldwyn-Mayer. Story: Al Boasberg, Sidney Lazarus. Scenario: Richard Schayer. Dialogue: Al Boasberg, Richard Schayer. Dances staged by: Sammy Lee. Words and Music: Edward Sedgwick, Howard Johnson, Joseph Meyer. Recording Director: Douglas Shearer. Art Director: Cedric Gibbons. Wardrobe: Vivian Baer. Photography: Leonard Smith. Editor: William LeVanway. Producer: Lawrence Weingarten. Director: Edward Sedgwick. Cast: Buster Keaton, Cliff Edwards, Sally Eilers, Edward Brophy, Victor Potel, Arnold Korff, Frank Mayo, Pitzy Katz, William Steele

Parlor, Bedroom and Bath (1931)
Released: February 28, 1931. A Buster Keaton Production. Produced and Distributed by: Metro-Goldwyn-Mayer. From the play by Charles W. Bell and Mark Swan. Dialogue Continuity: Richard Schayer. Additional Dialogue: Robert E. Hopkins. Recording Director: Douglas Shearer. Art Director: Cedric Gibbons. Wardrobe: Rene Hubert. Photography: Leonard Smith. Editor: William LeVanway. Producer: Lawrence Weingarten. Director: Edward Sedgwick. Cast: Buster Keaton, Charlotte Greenwood, Reginald Denny, Cliff Edwards, Dorothy Christy, Joan Peters, Sally Eilers, Natalie Moorhead, Edward Brophy, Walter Merrill, Sidney Bracy

Sidewalks of New York (1931)
Released: September 26, 1931. A Buster Keaton Production. Produced and Distributed by: Metro-Goldwyn-Mayer. Story: George Landy and Paul Gerard Smith. Dialogue: Robert E. Hopkins, Eric Hatch. Recording Director: Douglas Shearer. Art Director: Cedric Gibbons. Photography: Leonard Smith. Editor: Charles Hochberg. Producer: Lawrence Weingarten. Director: Jules White, Zion Myers. Cast: Buster Keaton, Anita Page, Cliff Edwards, Frank Rowan, Norman Phillips, Jr., Frank La Rue, Oscar Apfel, Syd Saylor, Clark Marshall

The Passionate Plumber (1932)
Released: February 6, 1932. A Buster Keaton Production. Produced and Distributed by: Metro-Goldwyn-Mayer. Adaptation: Laurence E. Johnson from the play *Her Cardboard Lover* by Jacques Deval. Dialogue: Ralph Spence. Recording Director: Douglas Shearer. Art Director: Cedric Gibbons. Photography: Norbert Brodine. Editor: William S. Gray. Producer: Harry Rapf. Director: Edward Sedgwick. Cast: Buster Keaton, Jimmy Durante, Polly Moran, Irene Purcell, Gilbert Roland, Mona Maris, Maude Eburne, Henry Armetta, Paul Porcasi, Jean Del Val, August Tollaire

Speak Easily (1932)
Released: August 13, 1932. A Buster Keaton Production. Produced and Distributed by: Metro-Goldwyn-Mayer. Adaptation: Ralph Spence, Laurence E. Johnson from the story *Footlights* by Clarence Budington Kelland. Recording Director: Douglas Shearer. Art Director: Cedric Gibbons. Photography: Harold Wenstrom. Editor: William LeVanway. Costumes: Arthur Appell. Producer: Lawrence Weingarten. Director: Edward Sedgwick. Cast: Buster Keaton, Jimmy Durante, Ruth Selwyn, Thelma Todd, Hedda Hopper, William Pawley, Sidney Toler, Lawrence Grant, Henry Armetta, Edward Brophy, Sidney Bracy

What—No Beer? (1933)
Released: February 10, 1933. Produced and Distributed by: Metro-Goldwyn-Mayer. Story: Robert E. Hopkins. Screenplay: Carey Wilson. Additional Dialogue: Jack Cluett. Recording Director: Douglas Shearer. Art Director: Cedric Gibbons. Photography: Harold Wenstrom. Editor: Frank Sullivan. Producer: Lawrence Weingarten. Director: Edward Sedgwick. Cast: Buster Keaton, Jimmy Durante, Roscoe Ates, Phyllis Barry, John Miljan, Henry Armetta, Edward Brophy, Charles Dunbar, Charles Giblyn

FOREIGN-MADE KEATON FEATURES

Le Roi des Champs-Elysées (1934)
(British title: The Champ of the Champs-Elysées)
Released: December 1934. Distributed by: Paramount (never released in the United States of America). Screenplay: Arnold Lipp. Additional Dialogue: Yves Mirande. Art Director: Hugues Laurent, Jacques-Laurent Atthalin. Music: Joe Hajos. Photography: Robert Le Febvre. Supervisor: Robert Siodmark. Producer: Seymour Nebenzal. Director: Max Nosseck. Cast: Buster Keaton, Paulette Dubost, Colette Darfeuil, Madeline Guitty, Lucien Callamand, Jacques Dumesnil, Pierre Pierade, Gaston Dupray

The Invader (1936)
(American title: *An Old Spanish Custom*)
Released: January 2, 1936. Distributed by: British and Continental Films (Metro-Goldwyn-Mayer). Screenplay: Edwin Greenwood. Music: John Greenwood, George Rubens. Recording Engineer: Denis Scanlan. Photography: Eugene Schuefftan, Eric L. Gross. Editor: Dan Birt. Assistant Director: Pelham Leigh Aman. Producers: Sam Spiegel and Harold Richman. Director: Adrian Brunel. Cast: Buster Keaton, Lupita Tovar, Esme Percy, Lyn Harding, Andrea Malandrinos, Hilda Moreno, Clifford Heatherley, Webster Booth

El Moderno Barba Azul (1946)
(American title: *Boom in the Moon*)
Released: August 2, 1946. Produced by: Alsa Films (Mexico). Script: Victor Trivas, Jaime Salvador. Photography: Agustin Jiminez. Producer: Alexander Salkind. Director: Jaime Salvador. Cast: Buster Keaton, Angel Garasa, Virginia Serret, Luis Barreiro, Fernando Sotto, Jorge Mondragon, Luis Mondragon

EDUCATIONAL SHORTS

The Gold Ghost (1934)
Released: March 16, 1934. Distributed by: Fox Film Corporation. Presented by: E. W. Hammons. Produced by: Educational Films Corporation of America. Story: Ewart Adamson, Nick Barrows. Adaptation/Continuity: Ernest Pagano, Charles Lamont. Producer: E. H. Allen. Director: Charles Lamont. Cast: Buster Keaton, Dorothy Dix, William Worthington, Lloyd Ingraham, Warren Hymer, Joe Young, Billy Engle, Al Thompson, Leo Willis

Allez Oop (1934)
Released: May 25, 1934. Distributed by: Fox Film Corporation. Presented by: E.W. Hammons. Produced by: Educational Films Corporation of America. Story: Ernest Pagano, Ewart Adamson. Photography: Dwight Warren. Producer: E. H. Allen. Director: Charles Lamont. Cast: Buster Keaton, Dorothy Sebastian, George Lewis, Harry Myers, The Flying Escalantes

Palooka from Paducah (1935)
Released: January 11, 1935. Distributed by: Fox Film Corporation. Presented by: E.W. Hammons. Produced by: Educational Films Corporation of America. Story: Glen Lambert. Photography: Dwight Warren. Producer: E. H. Allen. Director: Charles Lamont. Cast: Buster Keaton, Joe Keaton, Myra Keaton, Louise Keaton, Dewey Robinson, Bull Montana

One Run Elmer (1935)
Released: February 22, 1935. Distributed by: Fox Film Corporation. Presented by: E.W. Hammons. Produced by: Educational Films Corporation of America. Story: Glen Lambert. Photography: Dwight Warren. Producer: E. H. Allen. Director: Charles Lamont. Cast: Buster Keaton, Lona Andre, Dewey Robinson, Harold Goodwin, Jim Thorpe

Hayseed Romance (1935)
Released: March 15, 1935. Distributed by: Fox Film Corporation. Presented by: E.W. Hammons. Produced by: Educational Films Corporation of America. Story: Charles Lamont. Dialogue/Continuity: Glen Lambert. Photography: Dwight Warren. Producer: E. H. Allen. Director: Charles Lamont. Cast: Buster Keaton, Jane Jones, Dorothea Kent

Tars and Stripes (1935)
Released: May 3, 1935. Distributed by: Fox Film Corporation. Presented by: E.W. Hammons. Produced by: Educational Films Corporation of America. Story: Charles Lamont. Adaptation: Ewart Adamson. Photography: Dwight Warren. Producer: E. H. Allen. Director: Charles Lamont. Cast: Buster Keaton, Vernon Dent, Dorothea Kent, Jack Shutta

The E-Flat Man (1935)
Released: August 9, 1935. Distributed by: Fox Film Corporation. Presented by: E.W. Hammons. Produced by: Educational Films Corporation of America. Story: Glen Lambert, Charles Lamont. Photography: Dwight Warren. Producer: E. H. Allen. Director: Charles Lamont. Cast: Buster Keaton, Dorothea Kent, Broderick O'Farrell, Charles McAvoy, Si Jenks, Fern Emmett, Jack Shutta

The Timid Young Man (1935)
Released: October 25, 1935. Distributed by: Twentieth Century-Fox Film Corporation. Presented by: E.W. Hammons. Produced by: Educational Films Corporation of America. Photography: Dwight Warren. Producer/Director: Mack Sennett. Cast: Buster Keaton, Lona Andre, Stanley J. Sandford, Kitty McHugh, Harry Bowen

Three on a Limb (1936)
Released: January 3, 1936. Distributed by: Twentieth Century-Fox Film Corporation. Presented by: E.W. Hammons. Produced by: Educational Films Corporation of America.

Story: Vernon Smith. Photography: Gus Peterson. Producer: E. H. Allen. Director: Charles Lamont. Cast: Buster Keaton, Lona Andre, Harold Goodwin, Grant Withers, Barbara Bedford, John Ince, Fern Emmett, Phyllis Crane

Grand Slam Opera (1936)
Released: February 21, 1936. Distributed by: Twentieth Century-Fox Film Corporation. Presented by: E.W. Hammons. Produced by: Educational Films Corporation of America. Story: Buster Keaton, Charles Lamont. Photography: Gus Peterson. Producer: E. H. Allen. Director: Charles Lamont. Cast: Buster Keaton, Diana Lewis, Harold Goodwin, John Ince, Melrose Coakley, Bud Jamison

Blue Blazes (1936)
Released: August 21, 1936. Distributed by: Twentieth Century-Fox Film Corporation. Presented by: E.W. Hammons. Produced by: Educational Films Corporation of America. Story: David Freedman. Photography: George Webber. Producer: E. H. Allen. Director: Raymond Kane. Cast: Buster Keaton, Arthur Jarrett, Rose Kessner, Patty Willson, Marilyn Stuart

The Chemist (1936)
Released: October 9, 1936. Distributed by: Twentieth Century-Fox Film Corporation. Presented by: E.W. Hammons. Produced by: Educational Films Corporation of America. Story: David Freedman. Photography: George Webber. Producer/Director: Al Christie. Cast: Buster Keaton, Marlyn Stuart, Earl Gilbert, Don McBride, Herman Lieb

Mixed Magic (1936)
Released: November 20, 1936. Distributed by: Twentieth Century-Fox Film Corporation. Presented by: E.W. Hammons. Produced by: Educational Films Corporation of America. Story: Arthur Jarrett, Marcy Klauber. Photography: George Webber. Producer: E. H. Allen. Director: Raymond Kane. Cast: Buster Keaton, Eddie Lambert, Marlyn Stuart, Eddie Hall, Jimmy Fox

Jail Bait (1937)
Released: January 8, 1937. Distributed by: Twentieth Century-Fox Film Corporation. Presented by: E.W. Hammons. Produced by: Educational Films Corporation of America. Story: Paul Gerard Smith. Photography: Dwight Warren. Producer: E. H. Allen. Director: Charles Lamont. Cast: Buster Keaton, Harold Goodwin, Mathew Betz, Bud Jamison, Betty Andre

Ditto (1937)
Released: February 12, 1937. Distributed by: Twentieth Century-Fox Film Corporation. Presented by: E.W. Hammons. Produced by: Educational Films Corporation of America. Story: Paul Gerard Smith. Photography: Dwight Warren. Producer: E. H. Allen. Director: Charles Lamont. Cast: Buster Keaton, Harold Goodwin, Barbara and Gloria Brewster, Al Thompson, Bob Ellsworth, Lynton Brent

Love Nest on Wheels (1937)
Released: March 26, 1937. Distributed by: Twentieth Century-Fox Film Corporation. Presented by: E.W. Hammons. Produced by: Educational Films Corporation of America.

Story: William Hazlett Upson. Adaptation: Paul Gerard Smith. Photography: Dwight Warren. Producer: E. H. Allen. Director: Charles Lamont. Cast: Buster Keaton, Myra Keaton, Al St. John, Lynton Brent, Diana Lewis, Bud Jamison, Louise Keaton, Harry Keaton

COLUMBIA SHORTS

Pest from the West (1939)
Released: June 16, 1939. Produced and Distributed by: Columbia Pictures Corporation. Screenplay: Clyde Bruckman. Photography: Henry Freulich. Editor: Charles Nelson. Producer: Jules White. Director: Del Lord. Cast: Buster Keaton, Lorna Gray (later Adrian Booth), Gino Corrida, Richard Fiske

Mooching Through Georgia (1939)
Released: August 11, 1939. Produced and Distributed by: Columbia Pictures Corporation. Screenplay: Clyde Bruckman. Photography: John Stumar. Editor: Arthur Seid. Producer/Director: Jules White. Cast: Buster Keaton, Monty Collins, Jill Martin, Bud Jamison

Nothing but Pleasure (1940)
Released: January 19, 1940. Produced and Distributed by: Columbia Pictures Corporation. Screenplay: Clyde Bruckman. Photography: Henry Freulich. Editor: Arthur Seid. Producer/Director: Jules White. Cast: Buster Keaton, Dorothy Appleby, Beatrice Blinn

Pardon My Berth Marks (1940)
Released: March 22, 1940. Produced and Distributed by: Columbia Pictures Corporation. Screenplay: Clyde Bruckman. Photography: Benjamin Kline. Editor: Mel Thorsen. Producer/Director: Jules White. Cast: Buster Keaton, Dorothy Appleby, Richard Fiske, Vernon Dent, Clarice (parrot)

The Taming of the Snood (1940)
Released: June 28, 1940. Produced and Distributed by: Columbia Pictures Corporation. Screenplay: Ewart Adamson, Clyde Bruckman. Photography: Henry Freulich. Editor: Mel Thorsen. Producer/Director: Jules White. Cast: Buster Keaton, Elsie Ames, Dorothy Appleby

The Spook Speaks (1940)
Released: September 20, 1940. Produced and Distributed by: Columbia Pictures Corporation. Screenplay: Ewart Adamson, Clyde Bruckman. Photography: Henry Freulich. Editor: Mel Thorsen. Producer/Director: Jules White. Cast: Buster Keaton, Elsie Ames, Don Beddoe, Dorothy Appleby, Orson (penguin)

His Ex Marks the Spot (1940)
Released: December 13, 1940. Produced and Distributed by: Columbia Pictures Corporation. Screenplay: Felix Adler. Photography: Henry Freulich. Editor: Mel Thorsen. Producer/Director: Jules White. Cast: Buster Keaton, Elsie Ames, Matt McHugh, Dorothy Appleby

So You Won't Squawk (1941)
Released: February 21, 1941. Produced and Distributed by: Columbia Pictures Corporation. Screenplay: Elwood Ullman.

Photography: Benjamin Kline. Editor: Arthur Seid. Producer: Del Lord, Hugh McCollum. Director: Del Lord. Cast: Buster Keaton, Matt McHugh, Eddie Fetherstone

General Nuisance (1941)
Released: September 18, 1941. Produced and Distributed by: Columbia Pictures Corporation. Screenplay: Felix Adler, Clyde Bruckman. Photography: Benjamin Kline. Editor: Jerome Thoms. Producer/Director: Jules White. Cast: Buster Keaton, Elsie Ames, Dorothy Appleby, Monty Collins

She's Oil Mine (1941)
Released: November 20, 1941. Produced and Distributed by: Columbia Pictures Corporation. Screenplay: Felix Adler. Photography: Benjamin Kline. Editor: Jerome Thoms. Producer/Director: Jules White. Cast: Buster Keaton, Elsie Ames, Monty Collins, Eddie Laughton

FEATURE FILM APPEARANCES

Hollywood Cavalcade (1939)
Released: October 13, 1939. Distributed by: Twentieth Century-Fox. Screenplay: Ernest Pascal. Story: Hilary Lynn, Brown Holmes. Based on an idea by Lou Breslow. Photography: Ernest Palmer, Allen M. Davey. Editor: Walter Thompson. Keystone Kops sequences directed by: Mal. St. Clair. Technical Advisor: Mack Sennett. Producer: Darryl F. Zanuck. Director: Irving Cummings. Cast: Don Ameche, Alice Faye, Buster Keaton, J. Edward Bromberg, Alan Curtis, Stuart Erwin, Al Jolson, Mack Sennett, Ben Turpin, Chester Conklin, Harold Goodwin

The Villain Still Pursued Her (1940)
Released: October 11, 1940. Distributed by: RKO. Produced by: Franklin-Blank Productions. Screenplay: Elbert Franklin. Based on the play The Fallen Saved (also known as The Drunkard). Additional Dialogue: Ethel La Blanche. Music: Frank Tours. Photography: Lucien Ballard. Editor: Arthur Hilton. Producer: Harold B. Franklin. Director: Edward Cline. Cast: Hugh Herbert, Anita Louise, Alan Mowbray, Buster Keaton, Joyce Compton, Richard Cromwell, Billy Gilbert, Margaret Hamilton, Diane Fisher, Charles Judels

Li'l Abner (1940)
Released: November 1, 1940. Distributed by: RKO. Produced by: Vogue Pictures. Screenplay: Charles Kerr and Tyler Johnson. From an original story by Al Capp. Based on the United Features comic "Li'l Abner" by Al Capp. Art Director: Ralph Berger. Photography: Harry Jackson. Editor: Otto Ludwig, Donn Hayes. Produced by Astor Pictures Corporation for Vogue Pictures. Associate Producer: Herman Schlom. Director: Albert S. Rogell. Cast: Granville Owen, Martha O'Driscoll, Mona Ray, Johnnie Morris, Buster Keaton, Billie Seward, Edgar Kennedy, Lucien Littlefield, Chester Conklin, Al St. John, Eddie Gribbon, Hank Mann, Louise Keaton, Blanche Payson

Forever and a Day (1943)
Released: March 26, 1943. Distributed by: RKO. Produced by: Anglo-American Productions. Script: Charles Bennett, C. S. Forester, Lawrence Hazard, Michael Hogan, W. P. Lipscomb,

Alice Duer Miller, John Van Druten, Alan Campbell, Peter Godfrey, S. M. Herzig, Christopher Isherwood, Gene Lockhart, R. C. Sherriff, Claudine West, Norman Corwin, Jack Hatfield, James Hilton, Emmett Lavery, Frederick Lonsdale, Donald Ogden Stewart, Keith Winter. Music Director: Anthony Collins. Photography: Robert DeGrasse, Lee Garmes, Russell Metty, Nicholas Musuraca. Editors: Elmo J. Williams, George Crone. Production Supervisor: Lloyd Richards. Directors: René Clair, Edmund Goulding, Cedric Hardwicke, Frank Lloyd, Victor Saville, Robert Stevenson, Herbert Wilcox. Cast: Brian Aherne, Robert Cummings, Edmund Gwen, Cedric Hardwicke, Edward Everett Horton, Buster Keaton, Elsa Lanchester, Charles Laughton, Ida Lupino, Herbert Marshall, Victor McLaglen, Ray Milland, Anna Neagle, Merle Oberon, Claude Rains, C. Aubrey Smith, Roland Young

San Diego, I Love You (1944)
Released: September 29, 1944. Distributed by: Universal Pictures. Screenplay: Michael Fessier, Ernest Pagano. Story: Ruth McKenney, Richard Bransten. Photography: Hal Mohr. Music: H. J. Salter. Editor: Charles Maynard. Producer: Michael Fessier, Ernest Pagano. Director: Reginald Le Borg. Cast: Jon Hall, Louise Allbritton, Edward Everett Horton, Eric Blore, Buster Keaton

That's the Spirit (1945)
Released: June 1, 1945. Distributed by: Universal Pictures. Screenplay: Michael Fessier, Ernest Pagano. Photography: Charles Van Enger. Music: H. J. Salter. Editor: Fred R. Feitshans, Jr. Producer: Michael Fessier, Ernest Pagano. Director: Charles Lamont. Cast: Peggy Ryan, Jack Oakie, June Vincent, Gene Lockhart, Johnny Coy, Andy Devine, Buster Keaton, Arthur Treacher

That Night With You (1945)
Released: September 28, 1945. Distributed by: Universal Pictures. Screenplay: Michael Fessier, Ernest Pagano. Story: Arnold Belgard. Photography: Charles Van Enger. Musical Director: H. J. Salter. Editor: Fred R. Feitshans, Jr. Executive Producer: Howard Benedict. Producer: Michael Fessier, Ernest Pagano. Director: William A. Seiter. Cast: Franchot Tone, Susanna Foster, David Bruce, Louise Allbritton, Buster Keaton

God's Country (1946)
Released: May 18, 1946. Distributed by: Screen Guild Productions. Produced by: Action Pictures. Producer: William B. David. Director/Screenplay: Robert Tansey. Cast: Robert Lowery, Helen Gilbert, William Farnum, Buster Keaton

The Lovable Cheat (1949)
Released: May 11, 1949. Distributed by: Film Classics. Produced by: Skyline Pictures. Screenplay: Edward Lewis, Richard Oswald. Based on the play *Mercadet le Falseur* by Honoré de Balzac. Music: Karl Hajos. Editor: Douglas Bagier. Associate Producer: Rosario Castagna. Producer: Richard Oswald, Edward Lewis. Director: Richard Oswald. Cast: Charlie Ruggles, Peggy Ann Garner, Richard Ney, Alan Mowbray, Buster Keaton

In the Good Old Summertime (1949)
Released: July 29, 1949. Distributed by: Metro-Goldwyn-Mayer. Screenplay: Samson Raphaelson. Adaptation: Albert Hackett, Frances Goodrich, Ivan Tors. Based on the play *Parfumerie* by Miklos Laszlo. Photography: Harry Stradling. Editor: Adrienne Fazan. Producer: Joe Pasternak. Director: Robert Z. Leonard. Cast: Judy Garland, Van Johnson, S. Z. "Cuddles" Sakall, Spring Byington, Buster Keaton, Clinton Sundberg, Marcia Van Dyke, Lillian Bronson

Sunset Boulevard (1950)
Released: August 4, 1950. Distributed by: Paramount Pictures. Script: Charles Brackett, Billy Wilder, D. M. Marshman, Jr. Based on the story "A Can of Beans." Music: Franz Waxman. Photography: John F. Seitz. Editors: Doane Harrison, Arthur Schmidt. Producer: Charles Brackett. Director: Billy Wilder. Cast: William Holden, Gloria Swanson, Erich von Stroheim, Nancy Olson, Fred Clark, Jack Webb, Cecil B. De Mille, Hedda Hopper, Buster Keaton, Anna Q. Nilsson, H. B. Warner

Limelight (1952)
Released: October 23, 1952 (pre-release); February 6, 1953 (general release). Distributed by: United Artists. Screenplay: Charles Chaplin. Musical Score: Charles Chaplin. Photography: Karl Struss. Editor: Joe Inge. Assistant Director: Robert Aldrich. Producer/Director: Charles Chaplin. Cast: Charles Chaplin, Claire Bloom, Nigel Bruce, Buster Keaton, Sydney Chaplin, Norman Lloyd, Andre Eglevsky, Melissa Hayden, Marjorie Bennett, Wheeler Dryden, Charles Chaplin, Jr., Geraldine Chaplin, Michael Chaplin, Josephine Chaplin

L'Incantevole Nemica (1953)
Released: June 14, 1953 (not released in the United States of America). Distributed by: Orso Films (Rome), Lambar Films (Paris). Executive Producer: Ferruccio Biancini. Director: Claudio Gora. Cast: Silvana Pampanini, Robert Lamoureux, Carlo Campanini, Buster Keaton

Around the World in 80 Days (1956)
Released: October 17, 1956. Distributed by: United Artists. Screenplay: James Poe, John Farrow, S. J. Perelman. Adapted from the novel by Jules Verne. Music: Victor Young. Photography: Lionel Lindon. Editors: Gene Ruggiero, Howard Epstein, Paul Weatherwax. Producer: Michael Todd. Director: Michael Anderson. Cast: David Niven, Cantinflas, Robert Newton, Shirley MacLaine, Ronald Colman, Noel Coward, Marlene Dietrich, John Gielgud, Buster Keaton, Beatrice Lillie, Peter Lorre, Frank Sinatra

The Adventures of Huckleberry Finn (1960)
Released: June 17, 1960. Distributed by: Metro-Goldwyn-Mayer. Script: James Lee. Based on the novel by Mark Twain. Music: Jerome Moross. Photography: Ted McCord. Editor: Frederic Steinkamp. Producer: Samuel Goldwyn, Jr. Director: Michael Curtiz. Cast: Tony Randall, Eddie Hodges, Archie Moore, Patty McCormack, Neville Brand, Mickey Shaughnessy, Andy Devine, Buster Keaton, John Carradine

Ten Girls Ago (1962)
Never released. Produced by: Am-Cam Productions. Script: Peter Farrow, Diane Lampert. Music Director: Joseph

Harnell. Music/Lyrics: Diane Lampert, Sammy Fain. Choreography: Bill Foster. Photography: Lee Garmes, Jackson M. Samuels. Producer: Edward A. Gollin. Director: Harold Daniels. Cast: Bert Lahr, Buster Keaton, Eddie Foy, Jr., Dion DiMucci, Austin Willis, Risella Bain, Jennifer Billingsly, Jan Miner

It's a Mad, Mad, Mad, Mad World (1963)
Released: November 7, 1963. Distributed by: United Artists. Screenplay: William Rose, Tania Rose. Production Design: Rudolph Sternad. Music: Ernest Gold. Photography: Ernest Lazlo. Editor: Fred Knudtson. Assistant Director: Ivan Volkman. Producer/Director: Stanley Kramer. Cast: Spencer Tracy, Milton Berle, Sid Caesar, Buddy Hackett, Ethel Merman, Mickey Rooney, Dick Shawn, Phil Silvers, Terry-Thomas, Jonathan Winters, Joe E. Brown, Buster Keaton, ZaSu Pitts, Jimmy Durante

Pajama Party (1964)
Released: November 11, 1964. Distributed by: American International Pictures. Script: Louis M. Heyward. Music: Les Baxter. Photography: Floyd Crosby. Editors: Fred Feitshans, Eve Newman. Producer: James H. Nicholson, Samuel Z. Arkoff. Director: Don Weis. Cast: Tommy Kirk, Annette Funicello, Elsa Lanchester, Harvey Lembeck, Jesse White, Jody McCrea, Susan Hart, Bobbi Shaw, Buster Keaton, Dorothy Lamour, Don Rickles, Frankie Avalon

Beach Blanket Bingo (1965)
Released: April 15, 1965. Distributed by: American International Pictures. Script: William Asher, Leo Townsend. Music: Les Baxter. Photography: Floyd Crosby. Editors: Fred Feitshans, Eve Newman. Producer: James H. Nicholson, Samuel Z. Arkoff. Director: William Asher. Cast: Frankie Avalon, Annette Funicello, Deborah Walley, Harvey Lembeck, John Ashley, Jody McCrea, Donna Loren, Marta Kristen, Linda Evans, Timothy Carey, Don Rickles, Paul Lynde, Buster Keaton, Earl Wilson

How to Stuff a Wild Bikini (1965)
Released: July 14, 1965. Distributed by: American International Pictures. Script: William Asher, Leo Townsend. Music: Les Baxter. Photography: Floyd Crosby. Editors: Fred Feitshans, Eve Newman. Producer: James H. Nicholson, Samuel Z. Arkoff. Director: William Asher. Cast: Annette Funicello, Dwayne Hickman, Brian Donlevy, Harvey Lembeck, Beverly Adams, John Ashley, Jody McCrea, Len Lesser, Bobbi Shaw, Marianne Gaba, Irene Tsu, Buster Keaton, Mickey Rooney, Frankie Avalon, Elizabeth Montgomery

Sergeant Deadhead (1965)
Released: August 18, 1965. Distributed by: American International Pictures. Script: Louis M. Heyward. Music: Les Baxter. Photography: Floyd Crosby. Editors: Ronald Sinclair, Eve Newman, Fred Feitshans. Producers: James H. Nicholson, Samuel Z. Arkoff. Director: Norman Taurog. Cast: Frankie Avalon, Deborah Walley, Cesar Romero, Fred Clark, Gale Gordon, Harvey Lembeck, John Ashley, Buster Keaton, Reginald Gardiner, Pat Buttram, Eve Arden, Dwayne Hickman

A Funny Thing Happened on the Way to the Forum (1966)
Released: October 16, 1966. Distributed by: United Artists. Screenplay: Melvin Frank, Michael Pertwee. Based on the stage play produced by Harold S. Prince. Music/Lyrics: Stephen Sondheim. Book: Burt Shevelove, Larry Gelbart. Photography: Nicolas Roeg. Editor: John Victor Smith. Producer: Melvin Frank. Director: Richard Lester. Cast: Zero Mostel, Phil Silvers, Buster Keaton, Michael Crawford, Jack Gilford, Annette Andre, Michael Hordern, Leon Greene, Patricia Jessel

War Italian Style (1967)
(Italian Title: Due Marines e un Generale)
Released: January 18, 1967. Distributed by: American International Pictures. Script: Franco Castellano, Pipolo, Fulvio Lucisano. Music: Piero Umiliani. Photography: Fausto Zuccoli. Producer: Fulvio Lucisano. Director: Luigi Scattini. Cast: Buster Keaton, Franco Franchi, Ciccio Ingrassia, Fred Clark, Martha Hyer

MISCELLANEOUS AND UNCREDITED APPEARANCES

The Round Up (1920)
Released: October 10, 1920. Distributed by: Paramount Pictures. Produced by: Famous Players-Lasky Corp. Length: 7 reels. Scenario: Edmund Day, Tom Forman. Photography: Paul Perry. Producer/Director: George Melford. Cast: Roscoe Arbuckle, Tom Forman, Irving Cummings, Mabel Julienne Scott, Jean Acker, Lucien Littlefield, Wallace Beery, A. Edward Sutherland, Buster Keaton (as the Indian who is shot by Arbuckle)

Seeing Stars (1922)
Released: 1922. Produced by the Independent Screen Artists' Guild and Associated First National Pictures. Distributed by: First National. Length: 1 reel. A promotional film with footage of the formal dinner at the Ambassador Hotel, Los Angeles upon the formation of the Independent Screen Artists' Guild. Buster is shown acting as a waiter attending to Chaplin and Jackie Coogan. Cast: Charles Chaplin, Norma Talmadge, Constance Talmadge, Jackie Coogan, Buster Keaton, Thomas H. Ince, Marshall Neilan

The Iron Mule (1925)
Released: April 12, 1925. Distributed by: Educational Films Corporation of America. Produced by: Reel Comedies, Inc. Scenario: Roscoe Arbuckle. Director: Roscoe Arbuckle. Cast: Al St. John, Buster Keaton (as Indian)

The Baby Cyclone (1928)
Released: September 27, 1928. Distributed by: Metro-Goldwyn-Mayer. Scenario: F. Hugh Herbert. Based on a play by George M. Cohan. Director: A. Edward Sutherland. Cast: Lew Cody, Aileen Pringle, Robert Armstrong, Gwen Lee, Buster Keaton (as the stand-in for Lew Cody when he falls down the stairs)

The Voice of Hollywood, 10 (1930)
Released: April 28, 1930. Distributed by: Tiffany. Length: 1 reel. Director/Producer: Louis Lewyn. Cast: Lew Cody, Cliff Edwards, Buster Keaton, Al St. John, Raquel Torres

The Stolen Jools (1931)
Released: April 3, 1931. Distributed by: Paramount Pictures and National Screen Service. Length: 2 reels. Supervisor: E. K. Nadel. Producer: Pat Casey. Director: William McGann. Cast: Wallace Beery, Buster Keaton (as a policeman), Edward G. Robinson, Stan Laurel, Oliver Hardy, Our Gang, Norma Shearer, Joan Crawford, Gary Cooper, Maurice Chevalier, Mitzi Green

Hollywood on Parade, A-6 (1933)
Released January 8, 1933. Distributed by Paramount Pictures. Length: 1 reel. Producer/Director: Louis Lewyn. Cast: Richard Arlen, Talullah Bankhead, Lew Cody, Clark Gable, Buster Keaton

La Fiesta de Santa Barbara (1935)
Released: December 7, 1935. Distributed by: Metro-Goldwyn-Mayer. Length: 2 reels. Script: Alexander Van Dorn. Photography: Ray Rennahan. Narrator: Pete Smith. Producer/Director: Louis Lewyn. Cast: Gary Cooper, Andy Devine, the Garland Sisters (with Judy Garland), Buster Keaton, Ida Lupino, Harpo Marx, Gilbert Roland, Robert Taylor

Sunkist Stars at Palm Springs (1936)
Released: 1936. Distributed by: Metro-Goldwyn-Mayer. Length: 2 reels. Dialogue: John Kraft. Photography: Allen Davey, Aldo Ermini. Producer: Louis Lewyn. Director: Roy Rowland. Cast: Robert Benchley, Jackie Coogan, Betty Grable, Walter Huston, Buster Keaton, Claire Trevor, Johnny Weissmuller

New Moon (1940)
Released: 1940. Distributed by: Metro-Goldwyn-Mayer. Script: Jacques Deval, Robert Arthur. Photography: William Daniels. Producer/Director: Robert Z. Leonard. Cast: Jeanette MacDonald, Nelson Eddy, Mary Boland, H. B. Warner, Buster Keaton (as a background player)

Screen Snapshots: Seeing Hollywood (1940)
Released: March 29, 1940. Distributed by: Columbia Pictures Corporation. Photography: Robert Tobey. Producer/Director: Ralph Staub. Cast: Gloria and Barbara Brewster, Joe E. Brown, Gary Cooper, Bing Crosby, Rita Hayworth, Bob Hope, Buster Keaton, Harold Lloyd, Groucho Marx

Screen Snapshots: Keystone Party (1941)
Released: August 15, 1941. Distributed by: Columbia Pictures Corporation. Editor: Edmund Kimber. Producer/Director: Ralph Staub. Cast: Milton Berle, Barbara and Gloria Brewster, Errol Flynn, Billy Gilbert, Buster Keaton, Ken Murray, Cesar Romero, Lupe Velez

She Went to the Races (1945)
Released: November 1945. Distributed by: Metro-Goldwyn-Mayer. Screenplay: Lawrence Hazard. Based on a story by:

Alan Friedman and DeVallon Scott. Photography: Charles Salerno. Producer: Frederick Stephani. Director: Willis Goldbeck. Cast: James Craig, Francis Gifford, Ava Gardner, Edmund Gwenn, Buster Keaton (as a bellboy)

You're My Everything (1949)
Released: August 1949. Distributed by: Twentieth Century-Fox. Screenplay: Lamar Trotti, Will H. Hays, Jr. Original Story: George Jessel. Photography: Arthur E. Arling. Music: Alfred Newman. Editor: J. Watson Webb, Jr. Producer: Lamar Trotti. Director: Walter Lang. Cast: Dan Dailey, Anne Baxter, Anne Revere, Stanley Ridges, Alan Mowbray, Buster Keaton (as a butler)

OTHER SHORT FILMS AND INDUSTRIAL FILMS

Un Duel à Mort (1950)
Released: September 7, 1950 (not released in the United States of America). Produced by: Films Azur, Paris. Script: Pierre Blondy, Buster Keaton. Photography: Jacques Isnard. Music: Georges Van Parys. Producer: René Beanco, Louis Lefait. Director: Pierre Blondy. Cast: Buster Keaton, Antonin Berval

Paradise for Buster (1952)
Released: for private showings only. Produced by: Wilding Picture Productions. Made for the John Deere Company. Script: J. P. Prindle, John Grey, Harold Goodwin. Music: Albert Glasser. Photography: J. J. La Fleur, Robert Sable. Editor: William Minnerly. Supervisors: H. M. Railsback, G. M. Rohrbach. Director: Del Lord. Cast: Buster Keaton, Harold Goodwin

The Devil to Pay (1960)
Released: not released commercially. Produced by: Education Research Films for the National Association of Wholesalers. Production Company: Rodel Productions. Script: Cummins-Betts. Art Director: Peter Masters, Joseph W. Swanson. Sound: Nelson Funk. Photography: Del Ankers, Fritz Roland. Editor: Cummins-Betts. Director: Herb Skoble. Cast: Buster Keaton, Ralph Dunne, Ruth Gillette, Marion Morris, John Rodney

The Triumph of Lester Snapwell (1963)
Released: not released commercially. Produced by: Eastman Kodak Company. Director: James Cahoun. Cast: Buster Keaton, Sigrid Nelsson, Nina Varela

There's No Business Like No Business (1963)
Made for Maremont Exhaust and Gabriel Shocks Division/ Arvin Corporation. Cast: Buster Keaton

The Fall Guy (1965)
Made by U.S. Steel. Director: Darrel Bateman. Cast: Buster Keaton

Film (1965)
Released: September 1965. Distributed by: Grove Press. Produced by: Evergreen Theatre. Script: Samuel Beckett. Art Director: Burr Smidt. Camera Operator: Joe Coffey. Editor: Sidney Meyers. Photography: Boris Kaufman. Producer:

Barney Rosset. Director: Alan Schneider. Cast: Buster Keaton, Nell Harrison, James Karen, Susan Reed

The Railrodder (1965)
Released: October 2, 1965. Distributed by: National Film Board of Canada. Script: Gerald Potterton. Music: Eldon Rathburn. Sound Effects: Karl du Plessis. Sound Recording: George Croll, Ted Haley. Photography: Robert Humble. Editor: Jo Kirkpatrick, Gerald Potterton. Assistant Director: Jo Kirkpatrick. Producer: Julian Biggs. Director: Gerald Potterton. Cast: Buster Keaton

The Scribe (1966)
Released: January 8, 1966. Produced by: Film-Tele Productions for the Construction Safety Association of Ontario. Script: Paul Sutherland, Clifford Braggins. Music: Quartet Productions. Photography: Mike Lente. Editor: Kenneth Heely-Ray. Executive Producers: Raymond Walters, James Collier. Producers: Ann and Kenneth Heely-Ray. Director: John Sebert. Cast: Buster Keaton

OFFSCREEN FILM CREDITS

Life in Sometown, U.S.A. (1938)
Released: February 26, 1938. Distributed by: Metro-Goldwyn-Mayer. Narrator: Carey Wilson. Script: Carl Dudley, Richard Murphy. Director: Buster Keaton

Hollywood Handicap (1938)
Released: May 28, 1938. Distributed by: Metro-Goldwyn-Mayer. Producer: Louis Lewyn. Director: Buster Keaton. Cast: The Original Sing Band

Streamlined Swing (1938)
Released: September 10, 1938. Distributed by: Metro-Goldwyn-Mayer. Script: Marion Mack. Dialogue: John Kraft. Producer: Louis Lewyn. Director: Buster Keaton. Cast: The Original Sing Band

The Jones Family in Hollywood (1939)
Released: June 2, 1939. Distributed by: Metro-Goldwyn-Mayer. Script: Harold Tarshis. Original Story: Joseph Hoffman, Buster Keaton. Based on characters by Katherine Kavanaugh. Director: Mal St. Clair. Cast: Jed Prouty, Spring Byington, Ken Howell, June Carlson, Florence Roberts

The Jones Family in Quick Millions (1939)
Released: August 25, 1939. Distributed by: Metro-Goldwyn-Mayer. Script: Joseph Hoffman, Stanley Rauh. Original Story: Joseph Hoffman, Buster Keaton. Based on characters by Katherine Kavanaugh. Director: Mal St. Clair. Cast: Jed Prouty, Spring Byington, Ken Howell, June Carlson, Florence Roberts

The Buster Keaton Story (1957)
Released: May 1957. Distributed by: Paramount Pictures. Script: Sidney Sheldon, Robert Smith. Photography: Loyal Griggs. Editor: Archie Marshek. Costumes: Edith Head. Technical Adviser: Buster Keaton. Producers: Robert Smith,

Sidney Sheldon. Director: Sidney Sheldon. Cast: Donald O'Connor, Ann Blyth, Rhonda Fleming, Peter Lorre, Larry Keating, Richard Anderson, Dave Willock, Claire Carleton, Larry White, Jackie Coogan, Cecil B. De Mille

UNCREDITED GAGS AND TECHNICAL ADVICE

Splash! (1931)
Released: October 3, 1931. Distributed by: Metro-Goldwyn-Mayer. Director: Jules White, Zion Myers

Fast Company (1938)
Released: 1938. Distributed by: Metro-Goldwyn-Mayer. Director: Edward Buzzell. Cast: Melvyn Douglas, Florence Rice, Claire Dodd, Louis Calhern

Too Hot to Handle (1938)
Released: 1938. Distributed by: Metro-Goldwyn-Mayer. Director: Jack Conway. Cast: Clark Gable, Myrna Loy, Walter Pidgeon

Love Finds Andy Hardy (1938)
Released: 1938. Distributed by: Metro-Goldwyn-Mayer. Director: George Seitz. Cast: Mickey Rooney, Judy Garland, Lana Turner, Lewis Stone

At the Circus (1939)
Released: 1939. Distributed by: Metro-Goldwyn-Mayer. Director: Edward Buzzell. Cast: The Marx Brothers

Comrade X (1940)
Released: 1940. Distributed by: Metro-Goldwyn-Mayer. Director: King Vidor. Cast: Clark Gable, Hedy Lamarr, Felix Bressart, Eve Arden

Go West (1940)
Released: 1940. Distributed by: Metro-Goldwyn-Mayer. Director: Edward Buzzell. Cast: The Marx Brothers

Tales of Manhattan (1942)
Released: 1942. Distributed by: Twentieth Century-Fox. Director: Julien Duvivier. Cast: Henry Fonda, Rita Hayworth, Ginger Rogers, Charles Boyer, Edward G. Robinson, Charles Laughton

I Dood It (1943)
Released: 1943. Distributed by: Metro-Goldwyn-Mayer. Director: Vincente Minnelli. Cast: Red Skelton, Eleanor Powell, Lena Horne, John Hodiak

Bathing Beauty (1944)
Released: 1944. Distributed by: Metro-Goldwyn-Mayer. Director: George Sidney. Cast: Red Skelton, Esther Williams, Basil Rathbone

Nothing but Trouble (1945)
Released: 1945. Distributed by: Metro-Goldwyn-Mayer. Director: Sam Taylor. Cast: Stan Laurel, Oliver Hardy

The Equestrian Quiz (1946)
Released: 1946. Distributed by: Metro-Goldwyn-Mayer. A Pete Smith Specialty. Cast: Dave O'Brian, Chistiani Brothers

Easy to Wed (1946)
Released: 1946. Distributed by: Metro-Goldwyn-Mayer. Director: Edward Buzzell. Cast: Van Johnson, Esther Williams, Lucille Ball

Cynthia (1947)
Released: 1947. Distributed by: Metro-Goldwyn-Mayer. Director: Robert Z. Leonard. Cast: Elizabeth Taylor, Mary Astor, James Lydon, George Murphy, S. Z. "Cuddles" Sakall

It Happened in Brooklyn (1947)
Released: 1947. Distributed by: Metro-Goldwyn-Mayer. Director: Richard Whorf. Cast: Frank Sinatra, Jimmy Durante, Kathryn Grayson, Peter Lawford

Merton of the Movies (1947)
Released: 1947. Distributed by: Metro-Goldwyn-Mayer. Director: Robert Alton. Cast: Red Skelton, Gloria Grahame, Virginia O'Brien, Leon Ames, Alan Mowbray

A Southern Yankee (1948)
Released: 1948. Distributed by: Metro-Goldwyn-Mayer. Director: Edward Sedgwick. Cast: Red Skelton, Arlene Dahl

Neptune's Daughter (1949)
Released: 1949. Distributed by: Metro-Goldwyn-Mayer. Director: Edward Buzzell. Cast: Esther Williams, Red Skelton, Ricardo Montalban

Take Me Out to the Ball Game (1949)
Released: 1949. Distributed by: Metro-Goldwyn-Mayer. Director: Busby Berkeley. Cast: Frank Sinatra, Gene Kelly, Esther Williams

Watch the Birdie (1950)
Released: 1950. Distributed by: Metro-Goldwyn-Mayer. Director: Jack Donohoe. Cast: Red Skelton, Arlene Dahl, Ann Miller

The Yellow Cab Man (1950)
Released: 1950. Distributed by: Metro-Goldwyn-Mayer. Director: Jack Donohoe. Cast: Red Skelton, Gloria DeHaven

Excuse My Dust (1951)
Released: 1951. Distributed by: Metro-Goldwyn-Mayer. Director: Roy Rowland. Cast: Red Skelton, Sally Forrest, MacDonald Carey

TELEVISION

The Ed Wynn Show (1949)
30-minute variety, CBS. Air Date: December 22, 1949. Cast: Ed Wynn, Buster Keaton, Virginia O'Brien

The Buster Keaton Show (1949)
30-minute comedy, KTTV Hollywood. A local television program that ran 17 episodes. Premiered: December 22, 1949. Script: Clyde Bruckman, Henry Taylor. Producer: Joe Parker. Director: Philippe Delacy. Cast: Buster Keaton, Alan Reed, Leon Belasco, Ben Weldon, Dick Elliot, Shirley Tegge

Toast of the Town (1950)
(The Ed Sullivan Show)
60-minute variety, CBS. Host: Ed Sullivan. Air date: November 5, 1950

Four Star Revue (1950)
60-minute variety, NBC. Host: Ed Wynn. Air date: November 15 and December 13, 1950

The Buster Keaton Show (1950–51)
30-minute comedy, syndicated. Produced by: Consolidated Television. The program was renamed *Life with Buster Keaton* in syndication and later several episodes were strung together and released in Great Britain by British Lion in 1953 as a theatrical feature film called *The Misadventures of Buster Keaton*. Script: Carl Hittleman, Jay Sommers, Clyde Bruckman, Ben Perry, Harold Goodwin. Photography: Jackson Rose. Producers: Carl Hittleman, Clyde Bruckman, Jay Sommers. Directors: Arthur Hilton, Eddie Cline. Cast: Buster Keaton, Marcia Mae Jones, Dorothy Ford, Jack Reitzen, Philip Van Zandt, Eddie Gribbon, Eleanor Keaton. Episodes: "The Army Story," "The Bakery Story," "The Billboard Story," "The Collapsible Clerk," "The Detective Story," "The Fishing Story," "The Gymnasium Story," "The Haunted House," "The Little Theater," "The Shakespeare Story," "The Time Machine," "The Western Story," and "The Gorilla Story"

The Jack Carter Show (1951)
60-minute variety, NBC. Host: Jack Carter. Air date: February 24, 1951

All Star Revue (1951)
60-minute variety, NBC. Host: Ed Wynn. Air date: November 10, 1951

The Colgate Comedy Hour (1952)
60-minute variety, NBC. Host: Donald O'Connor. Air date: March 2, 1952

Ford Festival (1952)
60-minute musical variety, NBC. Air date: April 17, 1952

Kate Smith Presents: Matinee in New York (1952)
NBC. Air date: July 15, 1952

All Star Summer Review (1952)
60-minute variety, NBC. Air date: July 19, 1952

All Star Review (1952)
60-minute variety, NBC. Host: Walter O'Keefe. Air date: December 27, 1952

Douglas Fairbanks, Jr. Presents: The Rheingold Theatre (1954)
30-minute anthology, NBC. Air date: July 14, 1954. Episode title: "The Awakening." Story Supervision: Guy Morgan. Music: Bretton Byrd. Director of Photography: Ken Talbot. Screenplay: Larry Marcus. Based on "The Overcoat" by Nikolay Vasilyevich Gogol. Producer: Lance Comfort. Director: Michael McCarthy. Cast: Buster Keaton, James Hayter, Carl Jaffe, Lynne Cole, Geoffrey Keen

Best of Broadway (1954)
60-minute anthology, CBS. Air date: October 13, 1954. Episode title: "The Man Who Came to Dinner." Adaptation: Ronald Alexander. Based on the play by Kaufman and Hart. Music: David Broekman. Producer: Martin Manulis. Director: David Alexander. Cast: Monty Woolley, Joan Bennett, Catherine Doucet, Sylvia Field, Reginald Gardiner, Margaret Hamilton, Buster Keaton, Bert Lahr, Merle Oberon, ZaSu Pitts, William Prince, Howard St. John, Frank Tweddell

This is Your Life (1954)
30 minutes, NBC. Host: Ralph Edwards. Air date: November 3, 1954. Keaton appears with guest of honor Joe E. Brown

Make the Connection (1955)
30-minute quiz, NBC. Host: Jim McKay. Air date: August 18, 1955

The Dunninger Show (1955)
30-minute mind reading-audience participation, NBC. Host: Joseph Dunninger. Air date: August 20, 1955

Tonight (1955)
90-minute talk-variety, NBC. Host: Steve Allen. Air date: August 24, 1955

The Sunday Spectacular (1955)
NBC. Air date: October 9, 1955. Episode title: "Show Biz"

Eddie Cantor Theater (1955)
30-minute variety, ABC. Host: Eddie Cantor. Air date: October 10, 1955. Episode title: "The Square World of Alonzo Pennyworth"

Screen Director's Playhouse (1955)
30-minute anthology, NBC. Air date: December 21, 1955. Episode title: "The Silent Partner." Writer: Barbara Hammer (from a story by Barbara Hammer and George Marshall). Producer: Hal Roach. Director: George Marshall. Cast: Buster Keaton, ZaSu Pitts, Joe E. Brown, Evelyn Ankers, Jack Kruschen, Jack Elam, Percy Helton, Joseph Corey, Lyle Latell, Charles Horvath

The Martha Raye Show (1956)
60-minute comedy-variety, NBC. Host: Martha Raye. Air date: March 6, 1956. Guests: Buster Keaton, Paul Douglas, Harold Arlen, the Baird Marionettes

It Could Be You (1956)
30-minute quiz, NBC. Air date: June 7, 1956

Today (1956)
News-talk, NBC. Air date: September 14, 1956

Producer's Showcase (1956)
90-minute anthology, NBC. Air date: September 17, 1956. Episode title: "The Lord Don't Play Favorites." Adaptation: Jo Swerling. Based on a story by Patrick H. Maloy. Music/Lyrics: Hal Stanley. Choreography: Tony Charmoli. Producer: Hal Stanley. Cast: Buster Keaton, Robert Stack, Kay Starr, Dick Haymes, Louis Armstrong, Nejla Ates, Mike Ross, Arthur Q. Bryan, Oliver Blake, Barry Kelley, Jerry Maren

The Steve Allen Show (1956)
60-minute variety, NBC. Host: Steve Allen. Air date: December 30, 1956

The Lux Show Starring Rosemary Clooney (1956)
30-minute musical variety, NBC

Lux Video Theater (1956)
60-minute anthology, NBC

Do You Trust Your Wife? (1956) (*The Edgar Bergen Show*)
30-minute quiz-audience participation, CBS. Host: Edgar Bergen

The Johnny Carson Show (1956)
30-minute comedy-variety, CBS. Host: Johnny Carson

It Could Be You (1957)
30-minute quiz, NBC. Air date: March 19, 1957

This Is Your Life (1957)
30 minutes, NBC. Air date: April 3, 1957. Host: Ralph Edwards. Keaton appears as guest of honor

Today (1957)
News-talk, NBC. Air date: April 23, 1957

Tonight! America After Dark (1957)
105-minute talk-variety, NBC. Host: Jack Lescoulie. Air date: April 24, 1957

Club 60 (1957)
NBC. Air date: May 2, 1957

I've Got a Secret (1957)
30-minute quiz, CBS. Moderator: Garry Moore

What's My Line? (1957)
30-minute quiz, CBS. Moderator: John Daly

It Could Be You (1957)
30-minute quiz, NBC. Air date: December 23, 1957

Truth or Consequences (1958)
30-minute quiz, NBC. Air dates: January 3, 1958, January 10, 1958, January 13, 1958, January 15, 1958

The Betty White Show (1958)
30-minute variety, ABC. Air date: February 12, 1958. Host: Betty White

You Asked for It (1958)
30-minute audience request, ABC. Air date February 16, 1958. Host: Art Baker

The Adventures of Mr. Pastry (1958)
26-minute unsold pilot episode for ITV (Great Britain). Aired in 1958 (filmed in 1956). Screenplay: Angus MacPhail, Harold Kent. Director of Photography: Gerald Gibbs. Editor: Inman Hunter. Executive Producer: Hannah Weinstein. Associate Producer: Sidney Cole. Director: Ralph Smart. Cast: Richard Hearne, Buster Keaton, Peggy Mount

Playhouse 90 (1958)
90-minute anthology, CBS. Air date: June 5, 1958. Episode title: "The Innocent Sleep." Script: Tad Mosel. Director: Franklin Schaffner. Cast: Buster Keaton, Hope Lange, Dennis King, John Ericson, Hope Emerson

Telephone Time (1958)
30-minute anthology, ABC. Host: Dr. Frank Baxter

The Jack Paar Show (1958)
105-minute talk-variety, NBC. Host: Jack Paar. Air date: November 14, 1958

The Garry Moore Show (1958)
60-minute variety, CBS. Host: Garry Moore

The Donna Reed Show (1958)
30-minute sitcom, ABC. Air date: December 24, 1958. Episode title: "A Very Merry Christmas." Cast: Donna Reed, Carl Betz, Paul Peterson, Shelley Fabares, Buster Keaton

It Could Be You (1959)
30-minute quiz, NBC. Air date: October 26, 1959

Masquerade Party (1959)
30-minute quiz, CBS. Moderator: Bert Parks

Today (1960)
News-talk, NBC. Air date: January 20, 1960

Sunday Showcase (1960)
60-minute anthology/variety, NBC. Air date: February 7, 1960. Episode title: "After Hours." Script: Tony Webster. Director: Alex March. Cast: Buster Keaton, Christopher Plummer, Sally Ann Howes, Robert Emhardt, Philip Abbott, Natalie Schafer, John Fiedler

Masquerade Party (1960)
30-minute quiz, NBC. Air date: February 5, 1960. Host: Bert Parks

It Could Be You (1960)
30-minute quiz, NBC. Air date: March 3, 1960

Revlon Presents (1960)
60-minute variety, CBS. Air date: March 24, 1960. Cast: Paul Whiteman, Buster Keaton, Peggy Lee, James Karen

Oscar Night in Hollywood (1960)
Special, NBC. Air date: April 4, 1960

Play Your Hunch (1960)
30-minute quiz, NBC. Air date: August 19, 1960

It Could Be You (1961)
30-minute quiz, NBC. Air date: June 27, 1961

Candid Camera (1961)
30 minutes, CBS. Host: Allen Funt

Here's Hollywood (1961)
NBC. Air date: August 10, 1961

Twilight Zone (1961)
30-minute sci-fi anthology, CBS. Air date: December 15, 1961. Episode title: "Once Upon a Time." Host: Rod Serling. Script: Richard Matheson. Photography: George T. Clemens. Producer: Buck Houghton. Director: Norman Z. McLeod. Cast: Buster Keaton, Stanley Adams, Milton Parsons, Jesse White, Gil Lamb, James Flavin, Michael Ross, George E. Stone, Warren Parker

Your First Impression (1962)
NBC. Air date: January 12, 1962

Medicine Man (1962)
30-minute sitcom, Screen Gems. Episode title: "A Pony for Chris." Script: Jay Sommer, Joe Bigelow. Producer: Harry Ackerman. Director: Charles Barton. Cast: Ernie Kovacs, Buster Keaton, Kevin Brodie

Candid Camera (1962)
30 minutes, CBS. Host: Allen Funt

The Scene Stealers (1962)
60-minute comedy-drama, CBS. Distributed by March of Dimes. Air date: April 1962. Script: Johnny Bradford. Director: Jack Shea. Cast: Ed Wynn, Buster Keaton, Rosemary Clooney, Jimmy Durante, Ralph Edwards, James Garner, Lorne Greene, David Janssen, Eartha Kitt, Jack Lemmon

Your First Impression (1962)
NBC. Air date: August 29, 1962

Route 66 (1962)
60-minute adventure, CBS. Episode title: "Journey to Nineveh." Air date: September 28, 1962. Cast: George Maharis, Martin Milner, Buster Keaton, Joe E. Brown, Jenny Maxwell, Guy Raymond, John Astin, Edgar Buchanan, John Davis Chandler, John Durren

Mr. Smith Goes to Washington (1963)
30-minute sitcom, ABC. Air date: January 19, 1963. Episode title: "Think Mink." Cast: Fess Parker, Buster Keaton, Jesslyn Fax, Sandra Warner

Your First Impression (1963)
30 minutes. NBC. Air date: February 12, 1963

Truth or Consequences (1963)
30-minute quiz, NBC. Air date: March 7, 1963

Today (1963)
120-minute news-talk, NBC. Air date: April 26, 1963. Episode title: "Buster Keaton Revisited." Host: Hugh Downs

The Ed Sullivan Show (1963)
60-minute variety, CBS. Host: Ed Sullivan

The Greatest Show on Earth (1964)
60-minute drama, ABC. Air date: April 28, 1964. Episode title: "You're Alright, Ivy." Director: Jack Palance. Cast: Jack Palance, Stuart Erwin, Buster Keaton, Lynn Loring, Ted Bessell, Joe E. Brown, Joan Blondell, Betsy Jones-Moreland, Barbara Pepper, Larry Montaigne

Burke's Law (1964)
60-minute detective drama, ABC. Air date: May 8, 1964. Episode title: "Who Killed ½ of Glory Lee." Script: Harlan Ellison. Cast: Gene Barry, Gary Conway, Regis Toomey, Buster Keaton, Joan Blondell, Nina Foch, Anne Helm, Betty Hutton, Gisele Mackenzie

Hollywood Palace (1964)
60-minute variety, ABC. Host: Gene Barry. Air date: June 6, 1964

The Man Who Bought Paradise (1965)
60-minute comedy-drama, CBS. Air date: January 17, 1965. Script: Richard Alan Simmons. Producer/Director: Ralph Nelson. Cast: Buster Keaton, Robert Horton, Angie Dickinson, Paul Lukas, Ray Walston, Hoagy Carmichael, Dolores Del Rio, Cyril Richard, Walter Slezak

The Jonathan Winters Show (1965)
Comedy-variety, NBC. Host: Jonathan Winters. Air date: March 29, 1965

The Donna Reed Show (1965)
30-minute sitcom, ABC. Air date: February 11, 1965. Episode title: "Now You See It, Now You Don't." Director: Gene Nelson. Cast: Donna Reed, Ann McRea, Carl Betz, Bob Crane, Paul Peterson, Darryl Richard, Buster Keaton

Truth or Consequences (1965)
30-minute quiz, NBC. Air date: April 6, 1965

A Salute to Stan Laurel (1965)
60-minute special, CBS. Host: Dick Van Dyke. Air date: November 23, 1965. Cast: Lucille Ball, Fred Gwynne, Danny Kaye, Buster Keaton, Gregory Peck, Cesar Romero, Phil Silvers

COMMERCIALS

This listing of commercials does not include the many local commercials—primarily beer commercials—made by Keaton that remain unidentified.

1956:
Colgate Toothpaste

1958:
Alka-Seltzer
Northwest Orient Airlines
Simon Pure Beer

1959:
Shamrock Oil
7-Up
U.S. Steel

1960:
Wen Power Tools

1961:
Milky Way Candy Bar
Philips 66 Gasoline and Oil
Marlboro Cigarettes

1962:
Canadian Electric Razor
Ford Motor Company (five each year for three years)

1963:
Minute Rub

1964:
Georgia Oil
Ford Motor Company
U.S. Steel
Budweiser Beer
Salt Lake City Bank
Seneca Apple Juice

1965:
Pure Oil
Pepsi-Cola

DOCUMENTARY

Buster Keaton Rides Again (1965)
Released: October 30, 1965. Produced by: National Film Board of Canada. Commentary: Donald Brittain. Editors: John Spotton (picture), Malca Gillsom (music), Sidney Pearson (sound). Producer: Julian Biggs. Director/Photographer: John Spotton. Cast: Buster Keaton, Eleanor Keaton, Gerald Potterton

Index

Note: Page numbers in *italics* refer to illustration captions

Acknowledgments

This book could not have been possible without the full cooperation of Linda Mehr and other staff at the Margaret Herrick Library of the Academy of Motion Picture Arts and Sciences. I am especially grateful to Robert Cushman, Photograph Curator, who oversaw Eleanor Keaton's donation of her Buster-related photographs, papers, and artifacts into the Academy Foundation and later helped Eleanor and me through the amazing photographic holdings of that institution, making certain that this book is of a high pictorial standard. I am also appreciative of his kindly reading the manuscript and improving it with his suggestions.

Manoah Bowman printed all of the superb photographs for this book and served as photographic editor. More than that, he made sure that this book made it to publication and filled the collaborative void left by Eleanor's death. I am very grateful to him for his help.

I am grateful to Jon S. Bouker for his friendship and his numerous contributions to this project; to Kevin Brownlow for graciously providing the book's afterword; to David Shepard for assisting with picture permissions and for helpful suggestions with the manuscript; to David Robinson for his friendship and guidance with the manuscript; to Casey Shaw for his friendship and moral support, as well as his reminders of the things that are most important; and to James Karen for his constant encouragement and invaluable information deriving from his long friendship with Buster and Eleanor Keaton.

I thank my editor Elisa Urbanelli for her enthusiasm, patience, and judicious editing. I am also grateful to Kate Guyonvarch of Association Chaplin, Richard W. Bann, Robert S. Birchard, Marc Wanamaker of Bison Archives, Michael Schlesinger of Columbia Pictures, Melissa Talmadge Cox, Gary Dartnall and Tim Lanza of The Douris Corporation, Joel Goss, Lukas Hovorka, Phil Moad of The Kobal Collection, Bruce Levinson, Loyal T. Lucas, David Macleod, the late Roddy McDowall, Ann Lewis of Metro-Goldwyn-Mayer, Dean Riesner, Ruth Earl Silva, Anthony Slide, Kevin Eugene Smith, James Talmadge, Roger L. Mayer of Turner Entertainment, Sebastian Twardosz, and my family, particularly my mother Sandra Vance, for their support.

Photograph Credits

Editor: Elisa Urbanelli

Designer: Robert McKee

Library of Congress Cataloging-in-Publication Data

Keaton, Eleanor.
Buster Keaton remembered / by Eleanor Keaton and Jeffrey Vance;
afterword by Kevin Brownlow; photographs from the collection
of the Academy of Motion Picture Arts and Sciences; Manoah
Bowman, photographic editor.
     p. cm.
Includes bibliographical references and index.
ISBN 0–8109–4227–5
    1. Keaton, Buster, 1895–1966. 2. Keaton, Eleanor, 1918–1998.
3. Motion picture actors and actresses—United States—
Biography. 4. Comedians—United States—Biography. I.
Vance, Jeffery. II. Bowman, Manoah. III. Academy of Motion
Picture Arts and Sciences. IV. Title.

PN2287.K4 K43 2000
791.43'028'092—dc21
[B]   00–061853

Printed and bound in Japan

Harry N. Abrams, Inc.
100 Fifth Avenue
New York, N.Y. 10011
www.abramsbooks.com